Scott
ALLIE

EXURBIA

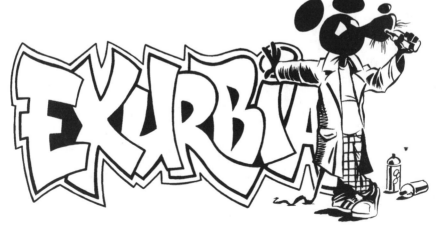

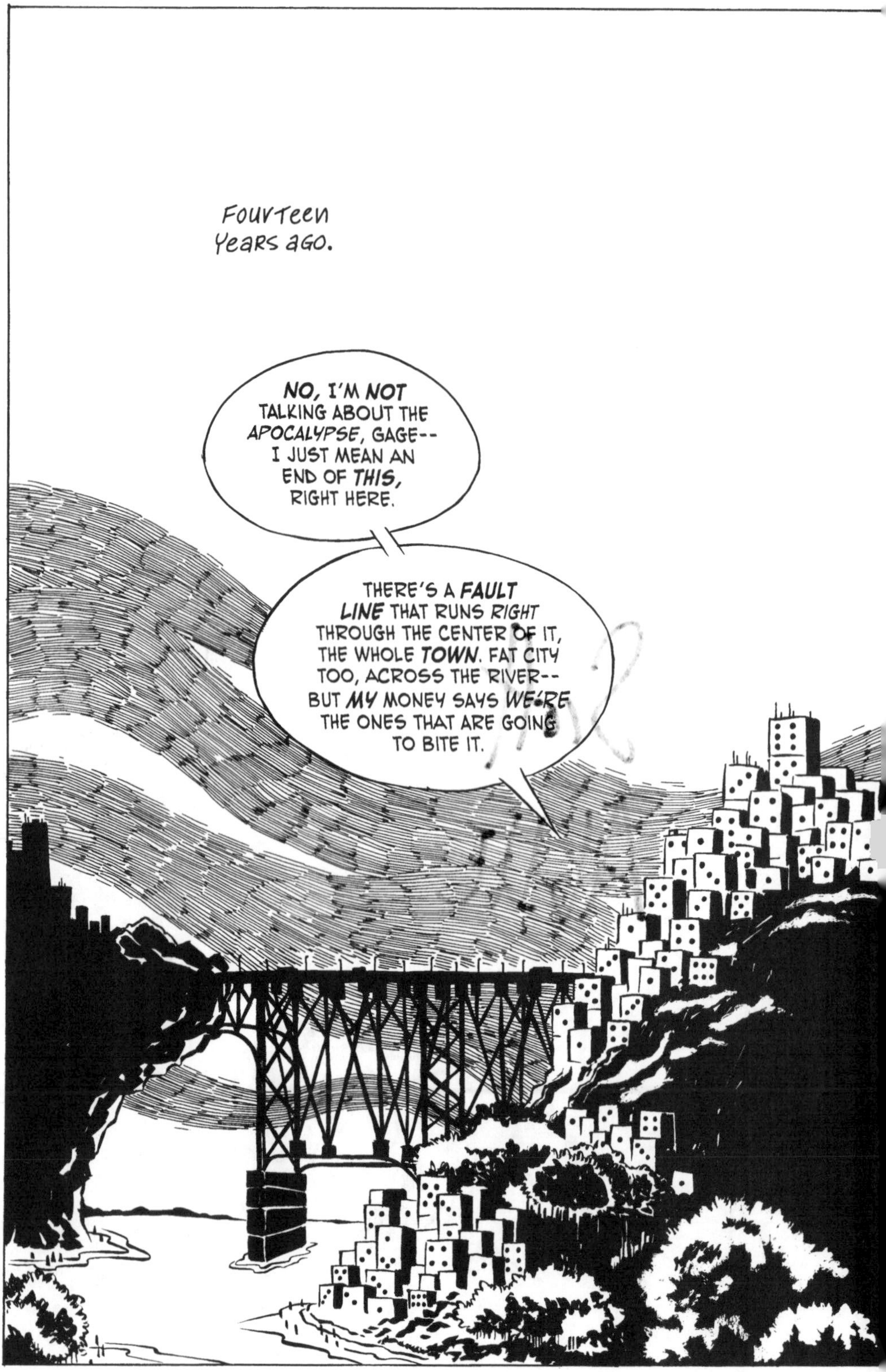
Fourteen years ago.
NO, I'M NOT TALKING ABOUT THE APOCALYPSE, GAGE-- I JUST MEAN AN END OF THIS, RIGHT HERE.
THERE'S A FAULT LINE THAT RUNS RIGHT THROUGH THE CENTER OF IT, THE WHOLE TOWN. FAT CITY TOO, ACROSS THE RIVER-- BUT MY MONEY SAYS WE'RE THE ONES THAT ARE GOING TO BITE IT.

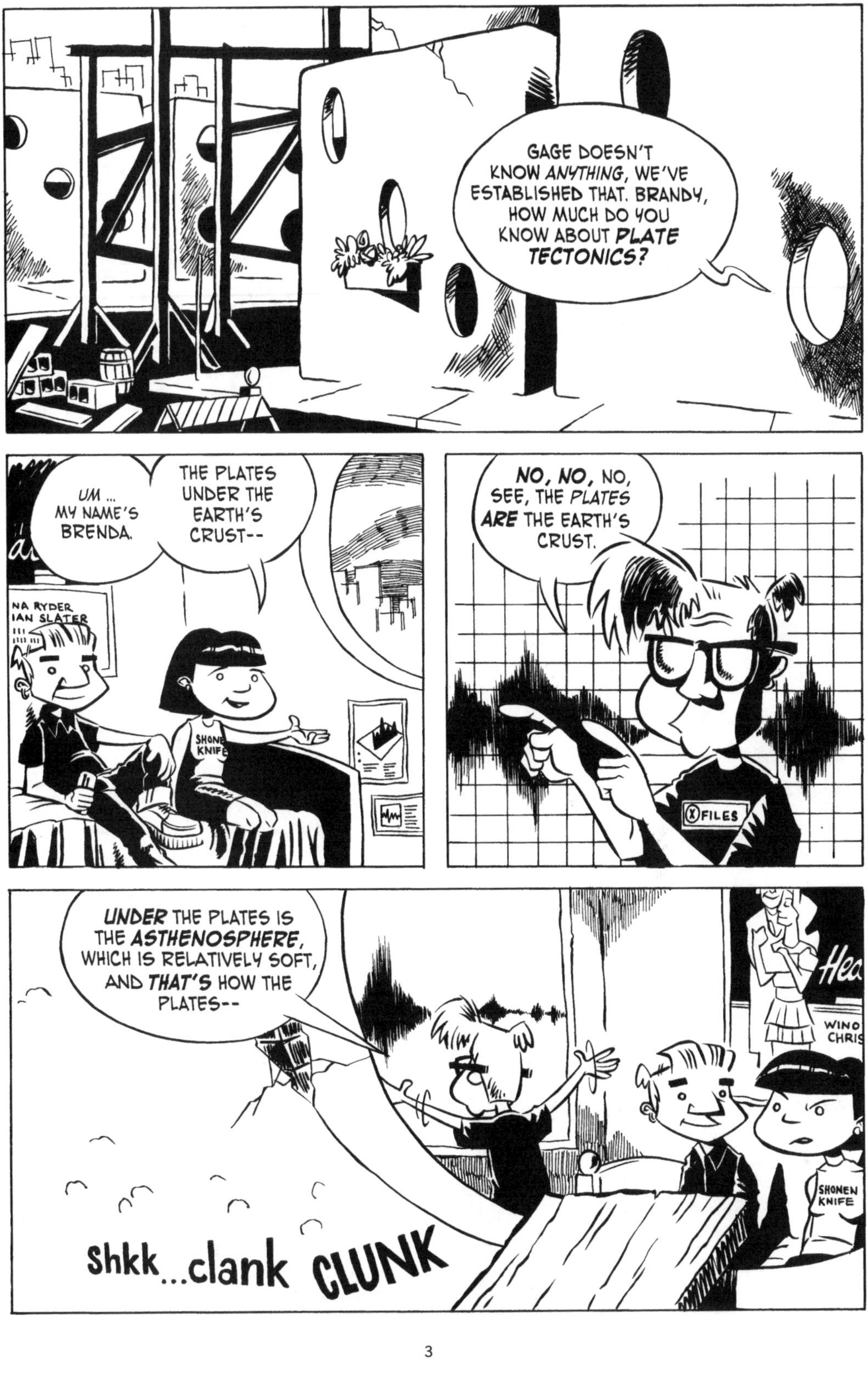
GAGE DOESN'T KNOW ANYTHING, WE'VE ESTABLISHED THAT. BRANDY, HOW MUCH DO YOU KNOW ABOUT PLATE TECTONICS?
UM ... MY NAME'S BRENDA.
THE PLATES UNDER THE EARTH'S CRUST--
NA RYDER
IAN SLATER
SHONE KNIFE
NO, NO, NO, SEE, THE PLATES ARE THE EARTH'S CRUST.
X FILES
UNDER THE PLATES IS THE ASTHENOSPHERE, WHICH IS RELATIVELY SOFT, AND THAT'S HOW THE PLATES--
WINO CHRIS
SHONEN KNIFE
Shkk...clank CLUNK

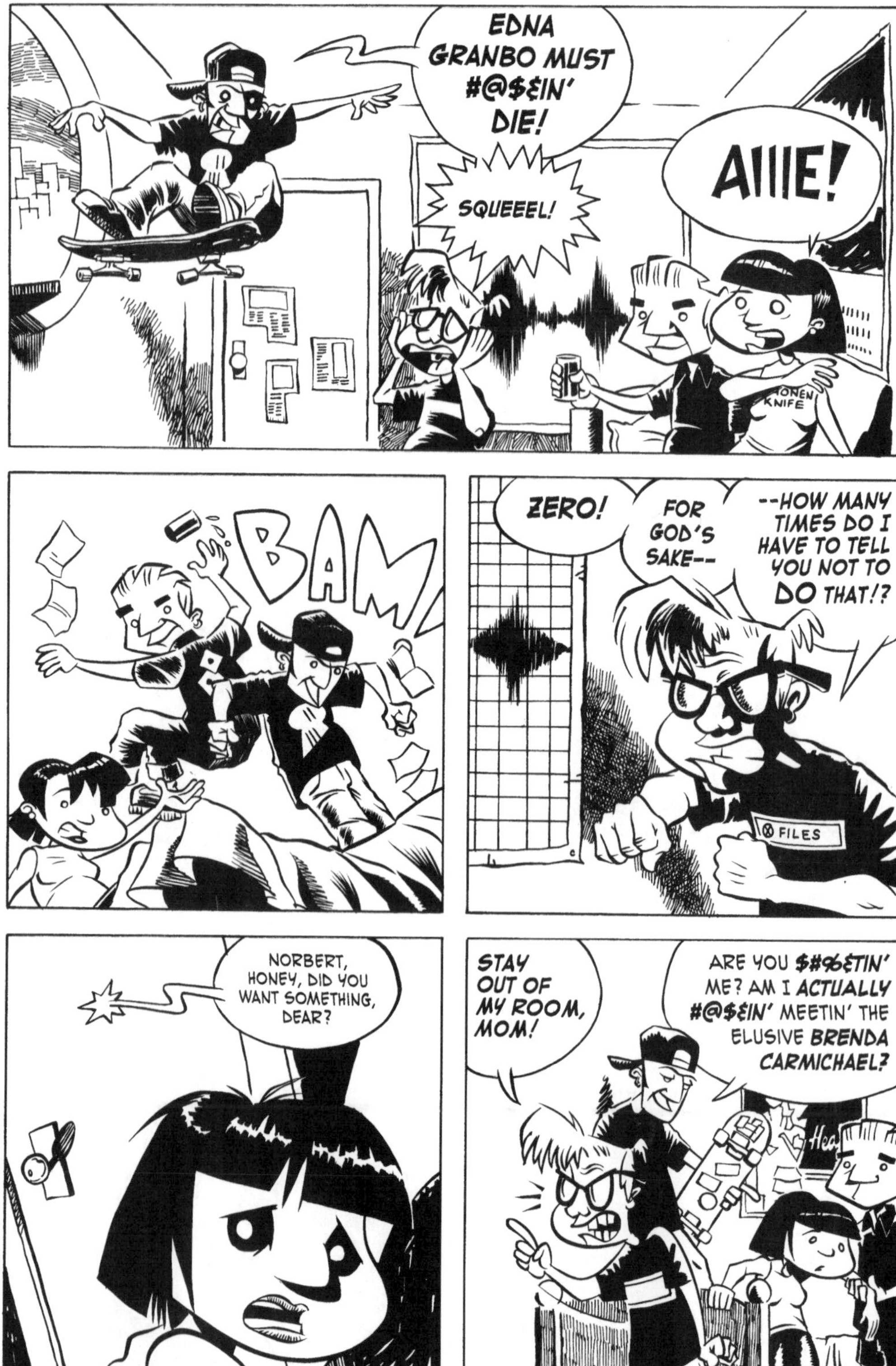
EDNA GRANBO MUST #@$&IN' DIE!
SQUEEEL!
AIIIE!
HONEN KNIFE
BAM!
ZERO!
FOR GOD'S SAKE--
--HOW MANY TIMES DO I HAVE TO TELL YOU NOT TO DO THAT!?
X FILES
NORBERT, HONEY, DID YOU WANT SOMETHING, DEAR?
STAY OUT OF MY ROOM, MOM!
ARE YOU $#%&TIN' ME? AM I ACTUALLY #@$&IN' MEETIN' THE ELUSIVE BRENDA CARMICHAEL?

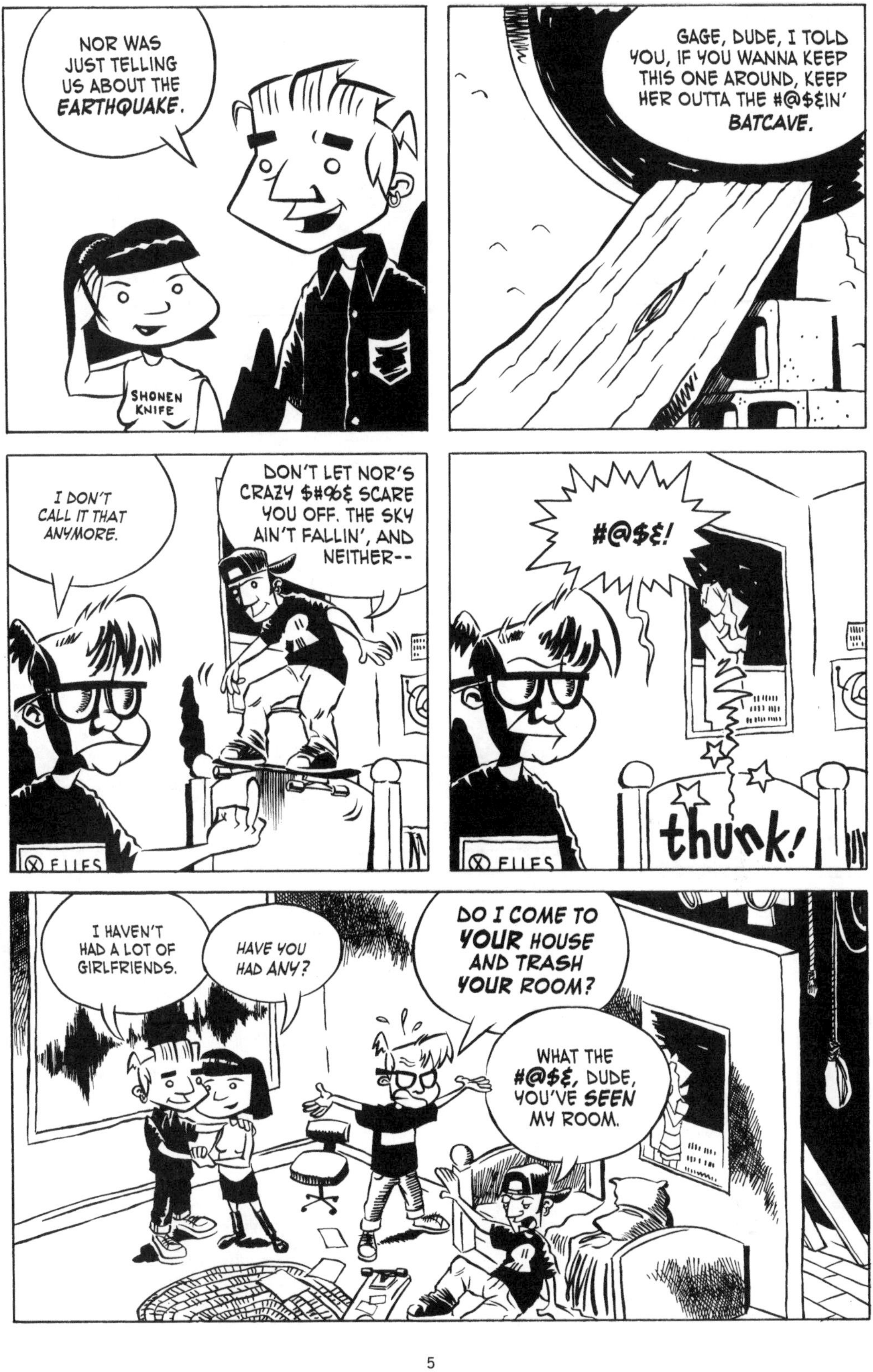
NOR WAS JUST TELLING US ABOUT THE EARTHQUAKE.
SHONEN KNIFE
GAGE, DUDE, I TOLD YOU, IF YOU WANNA KEEP THIS ONE AROUND, KEEP HER OUTTA THE #@$&IN' BATCAVE.
I DON'T CALL IT THAT ANYMORE.
DON'T LET NOR'S CRAZY $#%& SCARE YOU OFF. THE SKY AIN'T FALLIN', AND NEITHER--
X FILES
#@$&!
thunk!
X FILES
I HAVEN'T HAD A LOT OF GIRLFRIENDS.
HAVE YOU HAD ANY?
DO I COME TO YOUR HOUSE AND TRASH YOUR ROOM?
WHAT THE #@$&, DUDE, YOU'VE SEEN MY ROOM.

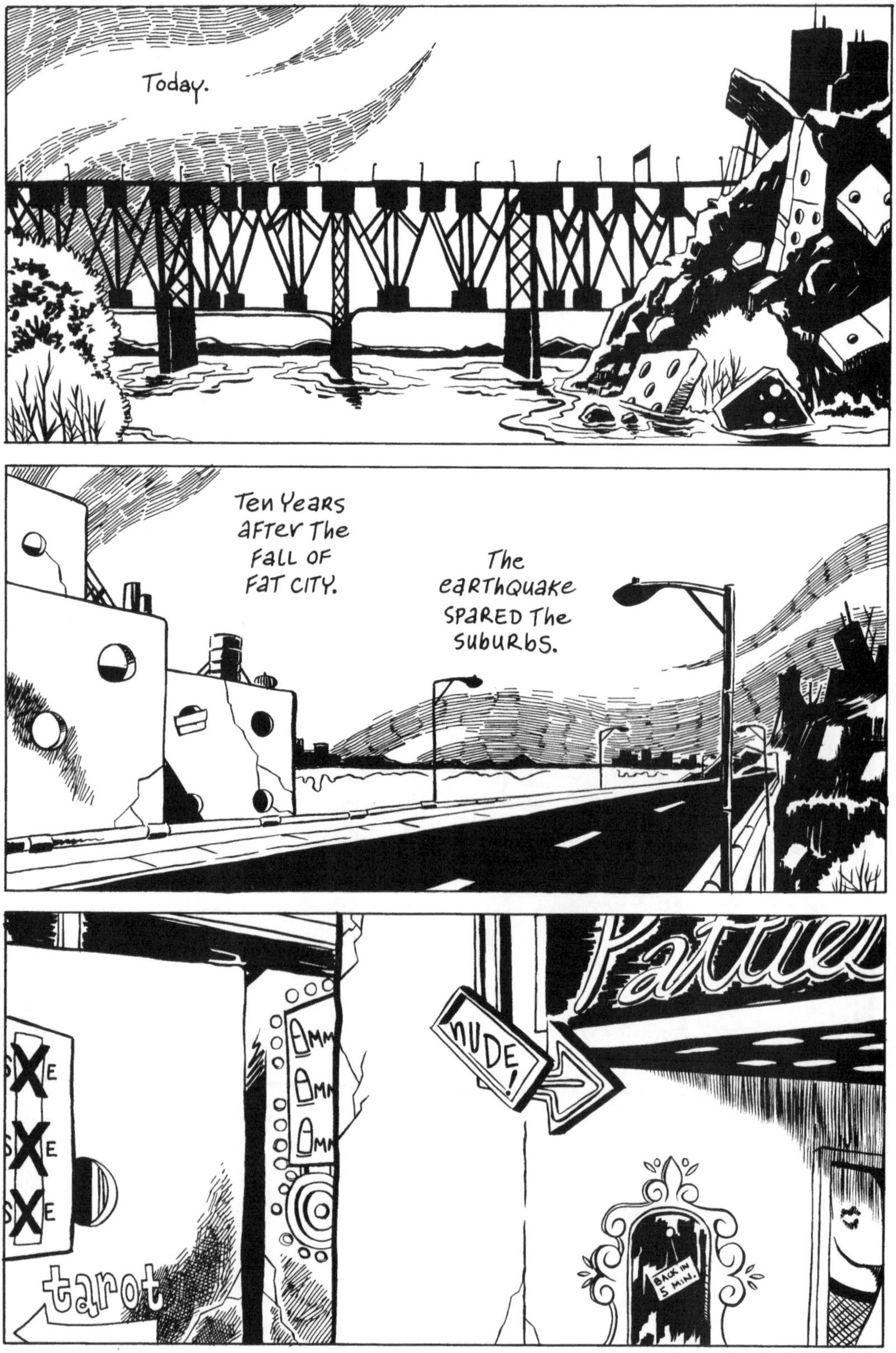
Today.
Ten Years After The Fall of Fat City.
The earthquake spared The suburbs.
NUDE!
tarot
BACK IN 5 MIN.

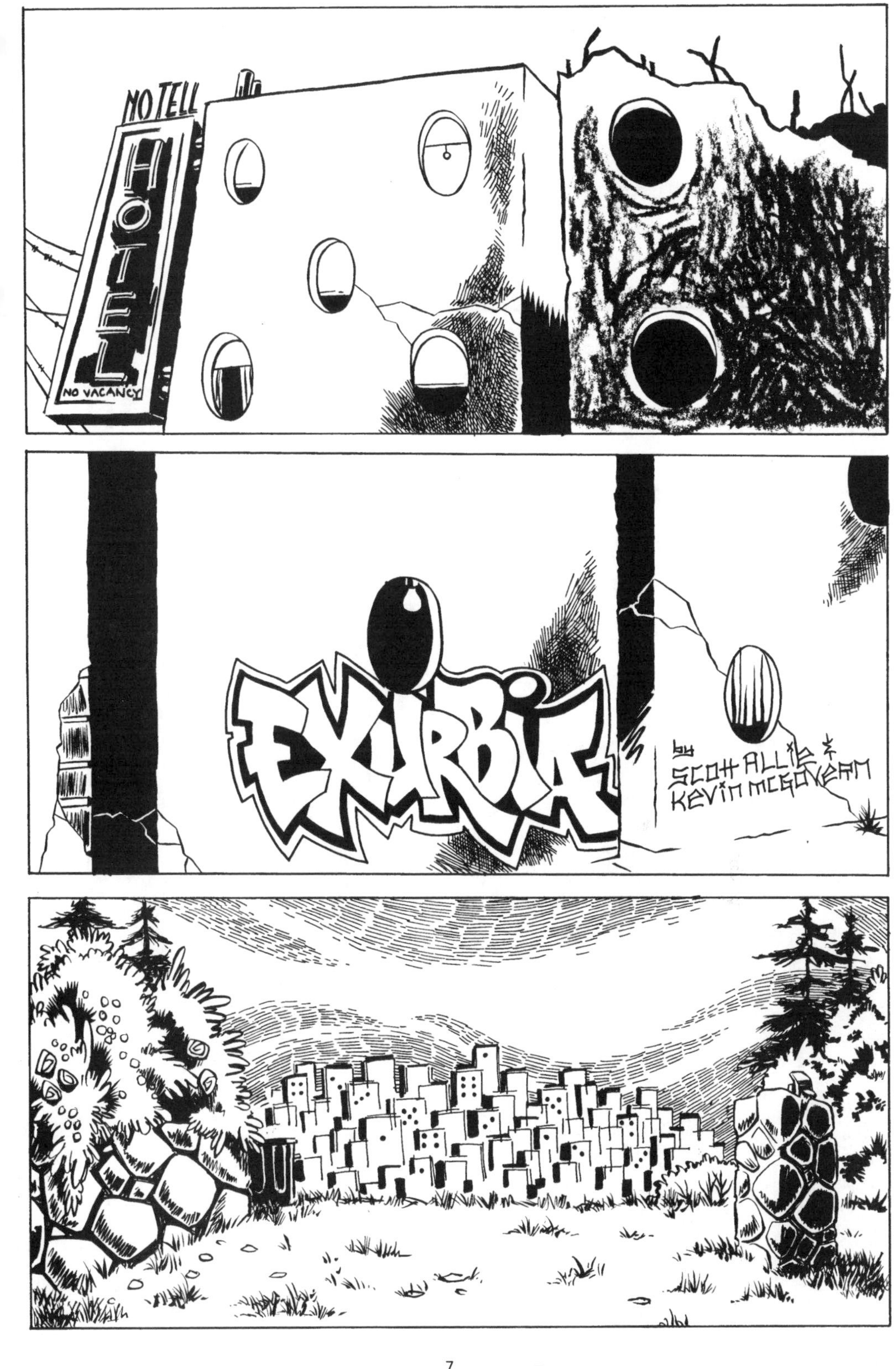
NO TELL
HOTEL
NO VACANCY
EXURBIA
by
Scott Allie &
Kevin McGovern

To find a comic shop in your area call the Comic Shop Locator Service toll-free at (888) 266-4226

First edition: October 2009 ▪ ISBN 978-1-59582-339-7

10 9 8 7 6 5 4 3 2 1 ▪ Printed in Canada

President and Publisher MIKE RICHARDSON Executive Vice President NEIL HANKERSON Chief Financial Officer TOM WEDDLE Vice President of Publishing RANDY STRADLEY Vice President of Business Development MICHAEL MARTENS Vice President of Marketing, Sales, and Licensing ANITA NELSON Vice President of Product Development DAVID SCROGGY Vice President of Information Technology DALE LAFOUNTAIN Director of Purchasing DARLENE VOGEL General Counsel KEN LIZZI Editorial Director DAVEY ESTRADA Senior Managing Editor SCOTT ALLIE Senior Books Editor CHRIS WARNER Executive Editor DIANA SCHUTZ Director of Design and Production CARY GRAZZINI Art Director LIA RIBACCHI Director of Scheduling CARA NIECE

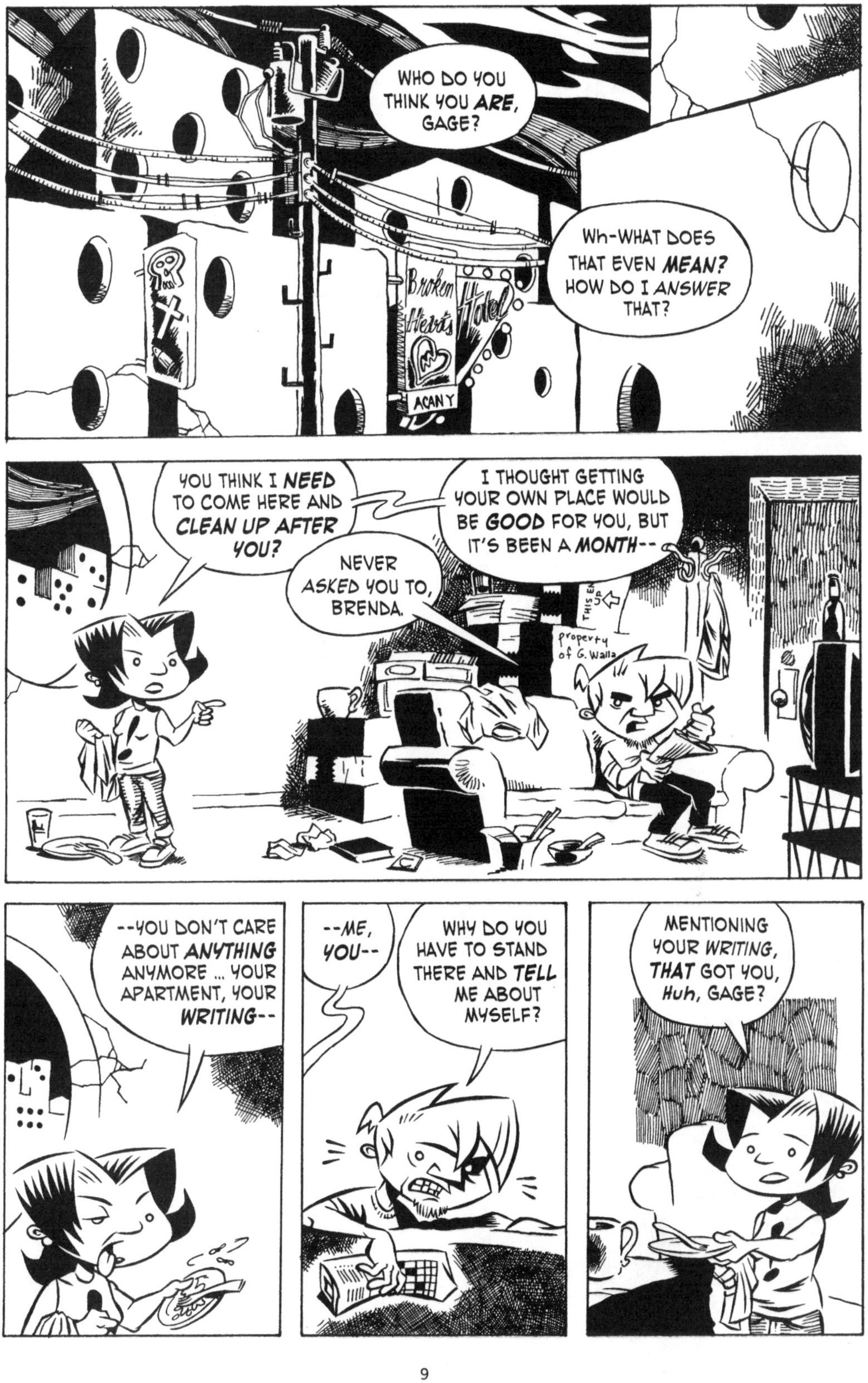
WHO DO YOU THINK YOU ARE, GAGE?
Wh-WHAT DOES THAT EVEN MEAN? HOW DO I ANSWER THAT?
Broken Hearts Hotel
ACANY
YOU THINK I NEED TO COME HERE AND CLEAN UP AFTER YOU?
NEVER ASKED YOU TO, BRENDA.
I THOUGHT GETTING YOUR OWN PLACE WOULD BE GOOD FOR YOU, BUT IT'S BEEN A MONTH--
THIS END UP
property of G. Walla
--YOU DON'T CARE ABOUT ANYTHING ANYMORE ... YOUR APARTMENT, YOUR WRITING--
--ME, YOU--
WHY DO YOU HAVE TO STAND THERE AND TELL ME ABOUT MYSELF?
MENTIONING YOUR WRITING, THAT GOT YOU, Huh, GAGE?

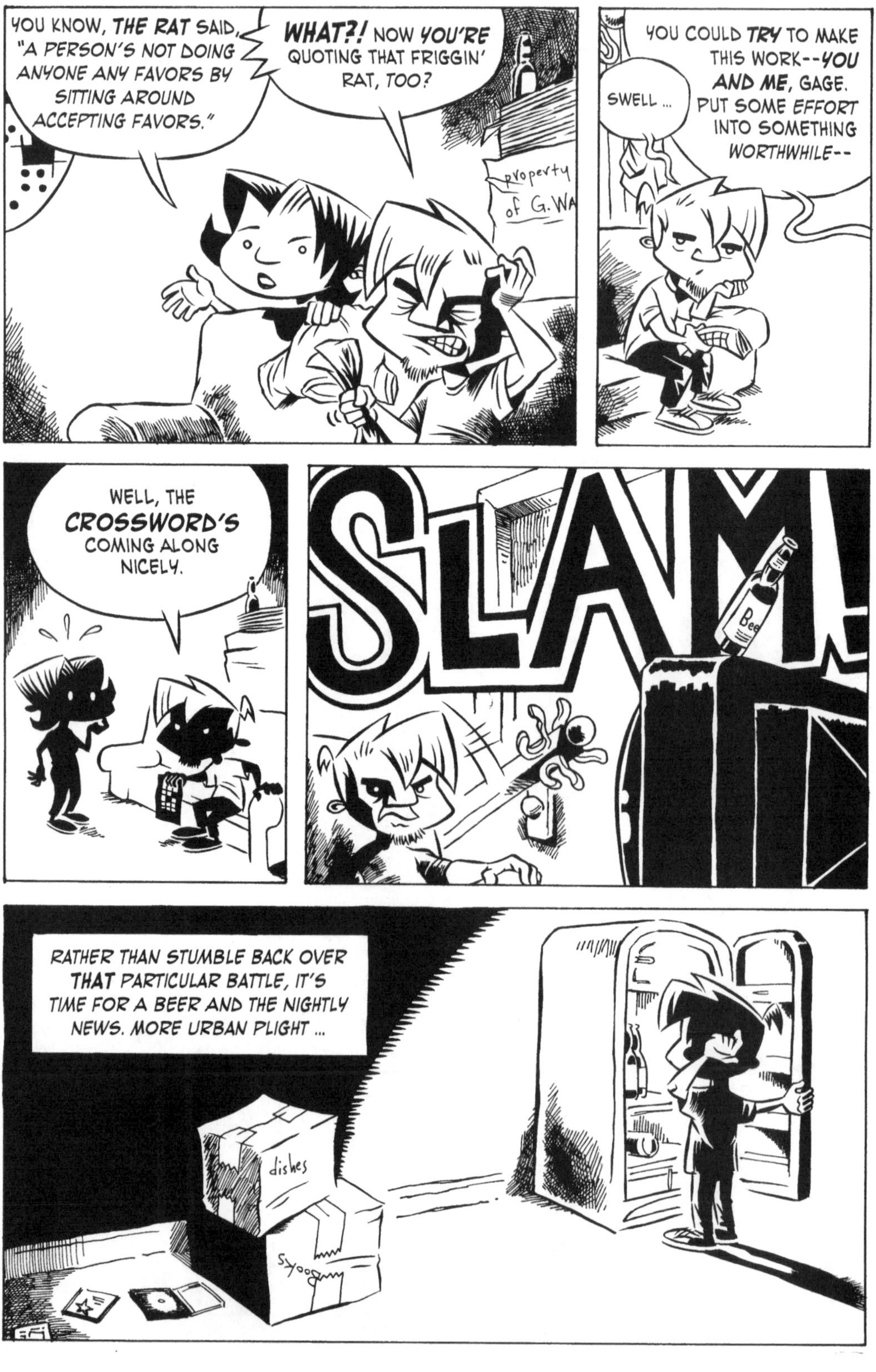
YOU KNOW, THE RAT SAID, "A PERSON'S NOT DOING ANYONE ANY FAVORS BY SITTING AROUND ACCEPTING FAVORS."
WHAT?! NOW YOU'RE QUOTING THAT FRIGGIN' RAT, TOO?
property of G. WA
YOU COULD TRY TO MAKE THIS WORK--YOU AND ME, GAGE. PUT SOME EFFORT INTO SOMETHING WORTHWHILE--
SWELL ...
WELL, THE CROSSWORD'S COMING ALONG NICELY.
SLAM!
Bee
RATHER THAN STUMBLE BACK OVER THAT PARTICULAR BATTLE, IT'S TIME FOR A BEER AND THE NIGHTLY NEWS. MORE URBAN PLIGHT ...
dishes
books

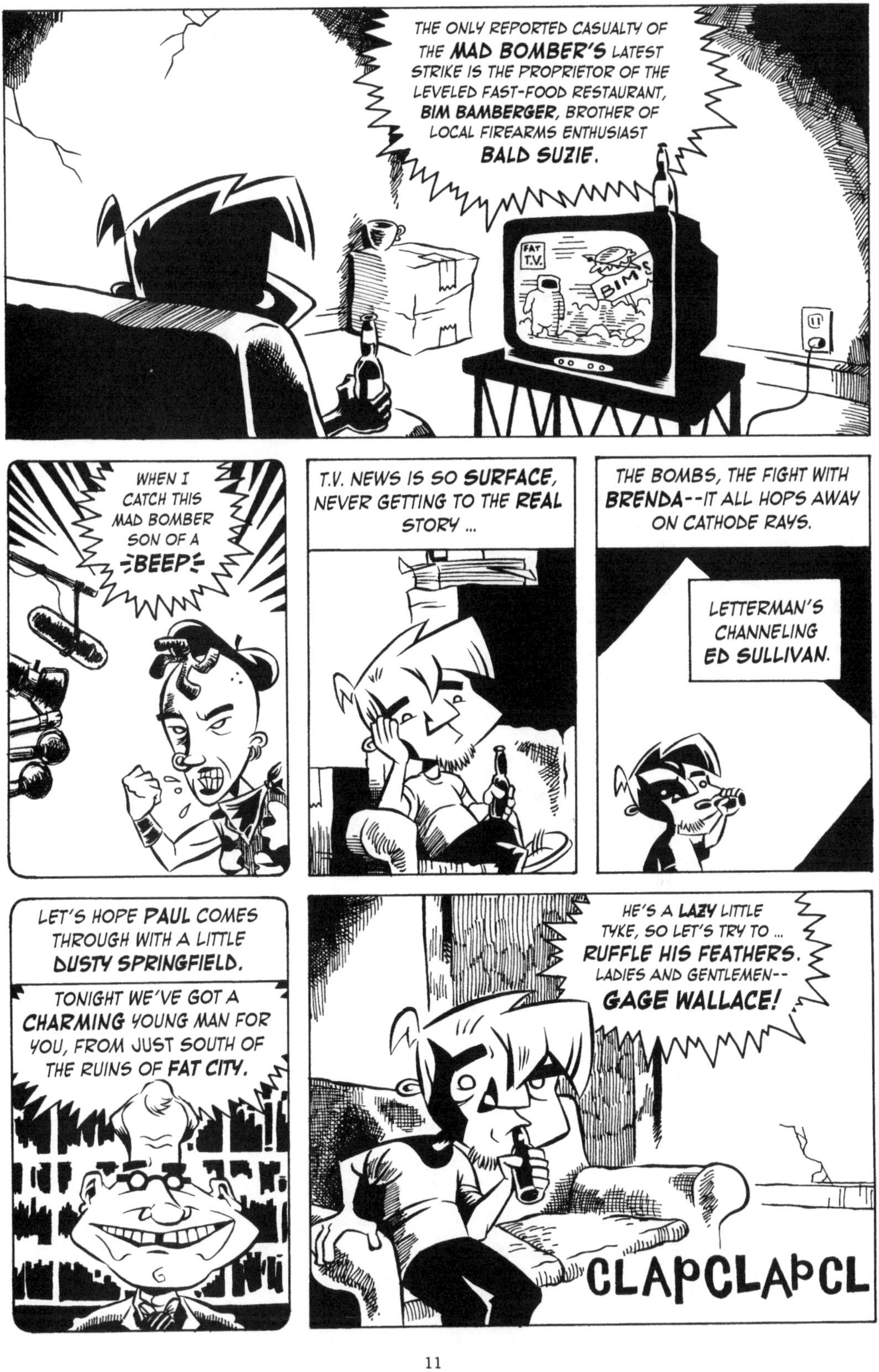
THE ONLY REPORTED CASUALTY OF THE MAD BOMBER'S LATEST STRIKE IS THE PROPRIETOR OF THE LEVELED FAST-FOOD RESTAURANT, BIM BAMBERGER, BROTHER OF LOCAL FIREARMS ENTHUSIAST BALD SUZIE.
FAT T.V.
BIM'S
WHEN I CATCH THIS MAD BOMBER SON OF A BEEP
T.V. NEWS IS SO SURFACE, NEVER GETTING TO THE REAL STORY ...
THE BOMBS, THE FIGHT WITH BRENDA--IT ALL HOPS AWAY ON CATHODE RAYS.
LETTERMAN'S CHANNELING ED SULLIVAN.
LET'S HOPE PAUL COMES THROUGH WITH A LITTLE DUSTY SPRINGFIELD.
TONIGHT WE'VE GOT A CHARMING YOUNG MAN FOR YOU, FROM JUST SOUTH OF THE RUINS OF FAT CITY.
HE'S A LAZY LITTLE TYKE, SO LET'S TRY TO ... RUFFLE HIS FEATHERS. LADIES AND GENTLEMEN-- GAGE WALLACE!
CLAPCLAPCL

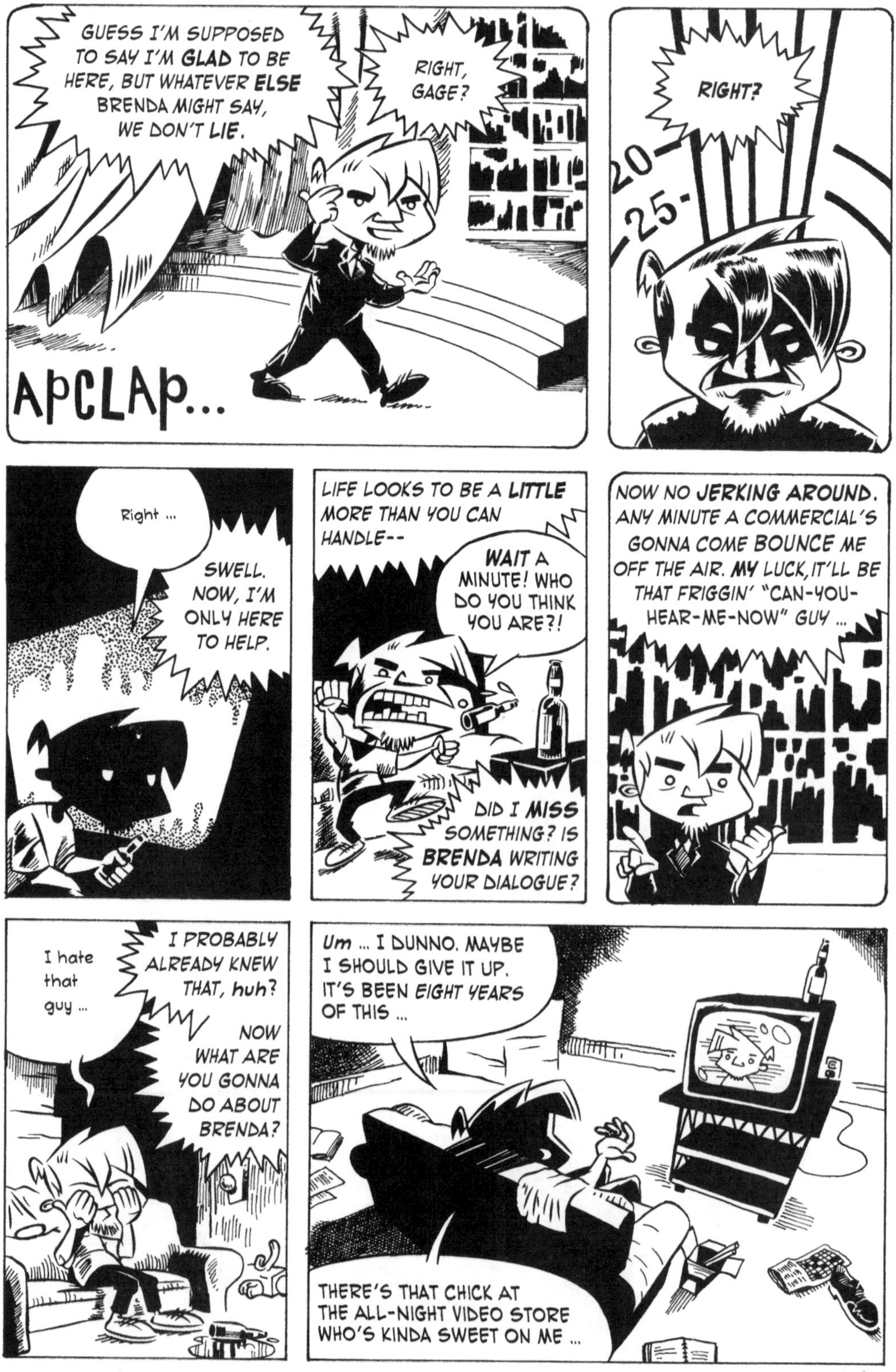
GUESS I'M SUPPOSED TO SAY I'M GLAD TO BE HERE, BUT WHATEVER ELSE BRENDA MIGHT SAY, WE DON'T LIE.
RIGHT, GAGE?
APCLAP...
RIGHT?
20-
25-
Right ...
SWELL. NOW, I'M ONLY HERE TO HELP.
LIFE LOOKS TO BE A LITTLE MORE THAN YOU CAN HANDLE--
WAIT A MINUTE! WHO DO YOU THINK YOU ARE?!
DID I MISS SOMETHING? IS BRENDA WRITING YOUR DIALOGUE?
NOW NO JERKING AROUND. ANY MINUTE A COMMERCIAL'S GONNA COME BOUNCE ME OFF THE AIR. MY LUCK, IT'LL BE THAT FRIGGIN' "CAN-YOU-HEAR-ME-NOW" GUY ...
I hate that guy ...
I PROBABLY ALREADY KNEW THAT, huh?
NOW WHAT ARE YOU GONNA DO ABOUT BRENDA?
Um ... I DUNNO. MAYBE I SHOULD GIVE IT UP. IT'S BEEN EIGHT YEARS OF THIS ...
THERE'S THAT CHICK AT THE ALL-NIGHT VIDEO STORE WHO'S KINDA SWEET ON ME ...

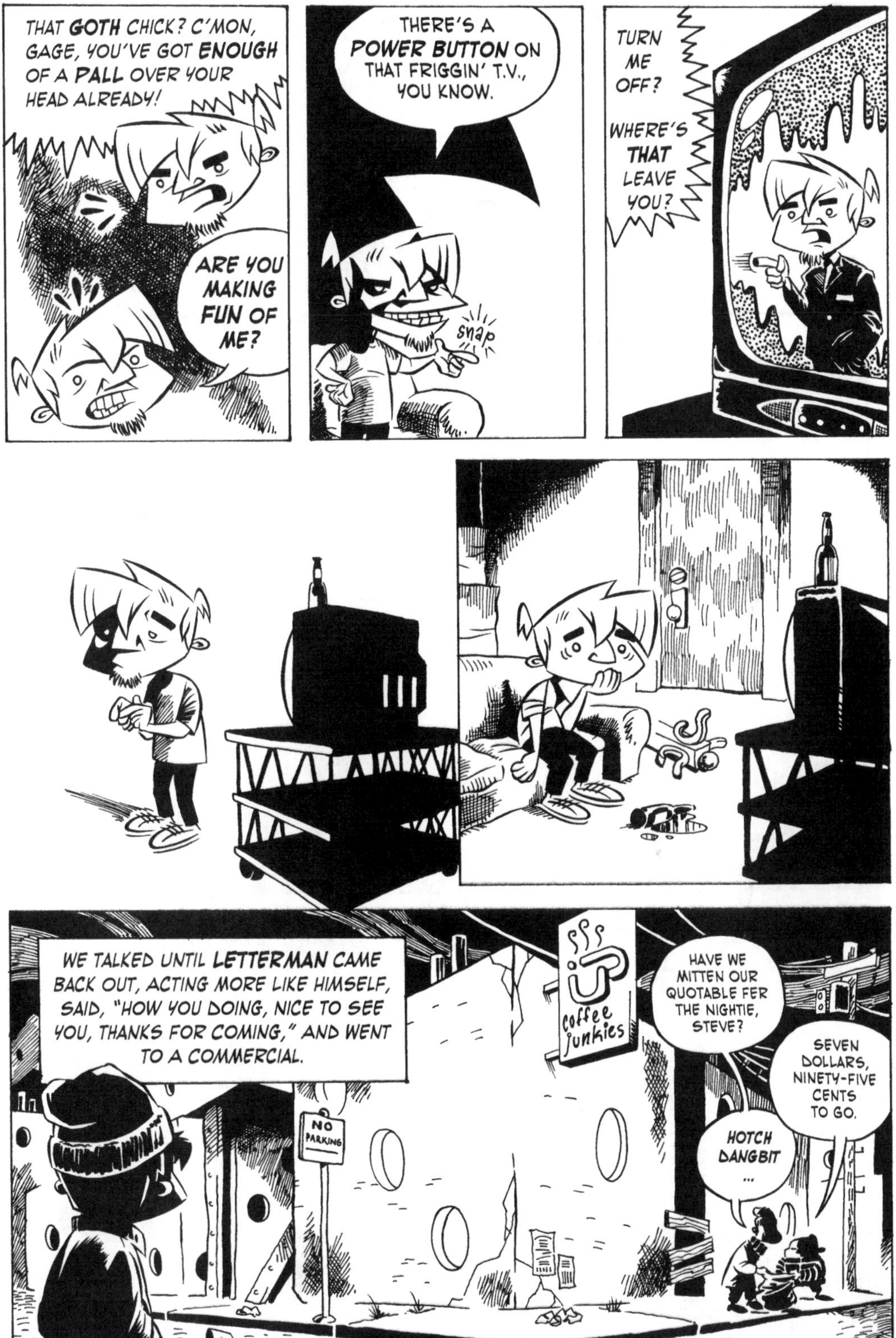
THAT GOTH CHICK? C'MON, GAGE, YOU'VE GOT ENOUGH OF A PALL OVER YOUR HEAD ALREADY!
ARE YOU MAKING FUN OF ME?
THERE'S A POWER BUTTON ON THAT FRIGGIN' T.V., YOU KNOW.
snap
TURN ME OFF?
WHERE'S THAT LEAVE YOU?
WE TALKED UNTIL LETTERMAN CAME BACK OUT, ACTING MORE LIKE HIMSELF, SAID, "HOW YOU DOING, NICE TO SEE YOU, THANKS FOR COMING," AND WENT TO A COMMERCIAL.
coffee junkies
NO PARKING
HAVE WE MITTEN OUR QUOTABLE FER THE NIGHTIE, STEVE?
SEVEN DOLLARS, NINETY-FIVE CENTS TO GO.
HOTCH DANGBIT ...

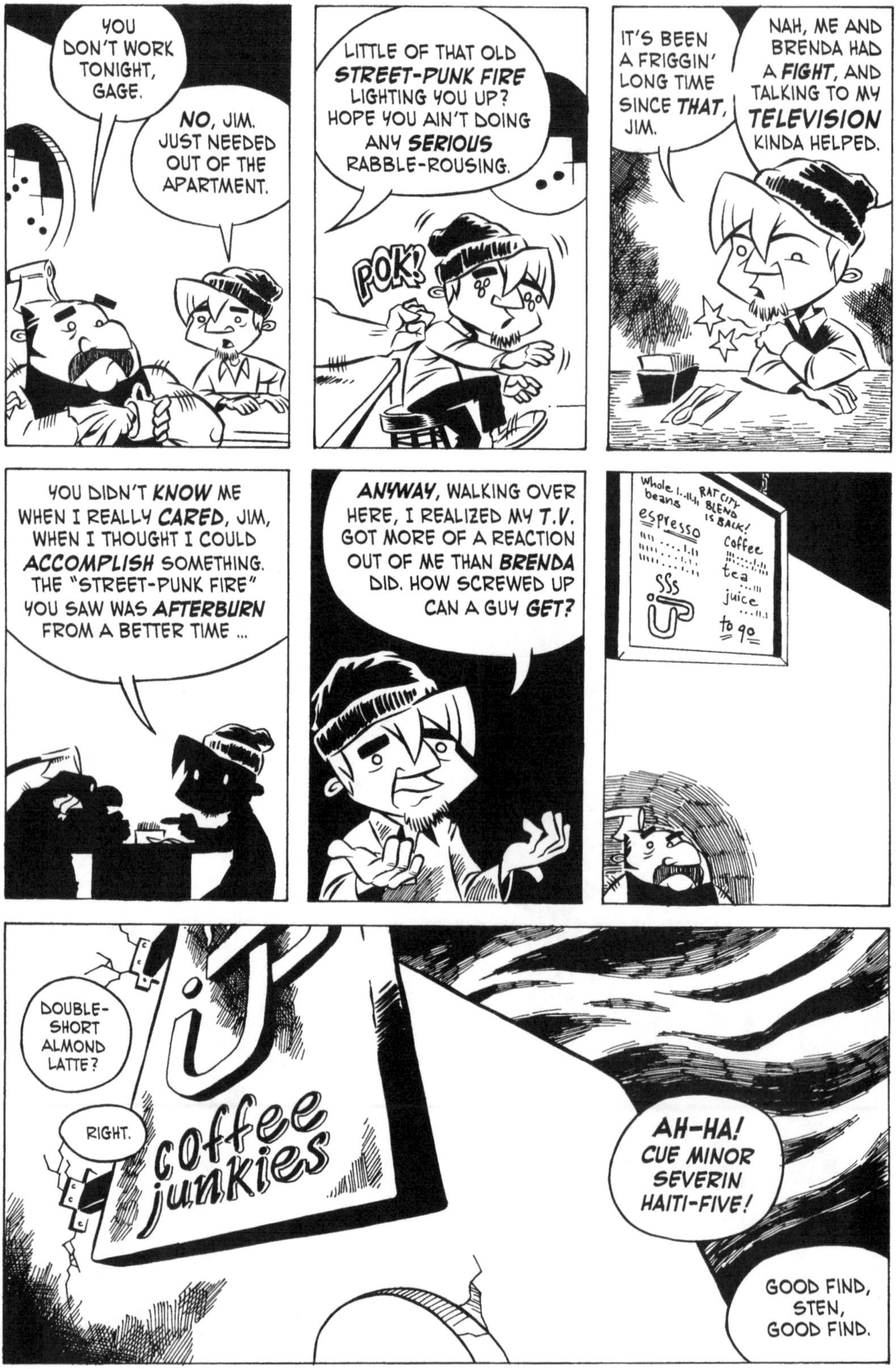
YOU DON'T WORK TONIGHT, GAGE.
NO, JIM. JUST NEEDED OUT OF THE APARTMENT.
LITTLE OF THAT OLD STREET-PUNK FIRE LIGHTING YOU UP? HOPE YOU AIN'T DOING ANY SERIOUS RABBLE-ROUSING.
POK!
IT'S BEEN A FRIGGIN' LONG TIME SINCE THAT, JIM.
NAH, ME AND BRENDA HAD A FIGHT, AND TALKING TO MY TELEVISION KINDA HELPED.
YOU DIDN'T KNOW ME WHEN I REALLY CARED, JIM, WHEN I THOUGHT I COULD ACCOMPLISH SOMETHING. THE "STREET-PUNK FIRE" YOU SAW WAS AFTERBURN FROM A BETTER TIME ...
ANYWAY, WALKING OVER HERE, I REALIZED MY T.V. GOT MORE OF A REACTION OUT OF ME THAN BRENDA DID. HOW SCREWED UP CAN A GUY GET?
Whole beans
RAT CITY BLEND IS BACK!
espresso
coffee
tea
juice
to go
DOUBLE-SHORT ALMOND LATTE?
RIGHT.
coffee junkies
AH-HA! CUE MINOR SEVERIN HAITI-FIVE!
GOOD FIND, STEN, GOOD FIND.

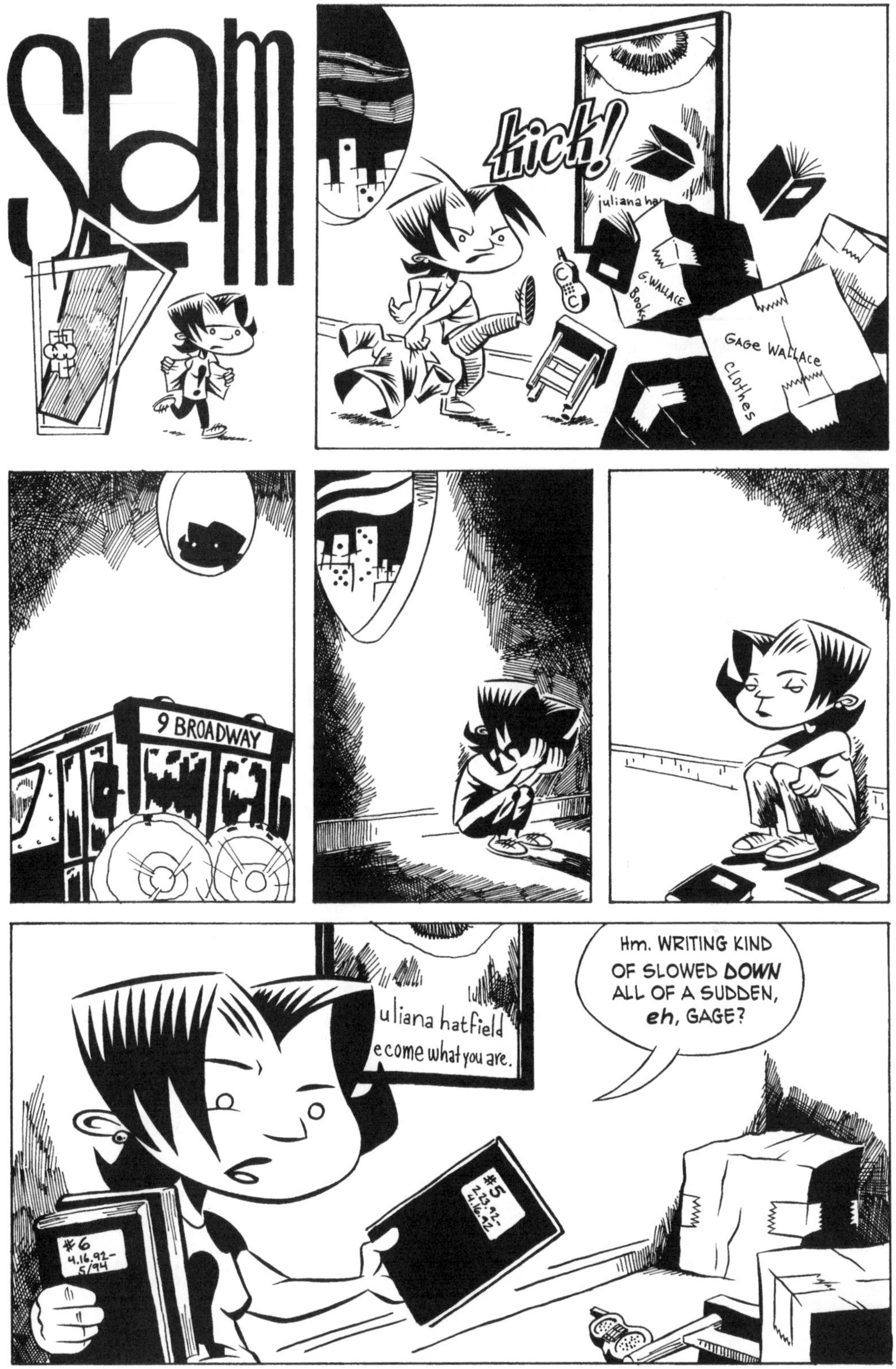
slam
kick!
juliana ha
G. WALLACE Books
GAGE WALLACE Clothes
9 BROADWAY
uliana hatfield
ecome what you are.
Hm. WRITING KIND OF SLOWED DOWN ALL OF A SUDDEN, eh, GAGE?
#6 4.16.92– 5/94
#5 2.23.92– 4.16.92

LET'S SEE ...

OKAY!

"... HITTING SEVENTEEN AND GETTING A GIRLFRIEND, SOMETHING HAS TURNED AROUND FOR ME. THIS LAST YEAR ..."

That's so *annoying*, Gage. Never cross out stuff in your *diary*.

"...HAVE TO BE CAREFUL, BUT I CAN'T HELP BUT PIN HIGH HOPES ON THIS **BRENDA CARMICHAEL**."

Oh, GAGE ...

"CONTINUED FROM JOURNAL NUMBER FIVE."

So *this'd* be before we met ...

"AFTER I BEGGED HIM FOR THREE DAYS, DAD **FINALLY** EXPLAINED TAXES, COMPLAINING THAT THEY COST HIM MORE THAN FOOD AND CLOTHES. BUT **WE'RE** MIDDLE CLASS. WHAT ABOUT ZERO'S FAMILY? NOR'S MOM?"

WHOOPS.

GAGE ... YOU WERE ONLY SIXTEEN ...

TAKE YER AXES TO TAXES

1040

TAX FORM

I CATS DON'T NEED TO BE CRIPPLED BY FEDERAL TAXES. MEET US AT THE CORNER OF FRONT AND MELVIN APRIL 22nd, 8PM
contact Gage Wallace at 291

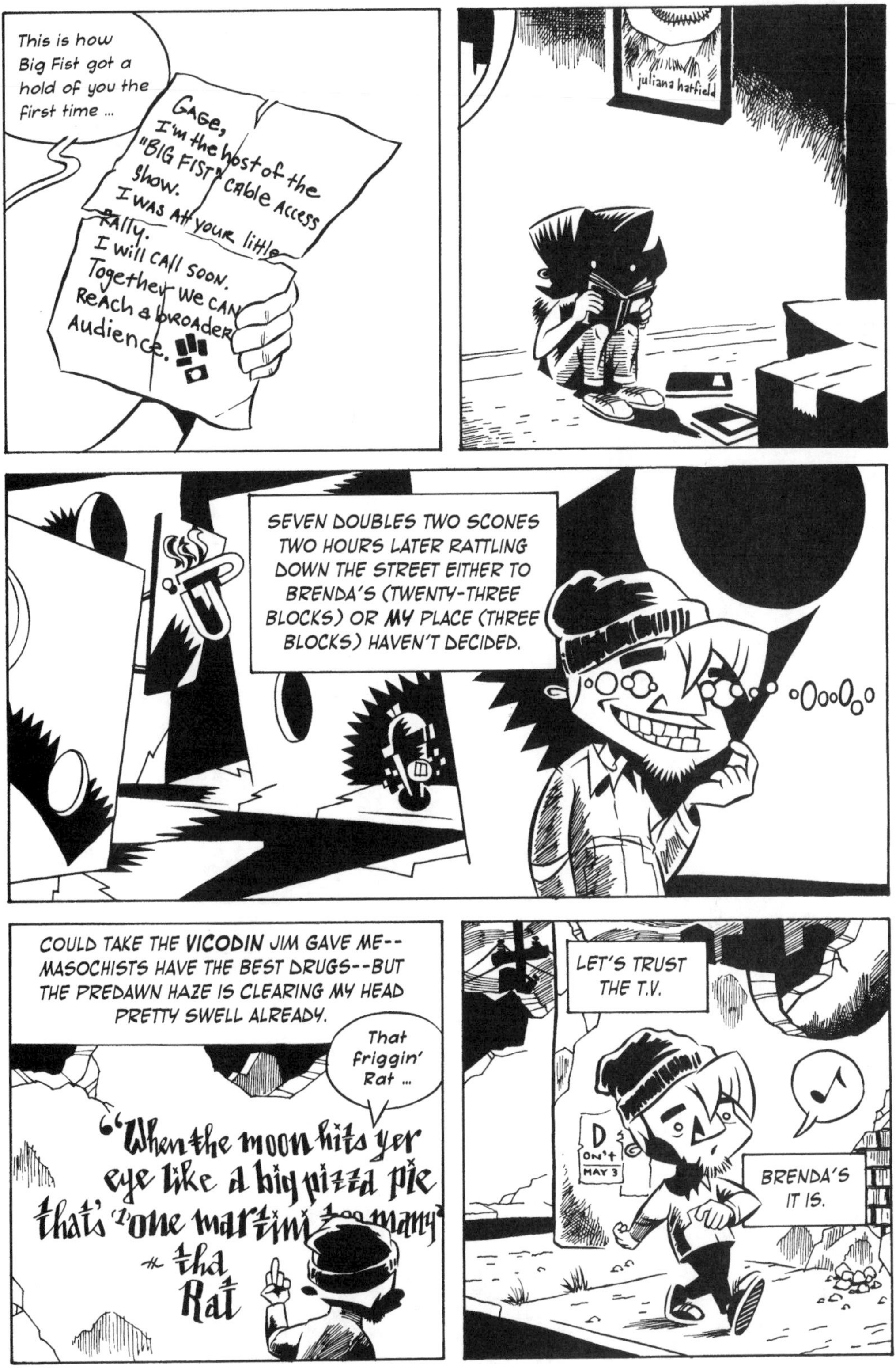
This is how Big Fist got a hold of you the first time ...
Gage, I'm the host of the "BIG FIST" cable access show. I was at your little rally. I will call soon. Together we can reach a broader audience.
juliana hatfield
SEVEN DOUBLES TWO SCONES TWO HOURS LATER RATTLING DOWN THE STREET EITHER TO BRENDA'S (TWENTY-THREE BLOCKS) OR MY PLACE (THREE BLOCKS) HAVEN'T DECIDED.
oOooOoo
COULD TAKE THE VICODIN JIM GAVE ME-- MASOCHISTS HAVE THE BEST DRUGS--BUT THE PREDAWN HAZE IS CLEARING MY HEAD PRETTY SWELL ALREADY.
That friggin' Rat ...
"When the moon hits yer eye like a big pizza pie that's 'one martini too many'" -- tha Rat
LET'S TRUST THE T.V.
D ON'T MAY 3
BRENDA'S IT IS.

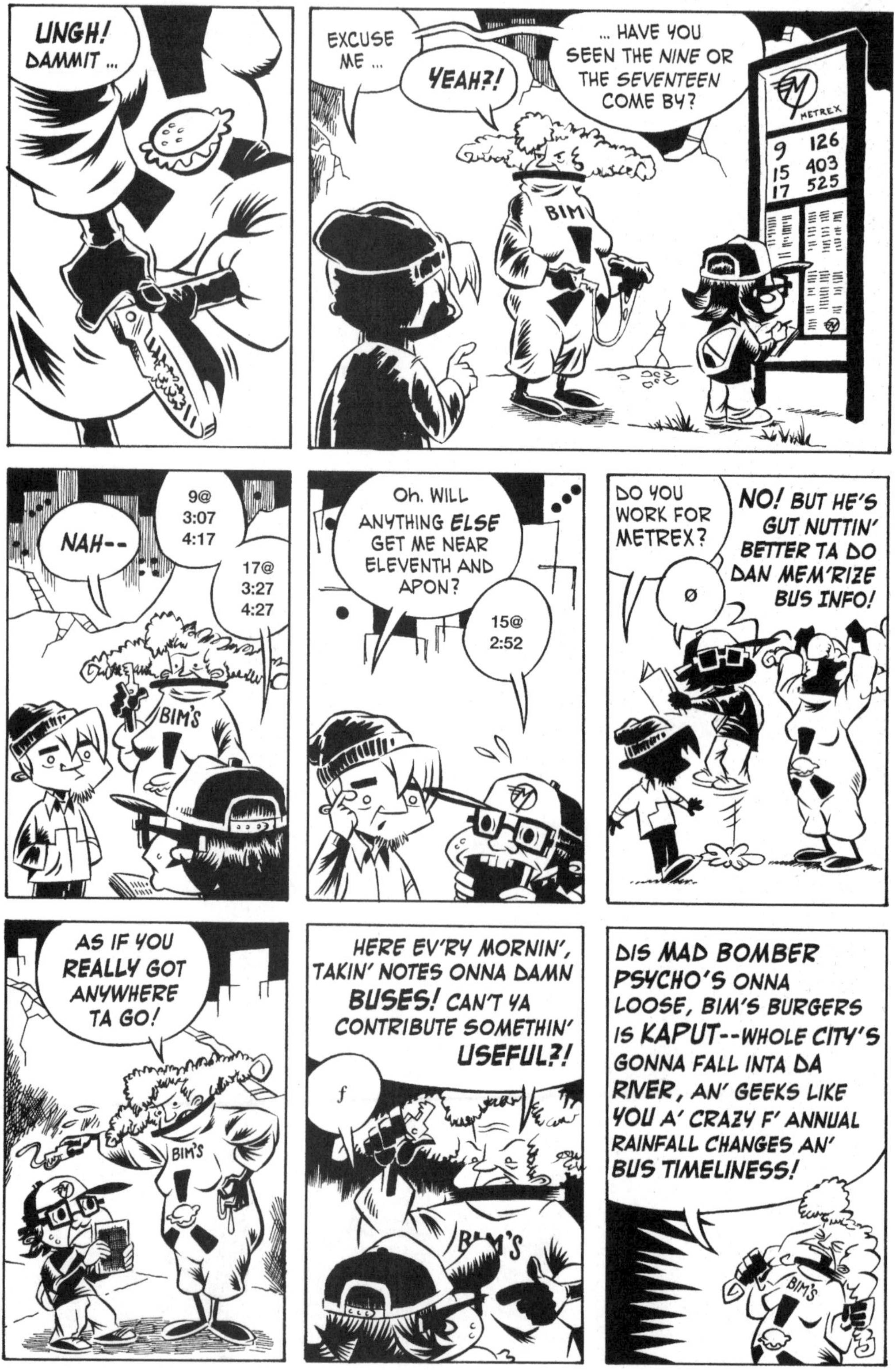
UNGH! DAMMIT ...
EXCUSE ME ...
YEAH?!
... HAVE YOU SEEN THE NINE OR THE SEVENTEEN COME BY?
METREX
9 126
15 403
17 525
BIM
NAH--
9@ 3:07 4:17
17@ 3:27 4:27
BIM'S
Oh. WILL ANYTHING ELSE GET ME NEAR ELEVENTH AND APON?
15@ 2:52
DO YOU WORK FOR METREX?
NO! BUT HE'S GUT NUTTIN' BETTER TA DO DAN MEM'RIZE BUS INFO!
ø
AS IF YOU REALLY GOT ANYWHERE TA GO!
BIM'S
HERE EV'RY MORNIN', TAKIN' NOTES ONNA DAMN BUSES! CAN'T YA CONTRIBUTE SOMETHIN' USEFUL?!
f
BIM'S
DIS MAD BOMBER PSYCHO'S ONNA LOOSE, BIM'S BURGERS IS KAPUT--WHOLE CITY'S GONNA FALL INTA DA RIVER, AN' GEEKS LIKE YOU A' CRAZY F' ANNUAL RAINFALL CHANGES AN' BUS TIMELINESS!
BIM'S

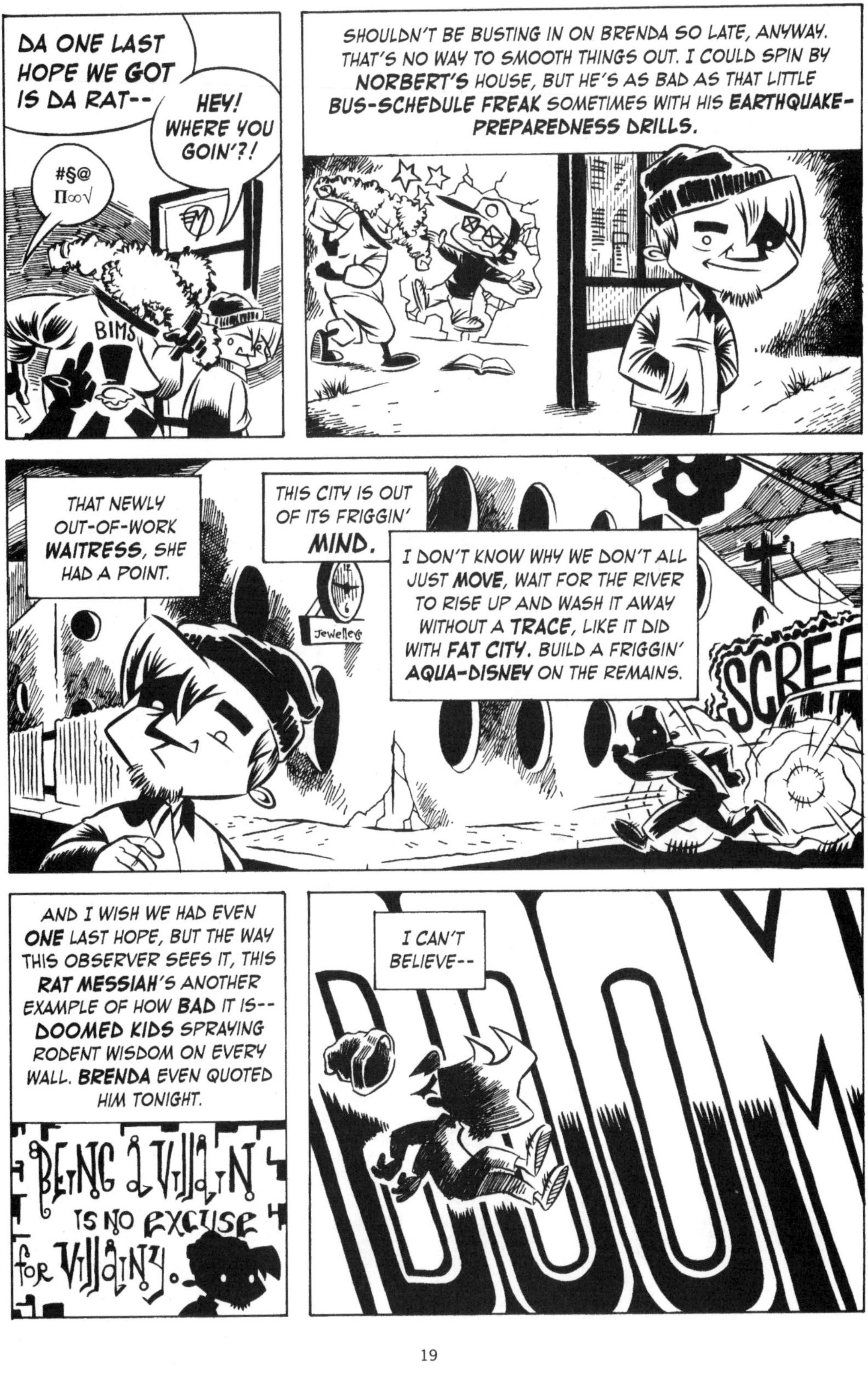
DA ONE LAST HOPE WE GOT IS DA RAT--
#§@ Π∞√
HEY! WHERE YOU GOIN'?!
BIMS
SHOULDN'T BE BUSTING IN ON BRENDA SO LATE, ANYWAY. THAT'S NO WAY TO SMOOTH THINGS OUT. I COULD SPIN BY NORBERT'S HOUSE, BUT HE'S AS BAD AS THAT LITTLE BUS-SCHEDULE FREAK SOMETIMES WITH HIS EARTHQUAKE-PREPAREDNESS DRILLS.
THAT NEWLY OUT-OF-WORK WAITRESS, SHE HAD A POINT.
THIS CITY IS OUT OF ITS FRIGGIN' MIND.
I DON'T KNOW WHY WE DON'T ALL JUST MOVE, WAIT FOR THE RIVER TO RISE UP AND WASH IT AWAY WITHOUT A TRACE, LIKE IT DID WITH FAT CITY. BUILD A FRIGGIN' AQUA-DISNEY ON THE REMAINS.
Jewellers
SCREE
AND I WISH WE HAD EVEN ONE LAST HOPE, BUT THE WAY THIS OBSERVER SEES IT, THIS RAT MESSIAH'S ANOTHER EXAMPLE OF HOW BAD IT IS-- DOOMED KIDS SPRAYING RODENT WISDOM ON EVERY WALL. BRENDA EVEN QUOTED HIM TONIGHT.
BEING A VILLAIN IS NO EXCUSE FOR VILLAINY.
I CAN'T BELIEVE--
BOOOM

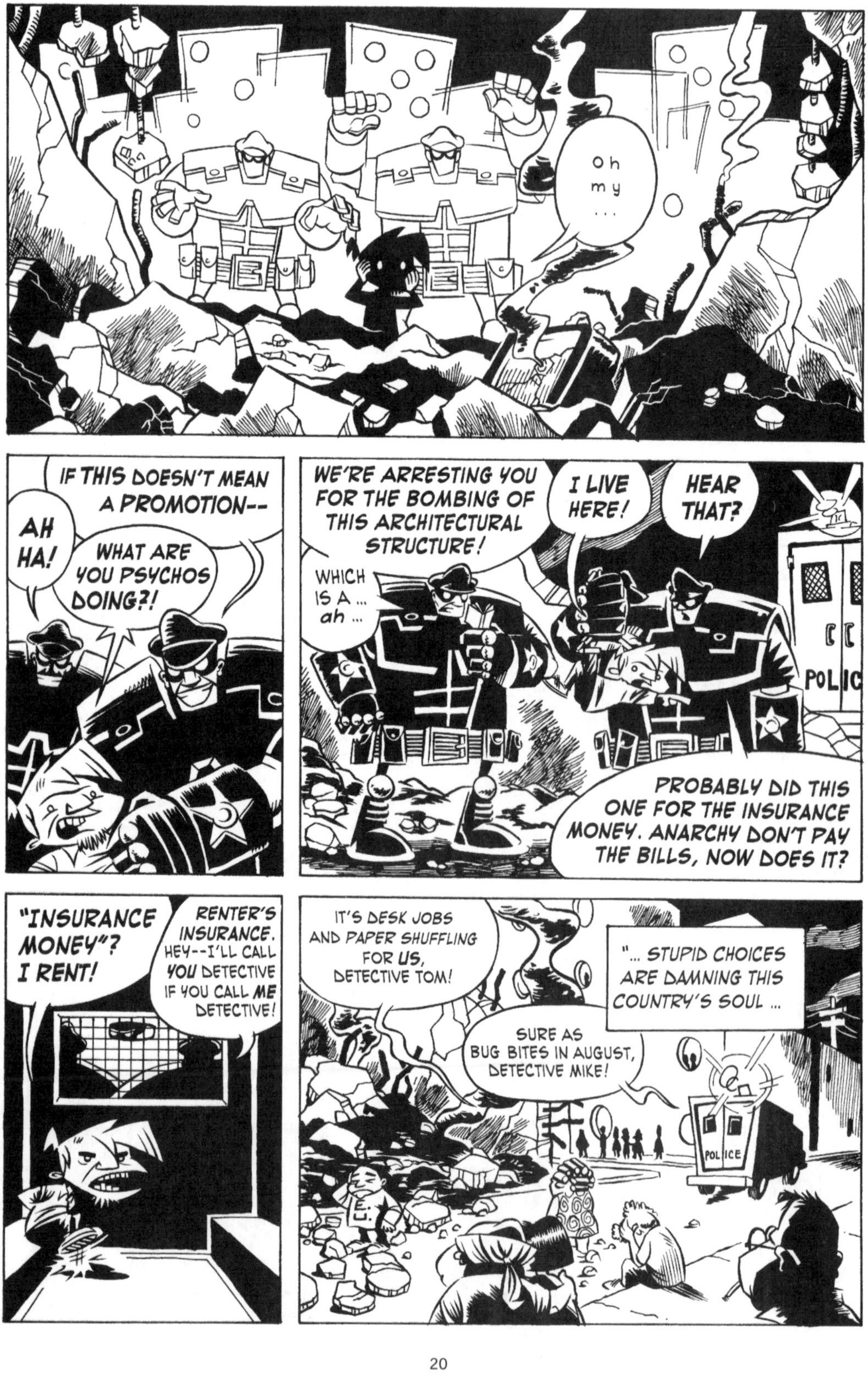
Oh my ...
IF THIS DOESN'T MEAN A PROMOTION--
AH HA!
WHAT ARE YOU PSYCHOS DOING?!
WE'RE ARRESTING YOU FOR THE BOMBING OF THIS ARCHITECTURAL STRUCTURE!
WHICH IS A ... ah ...
I LIVE HERE!
HEAR THAT?
POLIC
PROBABLY DID THIS ONE FOR THE INSURANCE MONEY. ANARCHY DON'T PAY THE BILLS, NOW DOES IT?
"INSURANCE MONEY"? I RENT!
RENTER'S INSURANCE. HEY--I'LL CALL YOU DETECTIVE IF YOU CALL ME DETECTIVE!
IT'S DESK JOBS AND PAPER SHUFFLING FOR US, DETECTIVE TOM!
"... STUPID CHOICES ARE DAMNING THIS COUNTRY'S SOUL ...
SURE AS BUG BITES IN AUGUST, DETECTIVE MIKE!
POLICE

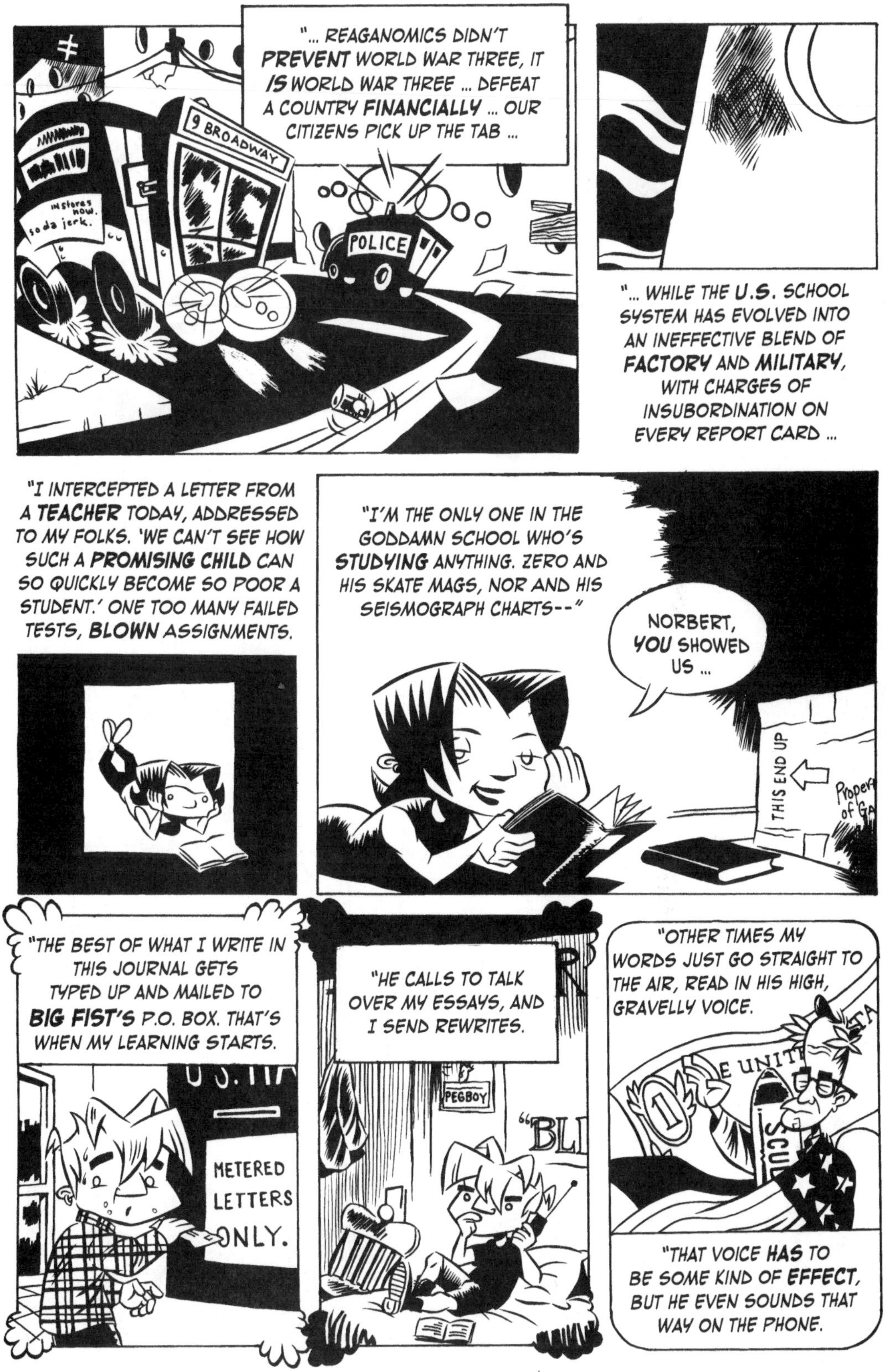
"... REAGANOMICS DIDN'T PREVENT WORLD WAR THREE, IT IS WORLD WAR THREE ... DEFEAT A COUNTRY FINANCIALLY ... OUR CITIZENS PICK UP THE TAB ...
9 BROADWAY
soda jerk.
POLICE
"... WHILE THE U.S. SCHOOL SYSTEM HAS EVOLVED INTO AN INEFFECTIVE BLEND OF FACTORY AND MILITARY, WITH CHARGES OF INSUBORDINATION ON EVERY REPORT CARD ...
"I INTERCEPTED A LETTER FROM A TEACHER TODAY, ADDRESSED TO MY FOLKS. 'WE CAN'T SEE HOW SUCH A PROMISING CHILD CAN SO QUICKLY BECOME SO POOR A STUDENT.' ONE TOO MANY FAILED TESTS, BLOWN ASSIGNMENTS.
"I'M THE ONLY ONE IN THE GODDAMN SCHOOL WHO'S STUDYING ANYTHING. ZERO AND HIS SKATE MAGS, NOR AND HIS SEISMOGRAPH CHARTS--"
NORBERT, YOU SHOWED US ...
THIS END UP
"THE BEST OF WHAT I WRITE IN THIS JOURNAL GETS TYPED UP AND MAILED TO BIG FIST'S P.O. BOX. THAT'S WHEN MY LEARNING STARTS.
METERED LETTERS ONLY.
"HE CALLS TO TALK OVER MY ESSAYS, AND I SEND REWRITES.
PEGBOY
"OTHER TIMES MY WORDS JUST GO STRAIGHT TO THE AIR, READ IN HIS HIGH, GRAVELLY VOICE.
"THAT VOICE HAS TO BE SOME KIND OF EFFECT, BUT HE EVEN SOUNDS THAT WAY ON THE PHONE.

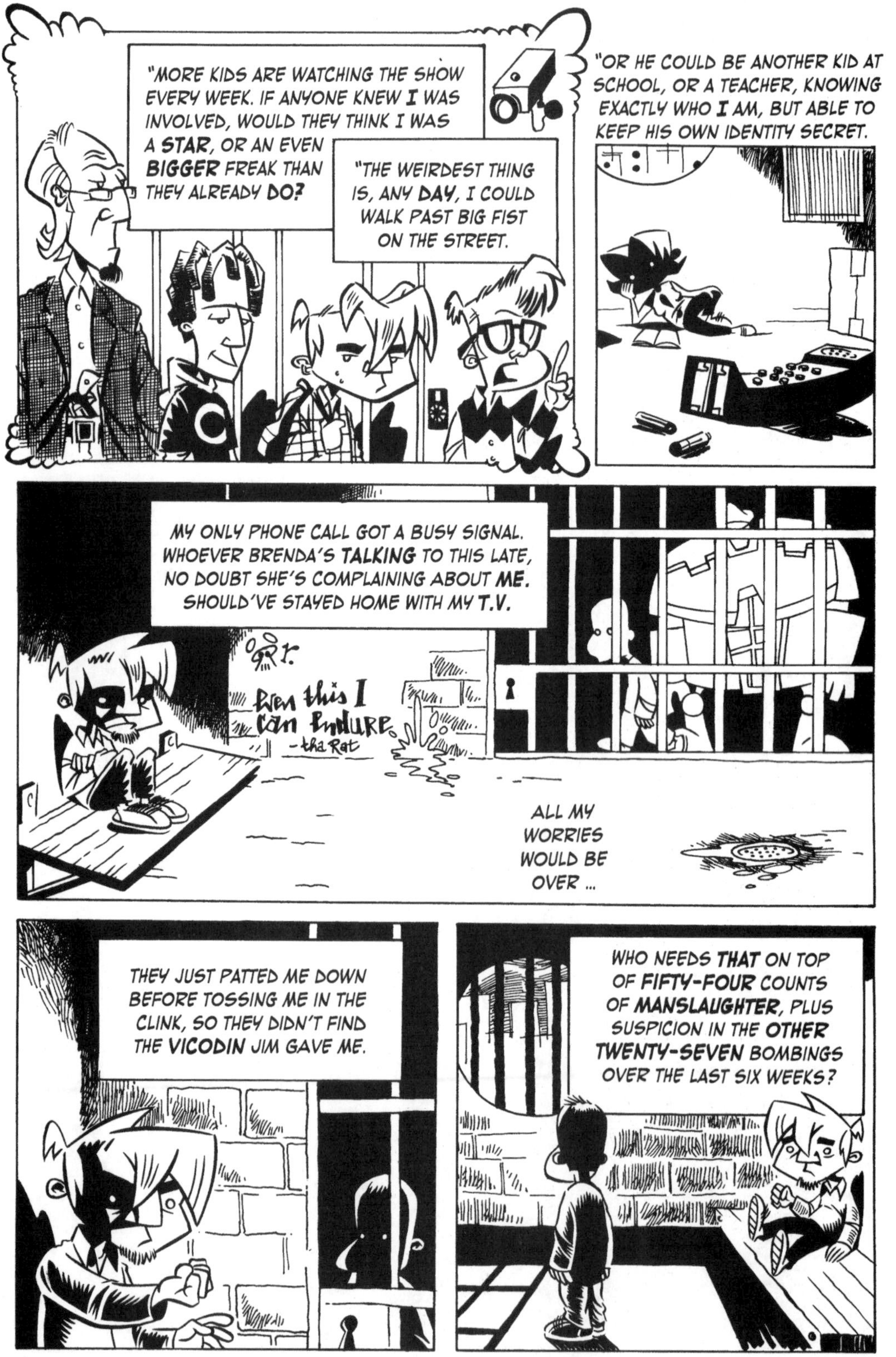
"MORE KIDS ARE WATCHING THE SHOW EVERY WEEK. IF ANYONE KNEW I WAS INVOLVED, WOULD THEY THINK I WAS A STAR, OR AN EVEN BIGGER FREAK THAN THEY ALREADY DO?
"THE WEIRDEST THING IS, ANY DAY, I COULD WALK PAST BIG FIST ON THE STREET.
"OR HE COULD BE ANOTHER KID AT SCHOOL, OR A TEACHER, KNOWING EXACTLY WHO I AM, BUT ABLE TO KEEP HIS OWN IDENTITY SECRET.
MY ONLY PHONE CALL GOT A BUSY SIGNAL. WHOEVER BRENDA'S TALKING TO THIS LATE, NO DOUBT SHE'S COMPLAINING ABOUT ME. SHOULD'VE STAYED HOME WITH MY T.V.
Even this I can Endure -tha Rat
ALL MY WORRIES WOULD BE OVER ...
THEY JUST PATTED ME DOWN BEFORE TOSSING ME IN THE CLINK, SO THEY DIDN'T FIND THE VICODIN JIM GAVE ME.
WHO NEEDS THAT ON TOP OF FIFTY-FOUR COUNTS OF MANSLAUGHTER, PLUS SUSPICION IN THE OTHER TWENTY-SEVEN BOMBINGS OVER THE LAST SIX WEEKS?

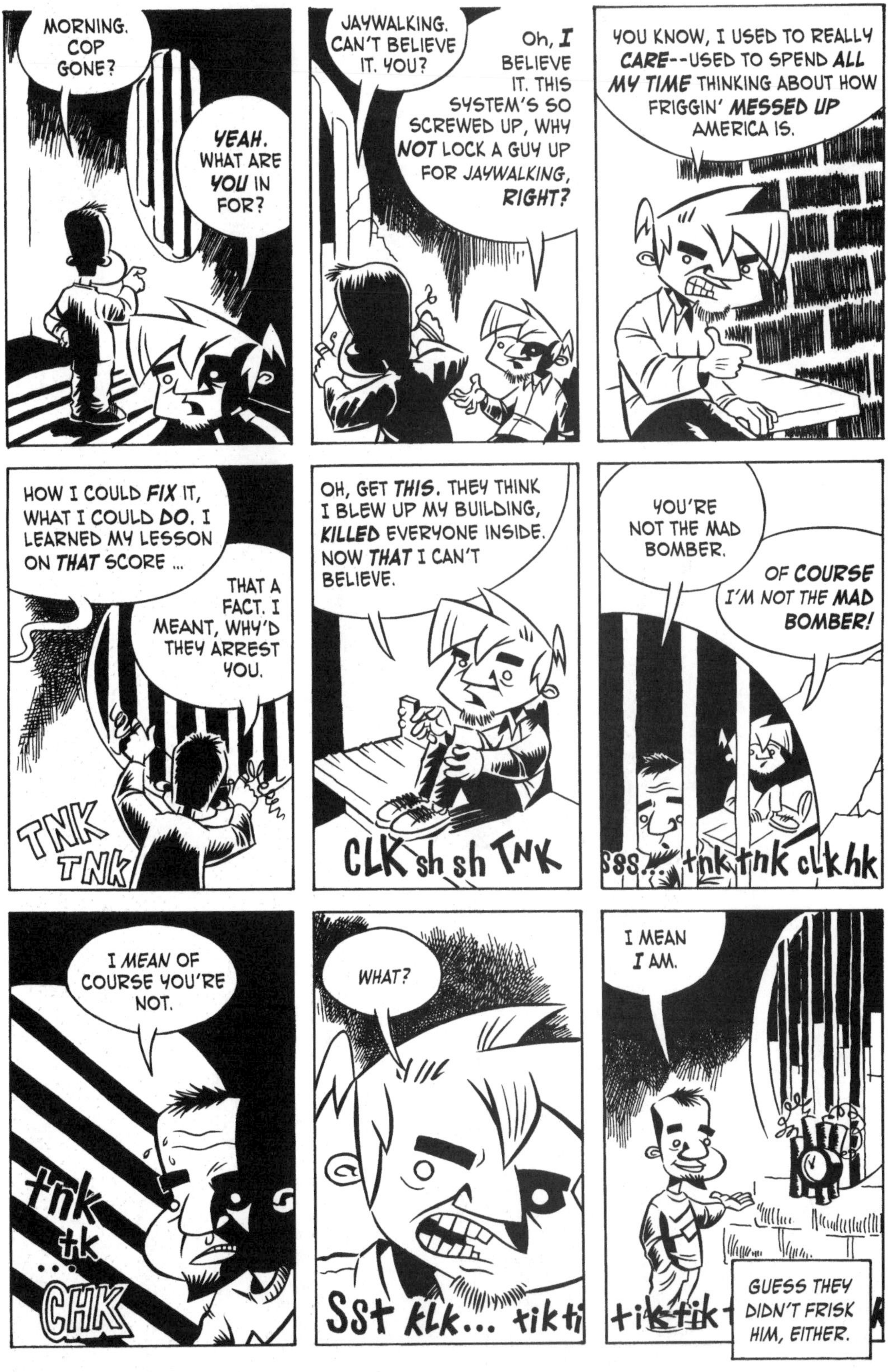
MORNING. COP GONE?
YEAH. WHAT ARE YOU IN FOR?
JAYWALKING. CAN'T BELIEVE IT. YOU?
Oh, I BELIEVE IT. THIS SYSTEM'S SO SCREWED UP, WHY NOT LOCK A GUY UP FOR JAYWALKING, RIGHT?
YOU KNOW, I USED TO REALLY CARE--USED TO SPEND ALL MY TIME THINKING ABOUT HOW FRIGGIN' MESSED UP AMERICA IS.
HOW I COULD FIX IT, WHAT I COULD DO. I LEARNED MY LESSON ON THAT SCORE ...
THAT A FACT. I MEANT, WHY'D THEY ARREST YOU.
TNK TNK
OH, GET THIS. THEY THINK I BLEW UP MY BUILDING, KILLED EVERYONE INSIDE. NOW THAT I CAN'T BELIEVE.
CLK sh sh TNK
YOU'RE NOT THE MAD BOMBER.
OF COURSE I'M NOT THE MAD BOMBER!
sss... tnk tnk clkhk
I MEAN OF COURSE YOU'RE NOT.
tnk tk ... CHK
WHAT?
Sst klk... tik ti
I MEAN I AM.
tik tik
GUESS THEY DIDN'T FRISK HIM, EITHER.

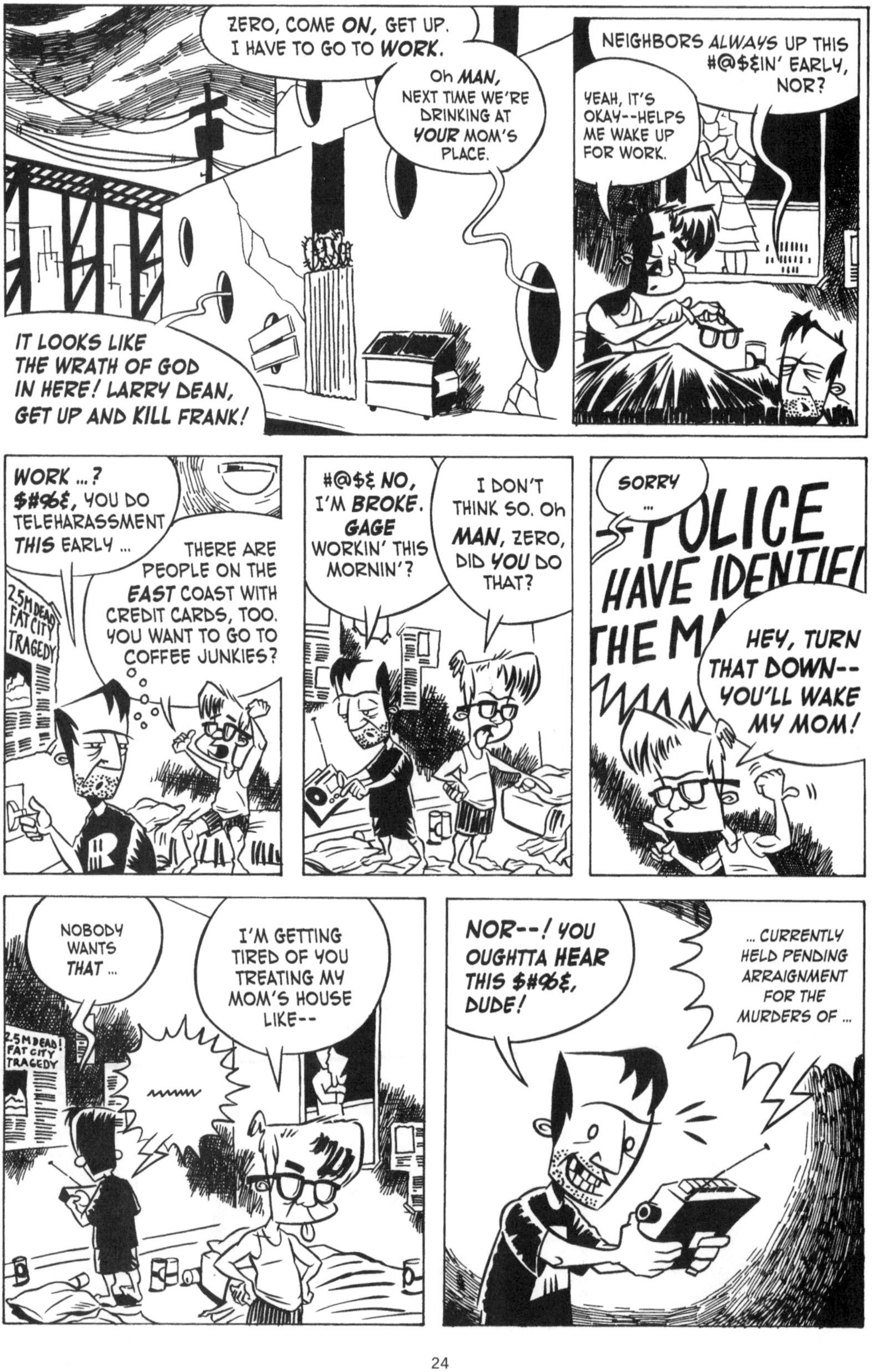

ZERO, COME ON, GET UP. I HAVE TO GO TO WORK.
Oh MAN, NEXT TIME WE'RE DRINKING AT YOUR MOM'S PLACE.
IT LOOKS LIKE THE WRATH OF GOD IN HERE! LARRY DEAN, GET UP AND KILL FRANK!
NEIGHBORS ALWAYS UP THIS #@$&IN' EARLY, NOR?
YEAH, IT'S OKAY--HELPS ME WAKE UP FOR WORK.
WORK ...? $#%&, YOU DO TELEHARASSMENT THIS EARLY ...
THERE ARE PEOPLE ON THE EAST COAST WITH CREDIT CARDS, TOO. YOU WANT TO GO TO COFFEE JUNKIES?
2.5M DEAD FAT CITY TRAGEDY
#@$& NO, I'M BROKE. GAGE WORKIN' THIS MORNIN'?
I DON'T THINK SO. Oh MAN, ZERO, DID YOU DO THAT?
SORRY ...
POLICE HAVE IDENTIFI THE M
HEY, TURN THAT DOWN--YOU'LL WAKE MY MOM!
NOBODY WANTS THAT ...
I'M GETTING TIRED OF YOU TREATING MY MOM'S HOUSE LIKE--
2.5M DEAD! FAT CITY TRAGEDY
NOR--! YOU OUGHTTA HEAR THIS $#%&, DUDE!
... CURRENTLY HELD PENDING ARRAIGNMENT FOR THE MURDERS OF ...

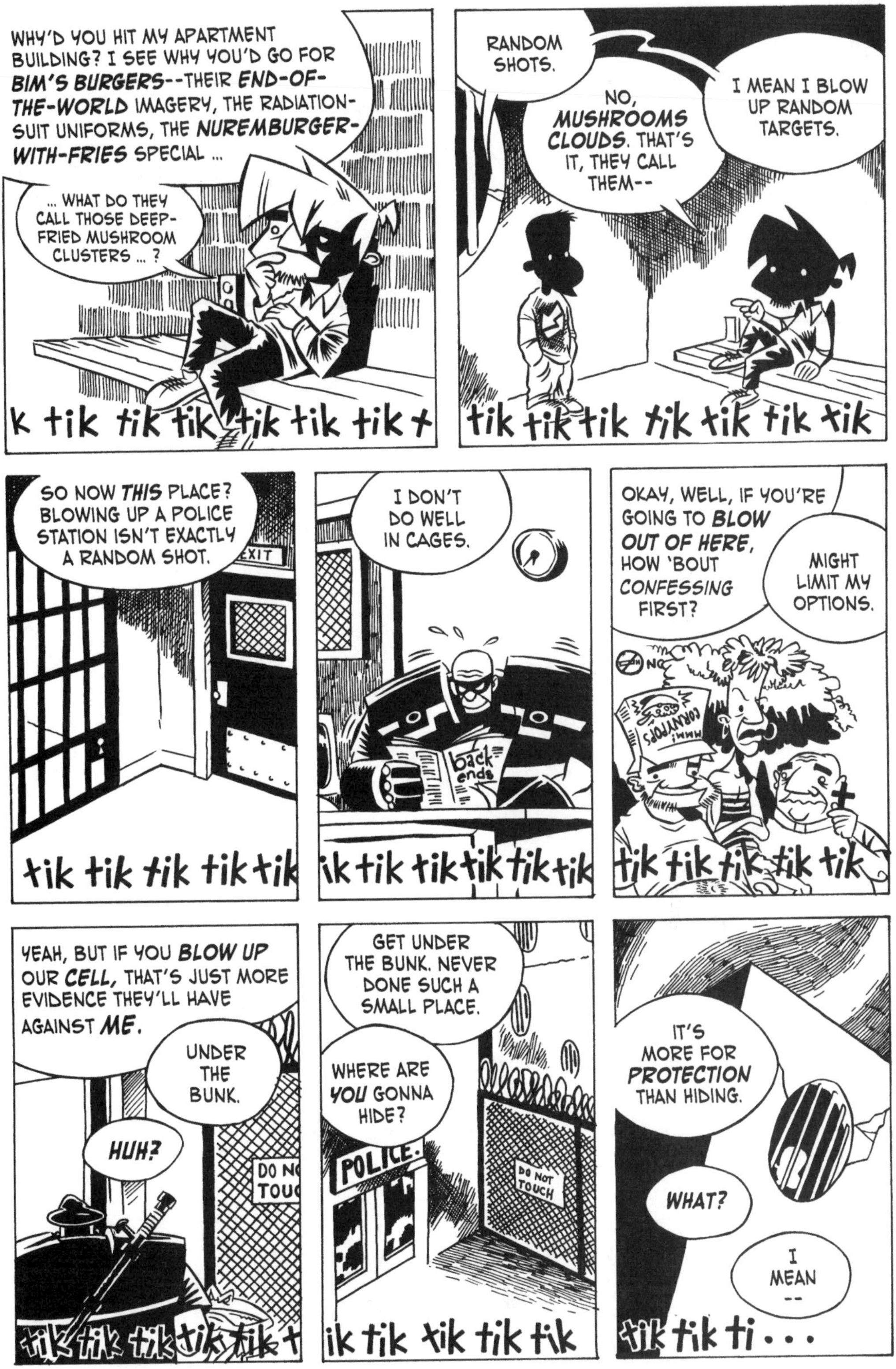
WHY'D YOU HIT MY APARTMENT BUILDING? I SEE WHY YOU'D GO FOR BIM'S BURGERS--THEIR END-OF-THE-WORLD IMAGERY, THE RADIATION-SUIT UNIFORMS, THE NUREMBURGER-WITH-FRIES SPECIAL ...
... WHAT DO THEY CALL THOSE DEEP-FRIED MUSHROOM CLUSTERS ... ?
k tik tik tik tik tik tik t
RANDOM SHOTS.
NO, MUSHROOMS CLOUDS. THAT'S IT, THEY CALL THEM--
I MEAN I BLOW UP RANDOM TARGETS.
tik tik tik tik tik tik tik
SO NOW THIS PLACE? BLOWING UP A POLICE STATION ISN'T EXACTLY A RANDOM SHOT.
EXIT
tik tik tik tik tik
I DON'T DO WELL IN CAGES.
back ends
ik tik tik tik tik tik
OKAY, WELL, IF YOU'RE GOING TO BLOW OUT OF HERE, HOW 'BOUT CONFESSING FIRST?
MIGHT LIMIT MY OPTIONS.
HMM! CORNYPOPS
tik tik tik tik tik
YEAH, BUT IF YOU BLOW UP OUR CELL, THAT'S JUST MORE EVIDENCE THEY'LL HAVE AGAINST ME.
UNDER THE BUNK.
HUH?
DO NO TOUC
tik tik tik tik tik t
GET UNDER THE BUNK. NEVER DONE SUCH A SMALL PLACE.
WHERE ARE YOU GONNA HIDE?
POLICE.
DO NOT TOUCH
ik tik tik tik tik
IT'S MORE FOR PROTECTION THAN HIDING.
WHAT?
I MEAN --
tik tik ti . . .

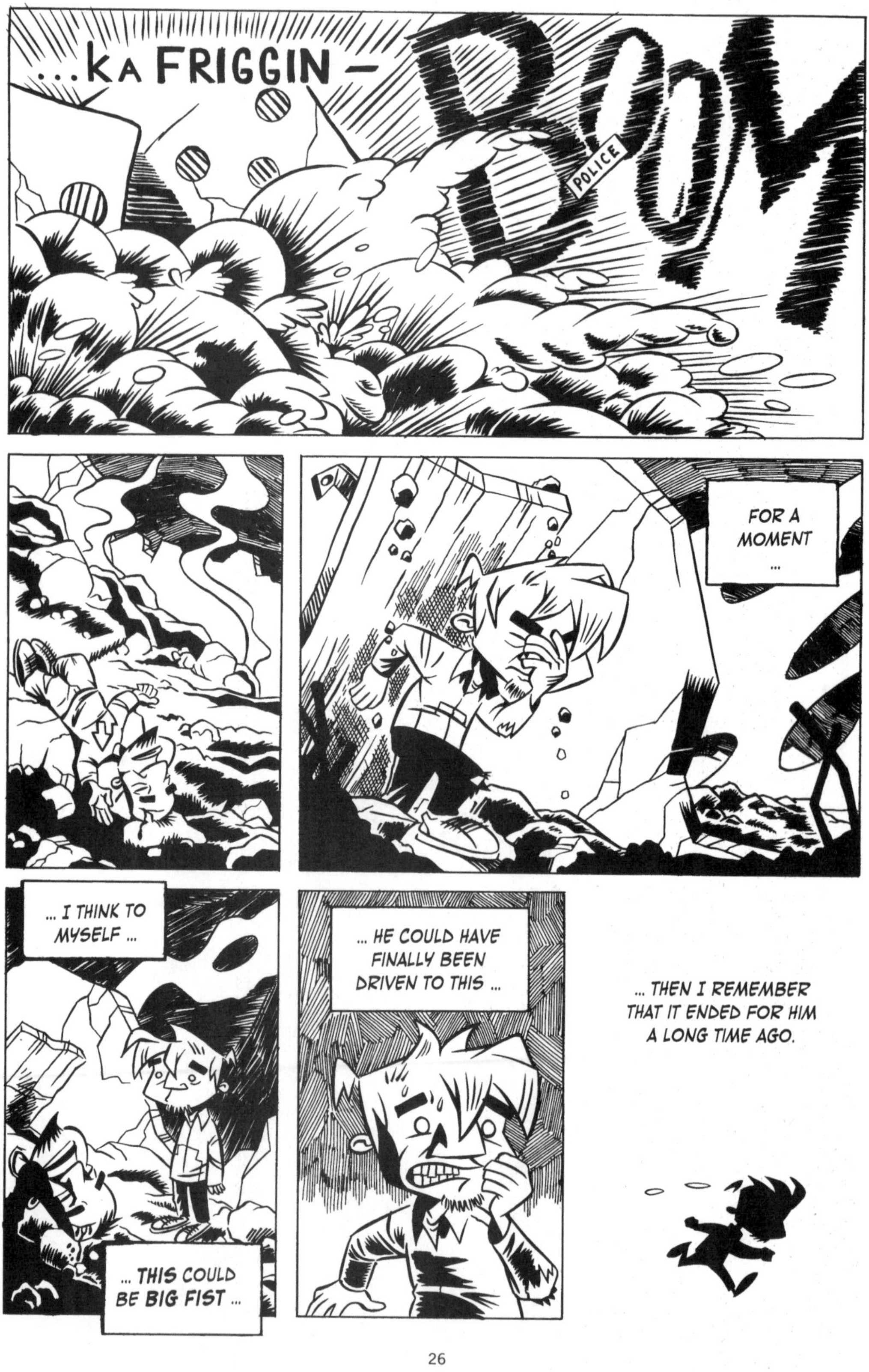
...KA FRIGGIN –
BOOM
POLICE
FOR A MOMENT ...
... I THINK TO MYSELF ...
... THIS COULD BE BIG FIST ...
... HE COULD HAVE FINALLY BEEN DRIVEN TO THIS ...
... THEN I REMEMBER THAT IT ENDED FOR HIM A LONG TIME AGO.

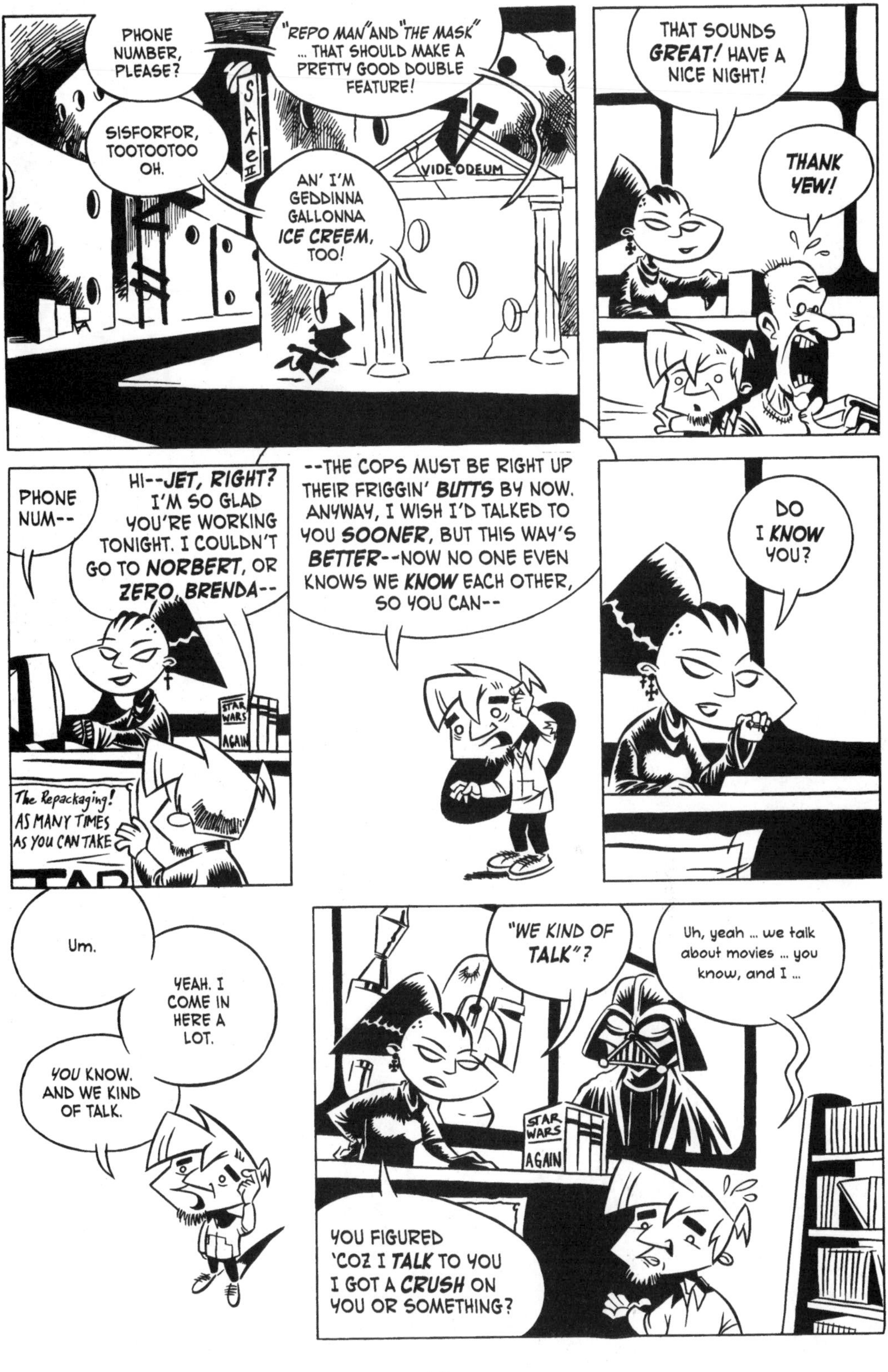

PHONE NUMBER, PLEASE?
"REPO MAN" AND "THE MASK" ... THAT SHOULD MAKE A PRETTY GOOD DOUBLE FEATURE!
SAKE II
VIDEODEUM
SISFORFOR, TOOTOOTOO OH.
AN' I'M GEDDINNA GALLONNA ICE CREEM, TOO!
THAT SOUNDS GREAT! HAVE A NICE NIGHT!
THANK YEW!
PHONE NUM--
HI--JET, RIGHT? I'M SO GLAD YOU'RE WORKING TONIGHT. I COULDN'T GO TO NORBERT, OR ZERO, BRENDA--
--THE COPS MUST BE RIGHT UP THEIR FRIGGIN' BUTTS BY NOW. ANYWAY, I WISH I'D TALKED TO YOU SOONER, BUT THIS WAY'S BETTER--NOW NO ONE EVEN KNOWS WE KNOW EACH OTHER, SO YOU CAN--
STAR WARS AGAIN
The Repackaging! AS MANY TIMES AS YOU CAN TAKE
DO I KNOW YOU?
Um.
YEAH. I COME IN HERE A LOT.
YOU KNOW. AND WE KIND OF TALK.
"WE KIND OF TALK"?
Uh, yeah ... we talk about movies ... you know, and I ...
STAR WARS AGAIN
YOU FIGURED 'COZ I TALK TO YOU I GOT A CRUSH ON YOU OR SOMETHING?

VIDEO RENTAL IS A *SERVICE INDUSTRY.* I'M *PAID* TO BE *NICE* TO CUSTOMERS.

I MADE SMALL TALK WITH *THAT FREAK* WHO JUST WALKED OUT. WITH A RELATIVELY *NORMAL-*LOOKING GUY LIKE YOU I FIGURE, WHY *NOT* CHAT ABOUT FILM-- BUT THEN THEY START THINKING ...

WAIT, YOU RENT ALL THAT *JAPANIMATION* AND THE OLD *COMEDIES,* RIGHT? *JESUS,* WHERE'D YOU GET THE IDEA--

LOOK, I'M NOT THINKING STRAIGHT, *OKAY?* I'M HAVING A FRIGGIN' WEIRD NIGHT, I NEED SOME HELP--

I WAS TALKING ABOUT *YOU* TO MY *T.V.* EARLIER TONIGHT --

THAT LINE *NEVER WORKS,* GAGE!

SHUT UP!

The Repackaging! AS MANY TIMES AS YOU CAN TAKE IT.

S̲T̲A̲R̲

HEY! YOU KNOW, *THE RAT* SAYS IF--

THE RAT?! *YOU'RE* GONNA TELL ME ABOUT THAT FRIGGIN' *RAT,* TOO?

he Repackaging! ANY TIMES AN TAKE IT

THE RAT IS ALL *AROUND* US! *POWERFUL* HE IS, AND IN *ALL LIVING THINGS* PRESENT.

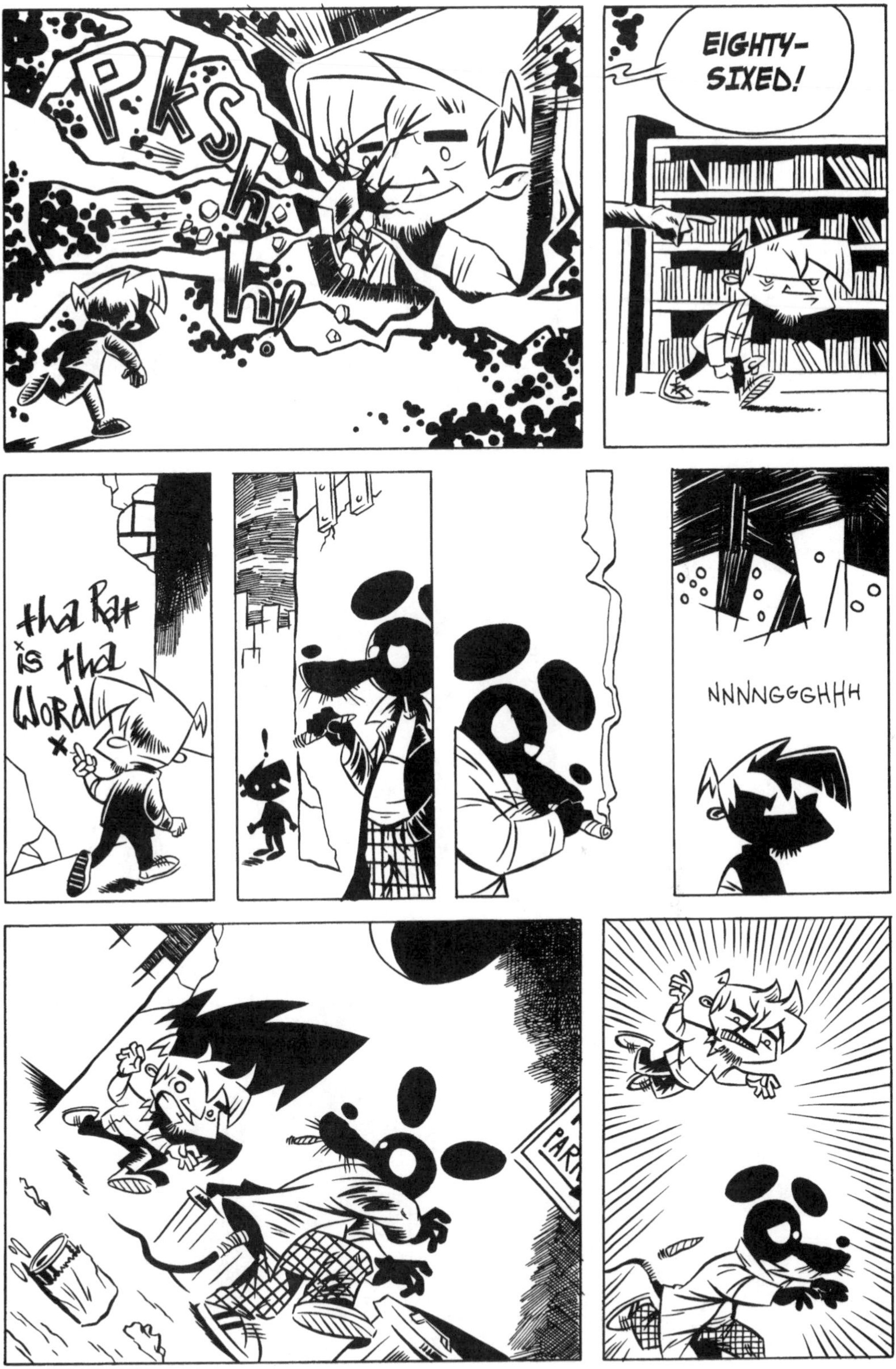
Pkshhh!
EIGHTY-SIXED!
tha Rat is tha Word
NNNNGGGHHH

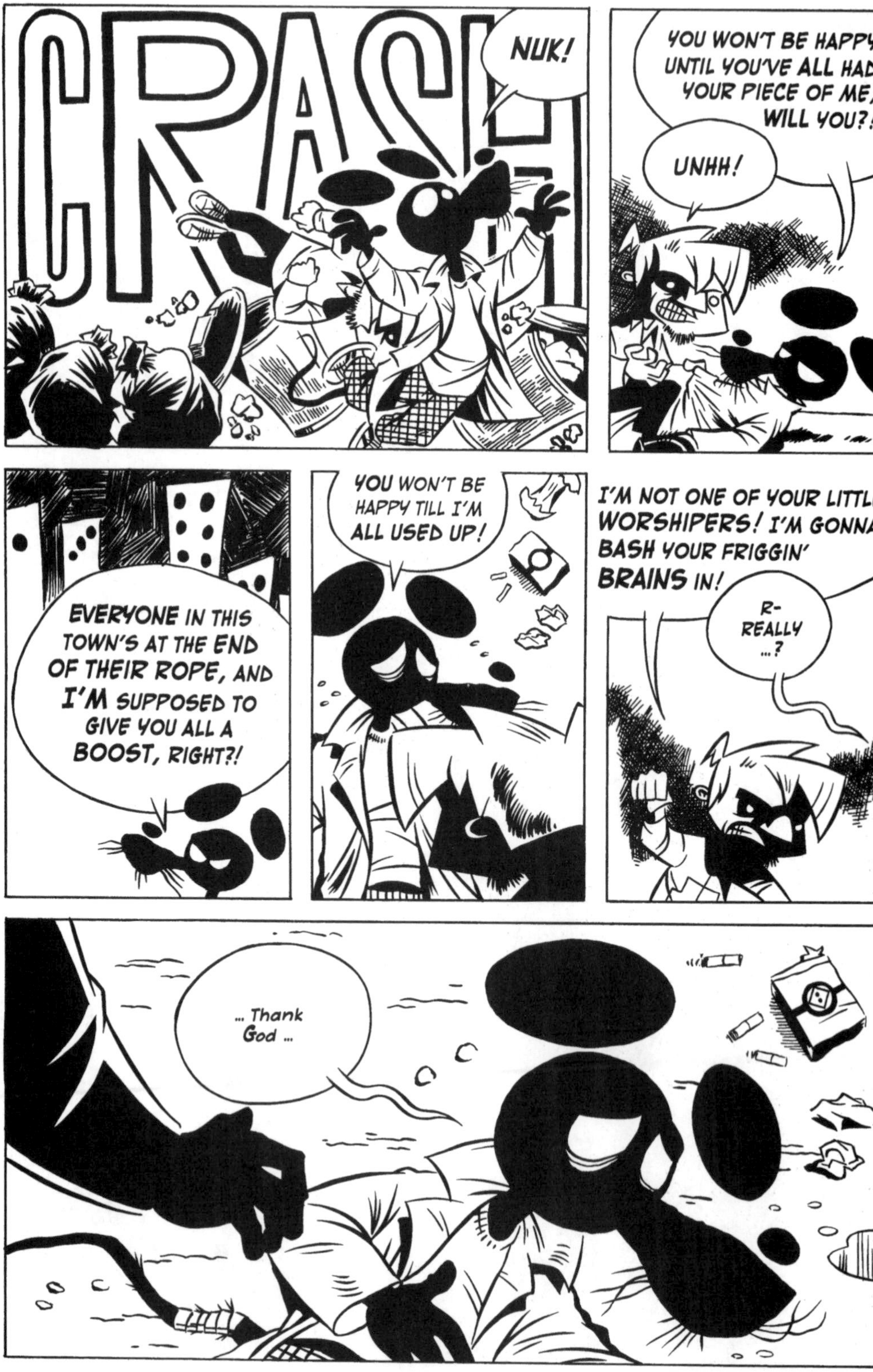
CRASH
NUK!
YOU WON'T BE HAPPY UNTIL YOU'VE ALL HAD YOUR PIECE OF ME, WILL YOU?!
UNHH!
EVERYONE IN THIS TOWN'S AT THE END OF THEIR ROPE, AND I'M SUPPOSED TO GIVE YOU ALL A BOOST, RIGHT?!
YOU WON'T BE HAPPY TILL I'M ALL USED UP!
I'M NOT ONE OF YOUR LITTLE WORSHIPERS! I'M GONNA BASH YOUR FRIGGIN' BRAINS IN!
R- REALLY ...?
... Thank God ...

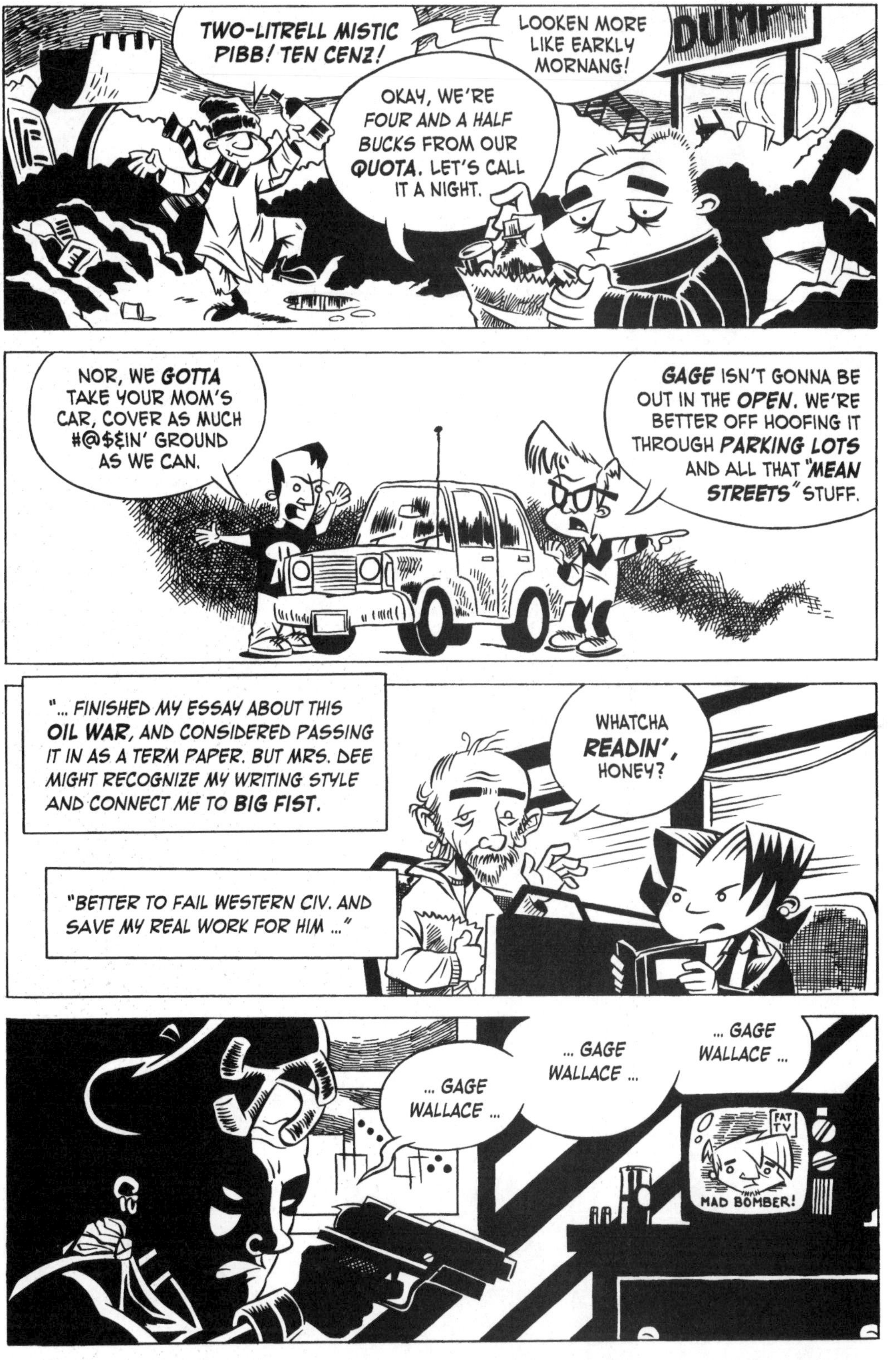
TWO-LITRELL MISTIC PIBB! TEN CENZ!
LOOKEN MORE LIKE EARKLY MORNANG!
OKAY, WE'RE FOUR AND A HALF BUCKS FROM OUR QUOTA. LET'S CALL IT A NIGHT.
DUMP
NOR, WE GOTTA TAKE YOUR MOM'S CAR, COVER AS MUCH #@$&IN' GROUND AS WE CAN.
GAGE ISN'T GONNA BE OUT IN THE OPEN. WE'RE BETTER OFF HOOFING IT THROUGH PARKING LOTS AND ALL THAT "MEAN STREETS" STUFF.
"... FINISHED MY ESSAY ABOUT THIS OIL WAR, AND CONSIDERED PASSING IT IN AS A TERM PAPER. BUT MRS. DEE MIGHT RECOGNIZE MY WRITING STYLE AND CONNECT ME TO BIG FIST.
WHATCHA READIN', HONEY?
"BETTER TO FAIL WESTERN CIV. AND SAVE MY REAL WORK FOR HIM ..."
... GAGE WALLACE ...
... GAGE WALLACE ...
... GAGE WALLACE ...
FAT TV
MAD BOMBER!

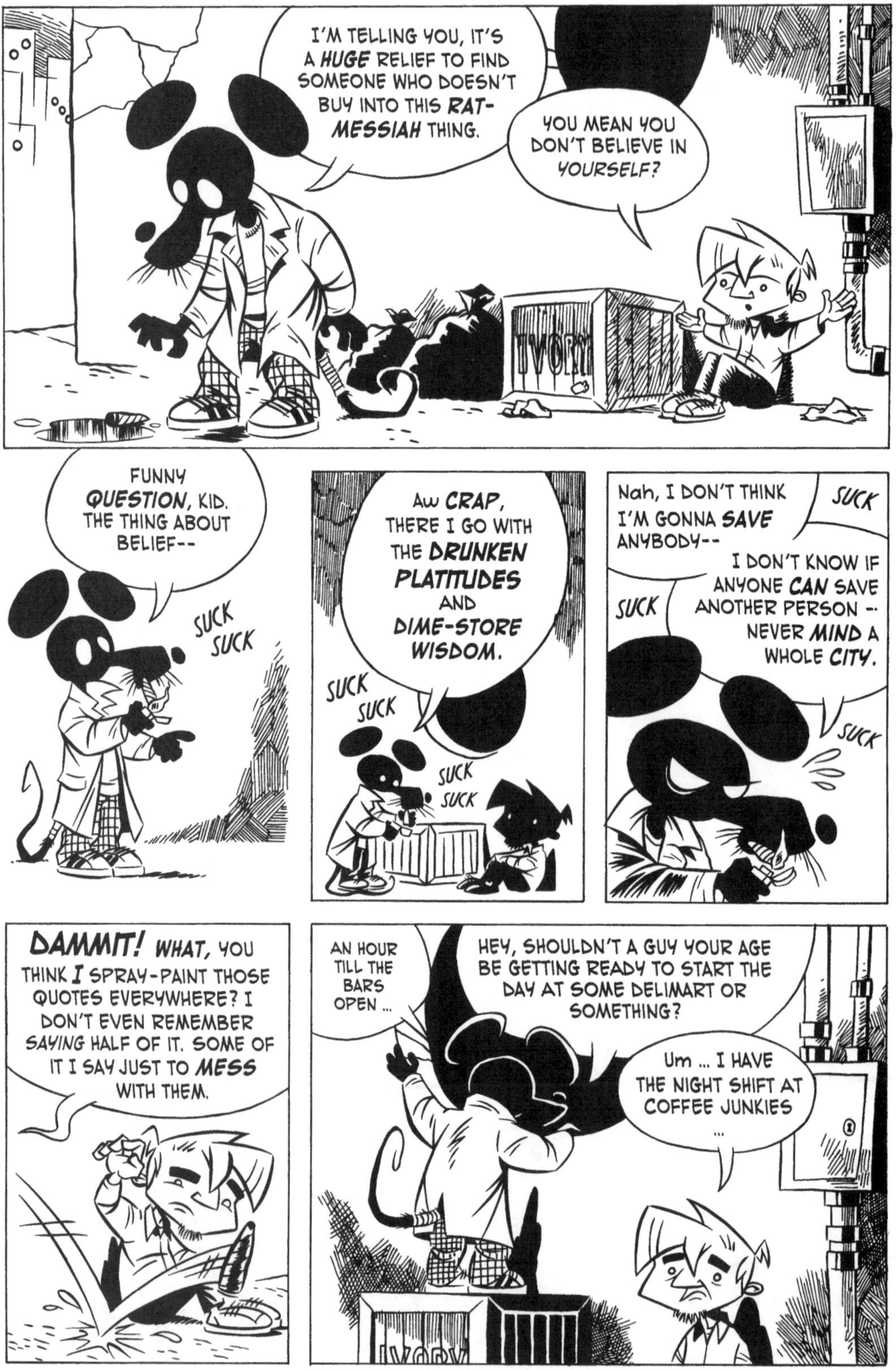
I'M TELLING YOU, IT'S A HUGE RELIEF TO FIND SOMEONE WHO DOESN'T BUY INTO THIS RAT-MESSIAH THING.
YOU MEAN YOU DON'T BELIEVE IN YOURSELF?
FUNNY QUESTION, KID. THE THING ABOUT BELIEF--
SUCK SUCK
Aw CRAP, THERE I GO WITH THE DRUNKEN PLATITUDES AND DIME-STORE WISDOM.
SUCK SUCK
SUCK SUCK
Nah, I DON'T THINK I'M GONNA SAVE ANYBODY--
SUCK
I DON'T KNOW IF ANYONE CAN SAVE ANOTHER PERSON -- NEVER MIND A WHOLE CITY.
SUCK
SUCK
DAMMIT! WHAT, YOU THINK I SPRAY-PAINT THOSE QUOTES EVERYWHERE? I DON'T EVEN REMEMBER SAYING HALF OF IT. SOME OF IT I SAY JUST TO MESS WITH THEM.
AN HOUR TILL THE BARS OPEN ...
HEY, SHOULDN'T A GUY YOUR AGE BE GETTING READY TO START THE DAY AT SOME DELIMART OR SOMETHING?
Um ... I HAVE THE NIGHT SHIFT AT COFFEE JUNKIES ...

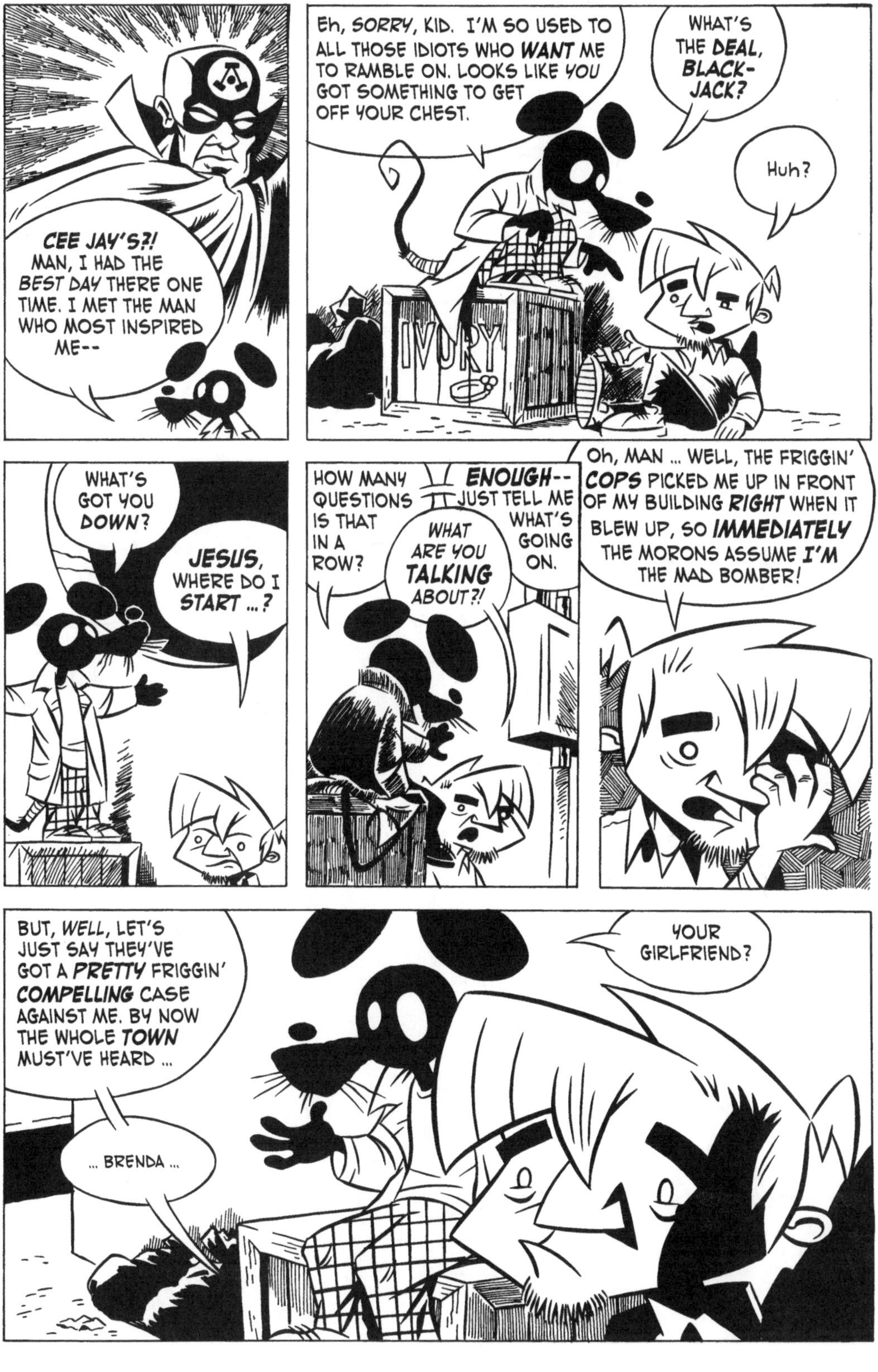
CEE JAY'S?! MAN, I HAD THE BEST DAY THERE ONE TIME. I MET THE MAN WHO MOST INSPIRED ME--
Eh, SORRY, KID. I'M SO USED TO ALL THOSE IDIOTS WHO WANT ME TO RAMBLE ON. LOOKS LIKE YOU GOT SOMETHING TO GET OFF YOUR CHEST.
WHAT'S THE DEAL, BLACK-JACK?
Huh?
IVORY
WHAT'S GOT YOU DOWN?
JESUS, WHERE DO I START ...?
HOW MANY QUESTIONS IS THAT IN A ROW?
ENOUGH-- JUST TELL ME WHAT'S GOING ON.
WHAT ARE YOU TALKING ABOUT?!
Oh, MAN ... WELL, THE FRIGGIN' COPS PICKED ME UP IN FRONT OF MY BUILDING RIGHT WHEN IT BLEW UP, SO IMMEDIATELY THE MORONS ASSUME I'M THE MAD BOMBER!
BUT, WELL, LET'S JUST SAY THEY'VE GOT A PRETTY FRIGGIN' COMPELLING CASE AGAINST ME. BY NOW THE WHOLE TOWN MUST'VE HEARD ...
YOUR GIRLFRIEND?
... BRENDA ...

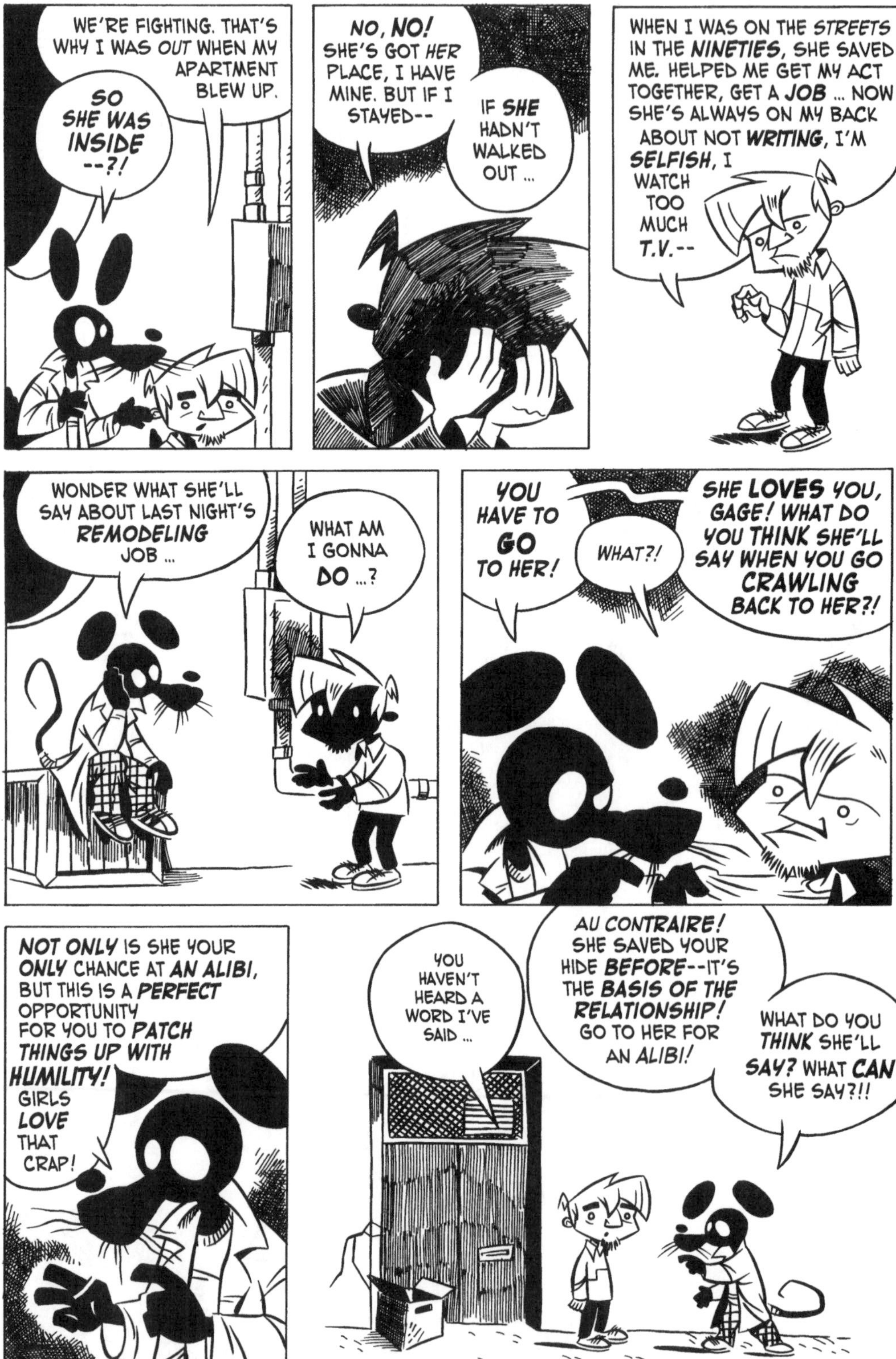
WE'RE FIGHTING. THAT'S WHY I WAS OUT WHEN MY APARTMENT BLEW UP.
SO SHE WAS INSIDE --?!
NO, NO! SHE'S GOT HER PLACE, I HAVE MINE. BUT IF I STAYED--
IF SHE HADN'T WALKED OUT ...
WHEN I WAS ON THE STREETS IN THE NINETIES, SHE SAVED ME. HELPED ME GET MY ACT TOGETHER, GET A JOB ... NOW SHE'S ALWAYS ON MY BACK ABOUT NOT WRITING, I'M SELFISH, I WATCH TOO MUCH T.V.--
WONDER WHAT SHE'LL SAY ABOUT LAST NIGHT'S REMODELING JOB ...
WHAT AM I GONNA DO ...?
YOU HAVE TO GO TO HER!
WHAT?!
SHE LOVES YOU, GAGE! WHAT DO YOU THINK SHE'LL SAY WHEN YOU GO CRAWLING BACK TO HER?!
NOT ONLY IS SHE YOUR ONLY CHANCE AT AN ALIBI, BUT THIS IS A PERFECT OPPORTUNITY FOR YOU TO PATCH THINGS UP WITH HUMILITY! GIRLS LOVE THAT CRAP!
YOU HAVEN'T HEARD A WORD I'VE SAID ...
AU CONTRAIRE! SHE SAVED YOUR HIDE BEFORE--IT'S THE BASIS OF THE RELATIONSHIP! GO TO HER FOR AN ALIBI!
WHAT DO YOU THINK SHE'LL SAY? WHAT CAN SHE SAY?!!

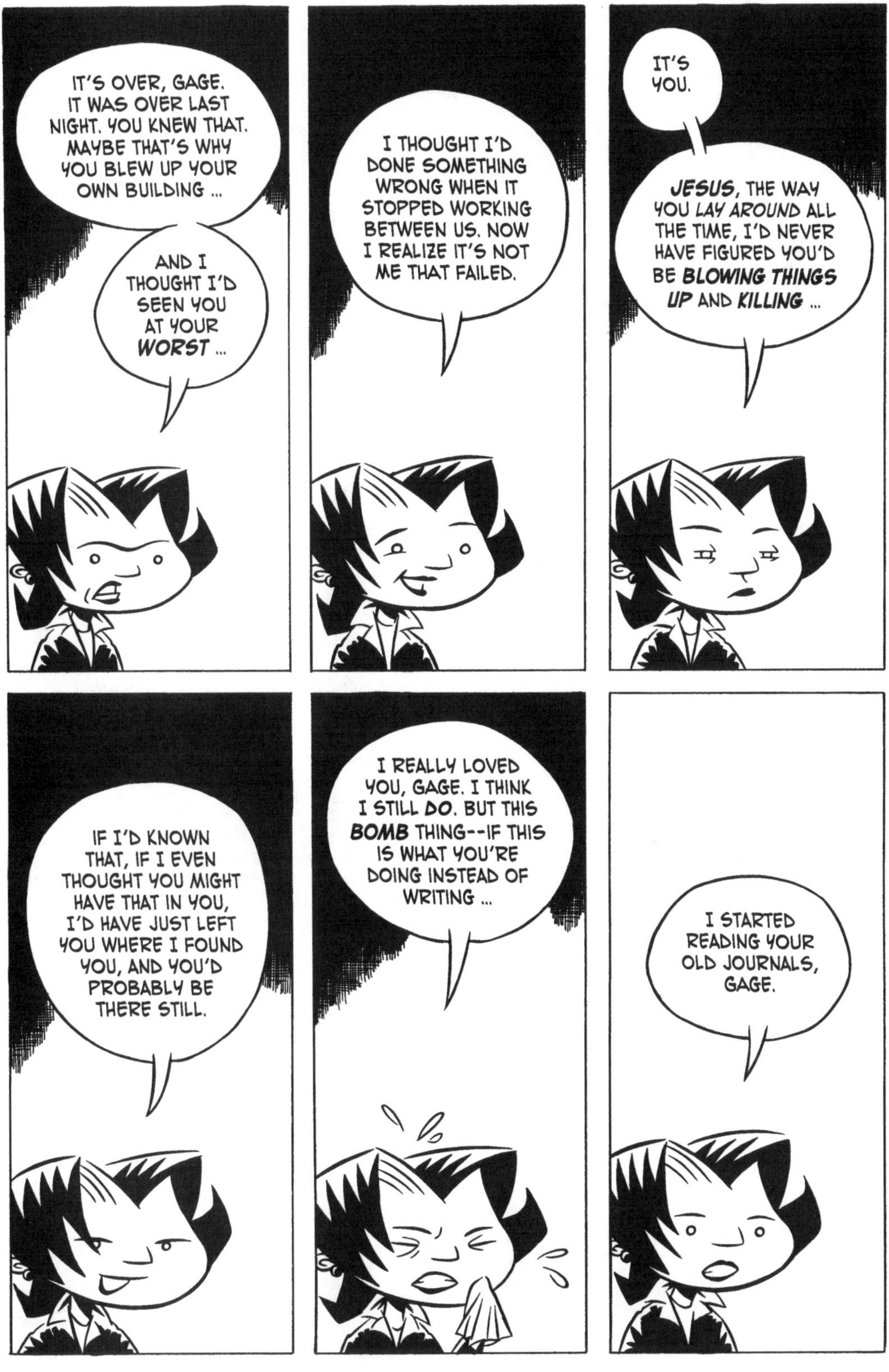
IT'S OVER, GAGE. IT WAS OVER LAST NIGHT. YOU KNEW THAT. MAYBE THAT'S WHY YOU BLEW UP YOUR OWN BUILDING ...
AND I THOUGHT I'D SEEN YOU AT YOUR WORST ...
I THOUGHT I'D DONE SOMETHING WRONG WHEN IT STOPPED WORKING BETWEEN US. NOW I REALIZE IT'S NOT ME THAT FAILED.
IT'S YOU.
JESUS, THE WAY YOU LAY AROUND ALL THE TIME, I'D NEVER HAVE FIGURED YOU'D BE BLOWING THINGS UP AND KILLING ...
IF I'D KNOWN THAT, IF I EVEN THOUGHT YOU MIGHT HAVE THAT IN YOU, I'D HAVE JUST LEFT YOU WHERE I FOUND YOU, AND YOU'D PROBABLY BE THERE STILL.
I REALLY LOVED YOU, GAGE. I THINK I STILL DO. BUT THIS BOMB THING--IF THIS IS WHAT YOU'RE DOING INSTEAD OF WRITING ...
I STARTED READING YOUR OLD JOURNALS, GAGE.

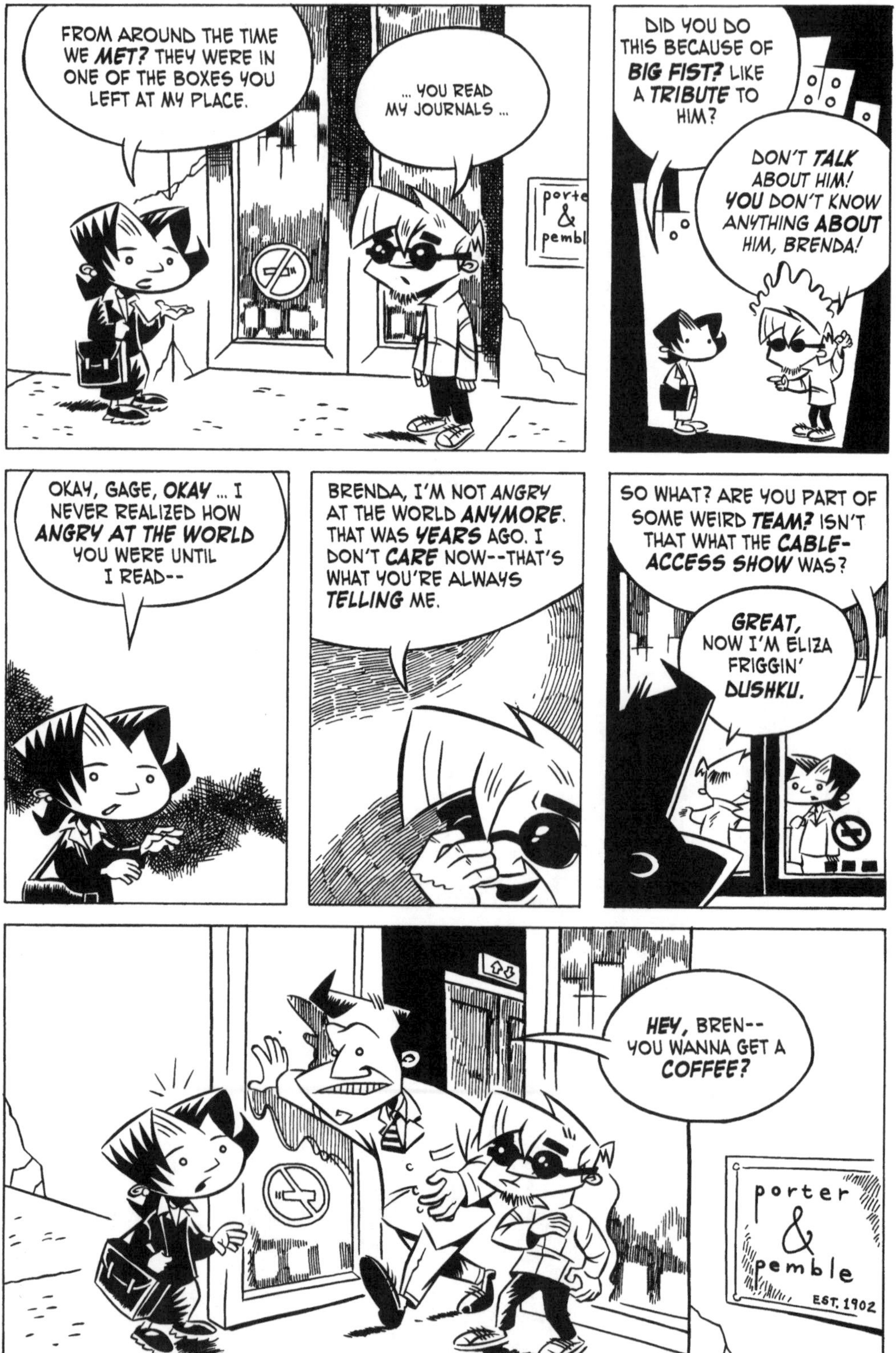
FROM AROUND THE TIME WE MET? THEY WERE IN ONE OF THE BOXES YOU LEFT AT MY PLACE.
... YOU READ MY JOURNALS ...
porte & pembl
DID YOU DO THIS BECAUSE OF BIG FIST? LIKE A TRIBUTE TO HIM?
DON'T TALK ABOUT HIM! YOU DON'T KNOW ANYTHING ABOUT HIM, BRENDA!
OKAY, GAGE, OKAY ... I NEVER REALIZED HOW ANGRY AT THE WORLD YOU WERE UNTIL I READ--
BRENDA, I'M NOT ANGRY AT THE WORLD ANYMORE. THAT WAS YEARS AGO. I DON'T CARE NOW--THAT'S WHAT YOU'RE ALWAYS TELLING ME.
SO WHAT? ARE YOU PART OF SOME WEIRD TEAM? ISN'T THAT WHAT THE CABLE-ACCESS SHOW WAS?
GREAT, NOW I'M ELIZA FRIGGIN' DUSHKU.
HEY, BREN-- YOU WANNA GET A COFFEE?
porter & pemble EST. 1902

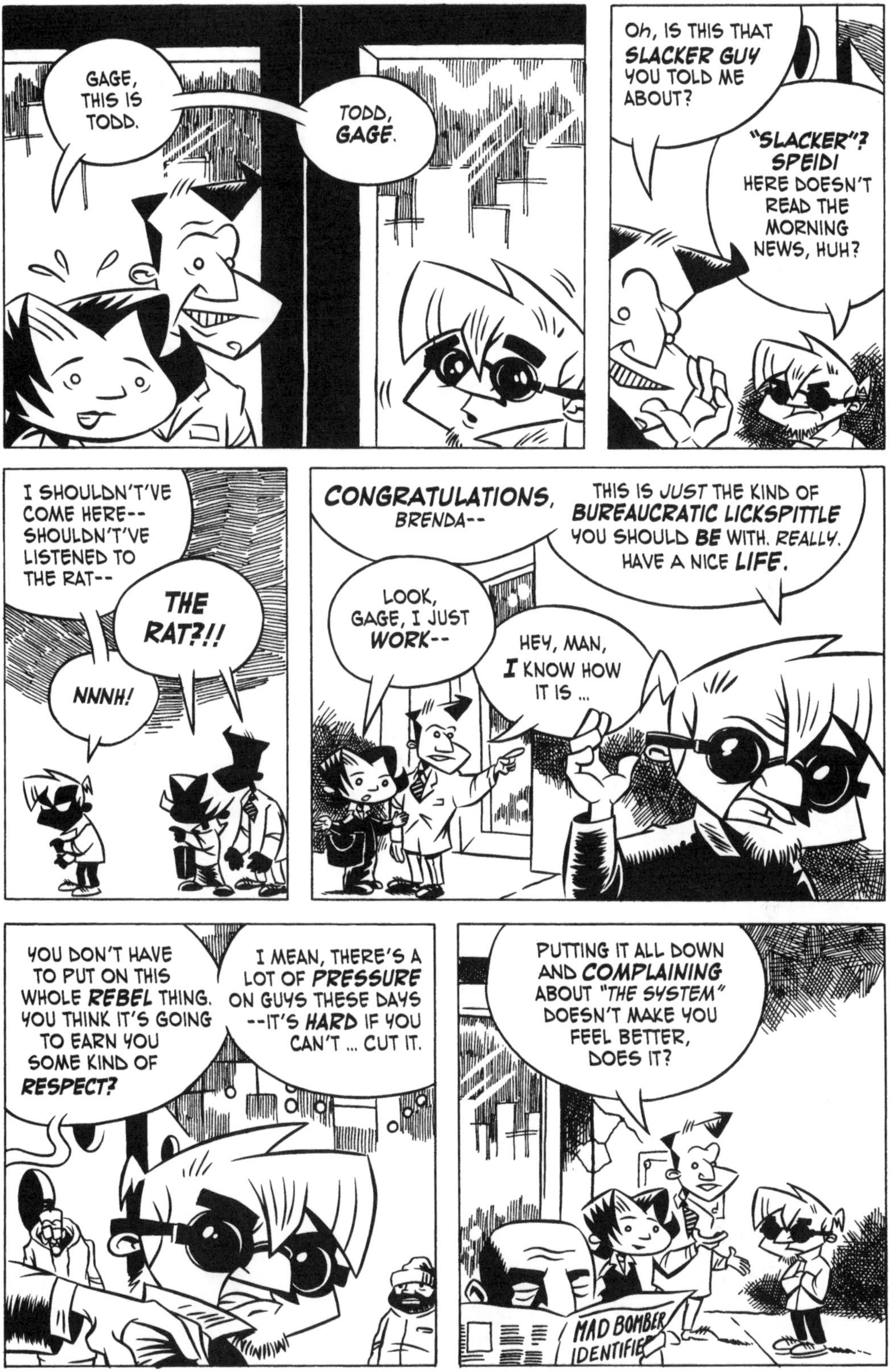
GAGE, THIS IS TODD.
TODD, GAGE.
Oh, IS THIS THAT SLACKER GUY YOU TOLD ME ABOUT?
"SLACKER"? SPEIDI HERE DOESN'T READ THE MORNING NEWS, HUH?
I SHOULDN'T'VE COME HERE-- SHOULDN'T'VE LISTENED TO THE RAT--
THE RAT?!!
NNNH!
CONGRATULATIONS, BRENDA--
THIS IS JUST THE KIND OF BUREAUCRATIC LICKSPITTLE YOU SHOULD BE WITH. REALLY. HAVE A NICE LIFE.
LOOK, GAGE, I JUST WORK--
HEY, MAN, I KNOW HOW IT IS ...
YOU DON'T HAVE TO PUT ON THIS WHOLE REBEL THING. YOU THINK IT'S GOING TO EARN YOU SOME KIND OF RESPECT?
I MEAN, THERE'S A LOT OF PRESSURE ON GUYS THESE DAYS --IT'S HARD IF YOU CAN'T ... CUT IT.
PUTTING IT ALL DOWN AND COMPLAINING ABOUT "THE SYSTEM" DOESN'T MAKE YOU FEEL BETTER, DOES IT?
MAD BOMBER IDENTIFIE

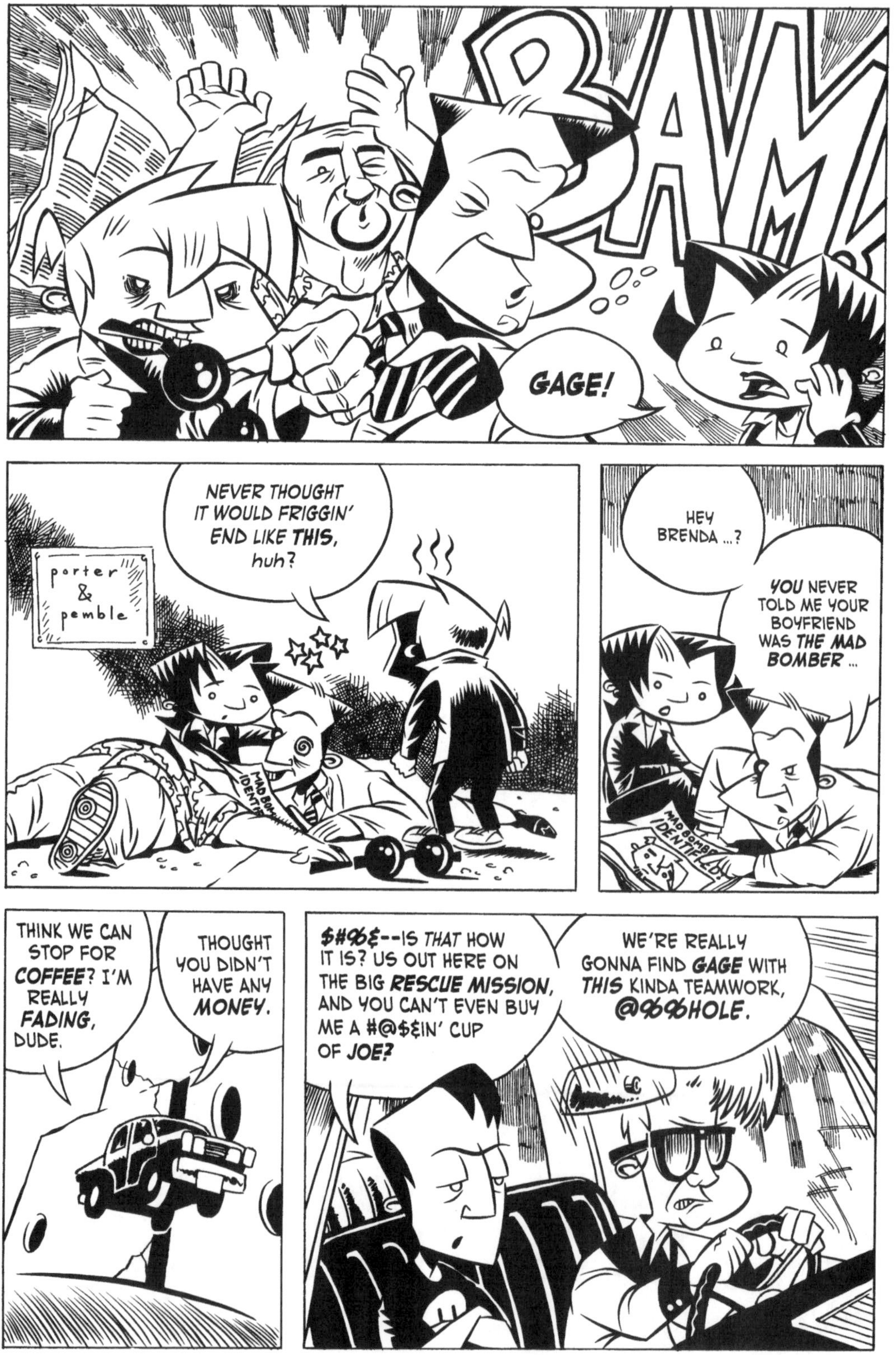
BAM
GAGE!
porter & pemble
NEVER THOUGHT IT WOULD FRIGGIN' END LIKE THIS, huh?
HEY BRENDA ...?
YOU NEVER TOLD ME YOUR BOYFRIEND WAS THE MAD BOMBER ...
MAD BOMBER IDENTIFIED
THINK WE CAN STOP FOR COFFEE? I'M REALLY FADING, DUDE.
THOUGHT YOU DIDN'T HAVE ANY MONEY.
$#%$--IS THAT HOW IT IS? US OUT HERE ON THE BIG RESCUE MISSION, AND YOU CAN'T EVEN BUY ME A #@$$IN' CUP OF JOE?
WE'RE REALLY GONNA FIND GAGE WITH THIS KINDA TEAMWORK, @%%HOLE.

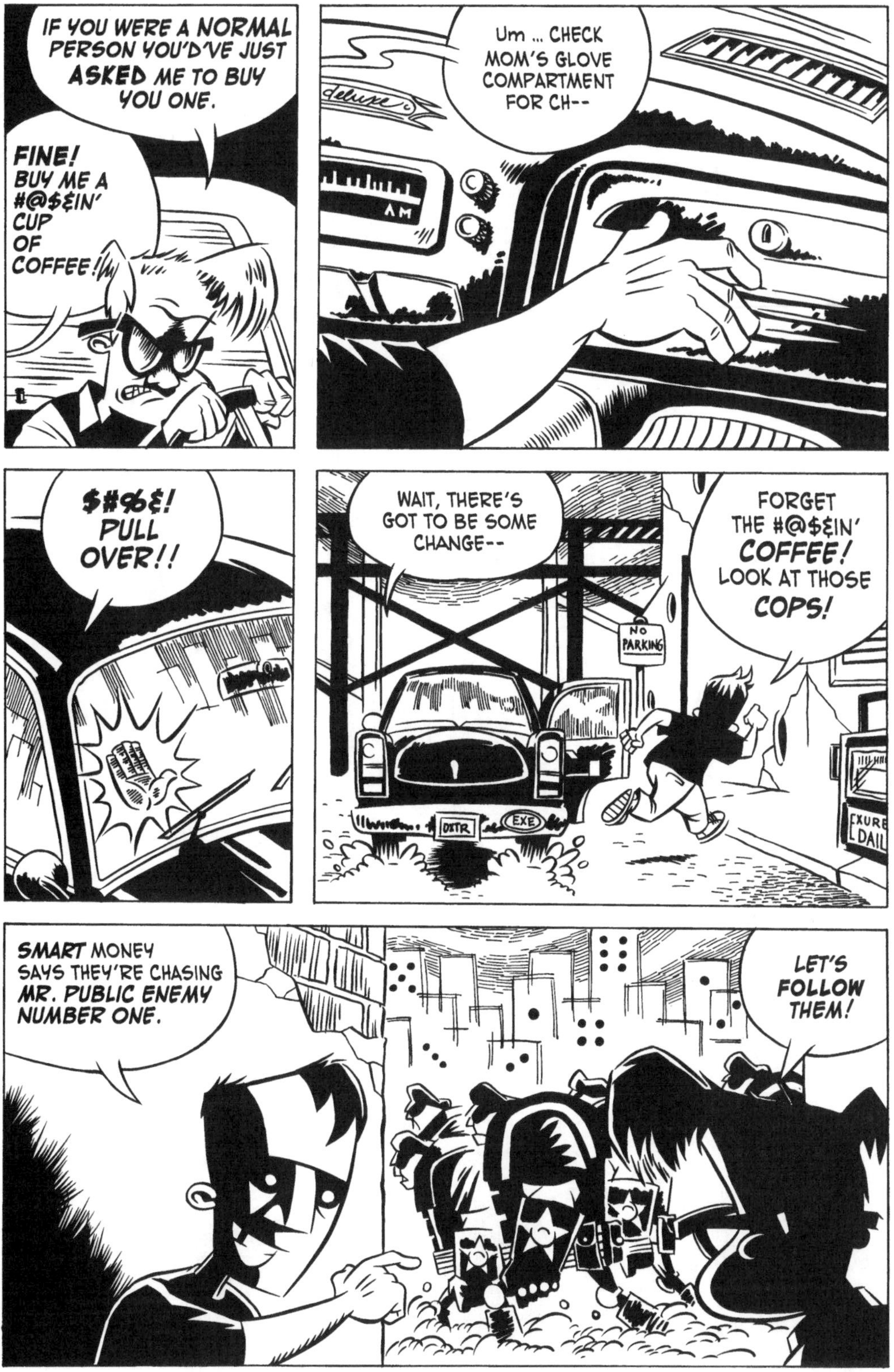
IF YOU WERE A NORMAL PERSON YOU'D'VE JUST ASKED ME TO BUY YOU ONE.
FINE! BUY ME A #@$&IN' CUP OF COFFEE!
Um ... CHECK MOM'S GLOVE COMPARTMENT FOR CH--
deluxe
AM
$#%&! PULL OVER!!
WAIT, THERE'S GOT TO BE SOME CHANGE--
FORGET THE #@$&IN' COFFEE! LOOK AT THOSE COPS!
NO PARKING
DXTR
EXE
SMART MONEY SAYS THEY'RE CHASING MR. PUBLIC ENEMY NUMBER ONE.
LET'S FOLLOW THEM!

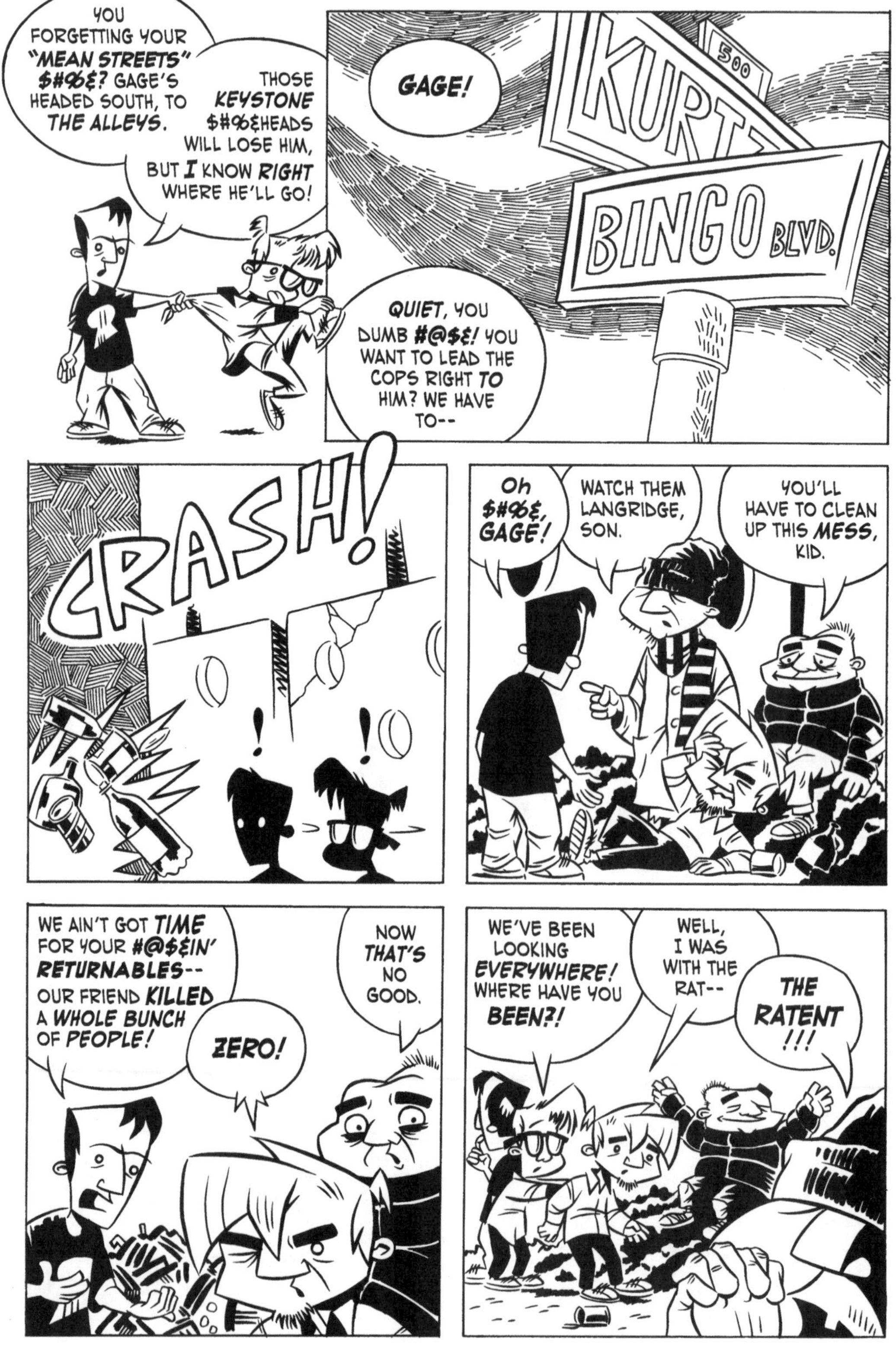
YOU FORGETTING YOUR "MEAN STREETS" $#%&? GAGE'S HEADED SOUTH, TO THE ALLEYS.
THOSE KEYSTONE $#%&HEADS WILL LOSE HIM, BUT I KNOW RIGHT WHERE HE'LL GO!
GAGE!
KURT
500
BINGO BLVD.
QUIET, YOU DUMB #@$&! YOU WANT TO LEAD THE COPS RIGHT TO HIM? WE HAVE TO--
CRASH!
Oh $#%&, GAGE!
WATCH THEM LANGRIDGE, SON.
YOU'LL HAVE TO CLEAN UP THIS MESS, KID.
WE AIN'T GOT TIME FOR YOUR #@$&IN' RETURNABLES-- OUR FRIEND KILLED A WHOLE BUNCH OF PEOPLE!
ZERO!
NOW THAT'S NO GOOD.
WE'VE BEEN LOOKING EVERYWHERE! WHERE HAVE YOU BEEN?!
WELL, I WAS WITH THE RAT--
THE RATENT !!!

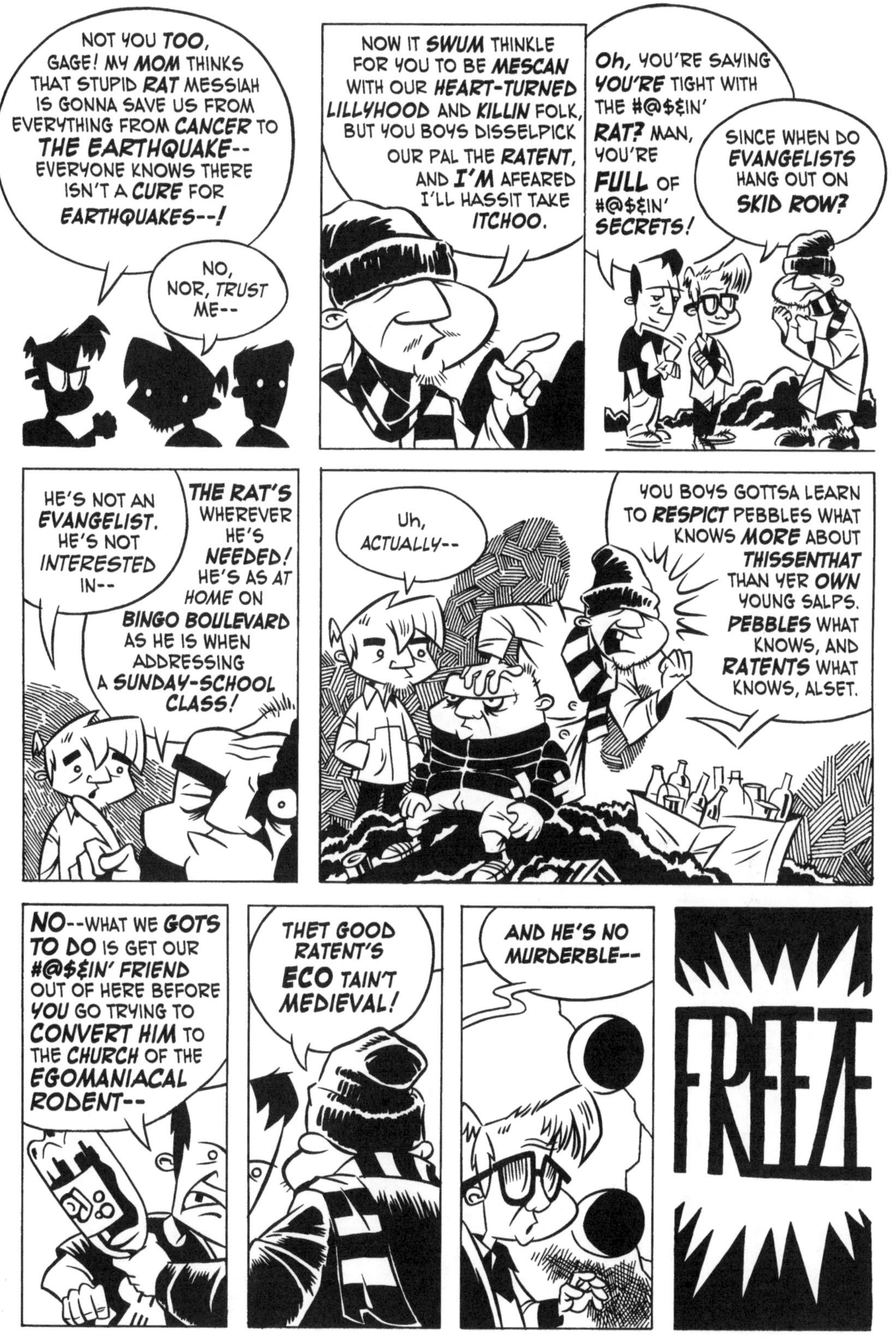
NOT YOU TOO, GAGE! MY MOM THINKS THAT STUPID RAT MESSIAH IS GONNA SAVE US FROM EVERYTHING FROM CANCER TO THE EARTHQUAKE-- EVERYONE KNOWS THERE ISN'T A CURE FOR EARTHQUAKES--!
NO, NOR, TRUST ME--
NOW IT SWUM THINKLE FOR YOU TO BE MESCAN WITH OUR HEART-TURNED LILLYHOOD AND KILLIN FOLK, BUT YOU BOYS DISSELPICK OUR PAL THE RATENT, AND I'M AFEARED I'LL HASSIT TAKE ITCHOO.
Oh, YOU'RE SAYING YOU'RE TIGHT WITH THE #@$&IN' RAT? MAN, YOU'RE FULL OF #@$&IN' SECRETS!
SINCE WHEN DO EVANGELISTS HANG OUT ON SKID ROW?
HE'S NOT AN EVANGELIST. HE'S NOT INTERESTED IN--
THE RAT'S WHEREVER HE'S NEEDED! HE'S AS AT HOME ON BINGO BOULEVARD AS HE IS WHEN ADDRESSING A SUNDAY-SCHOOL CLASS!
Uh, ACTUALLY--
YOU BOYS GOTTSA LEARN TO RESPICT PEBBLES WHAT KNOWS MORE ABOUT THISSENTHAT THAN YER OWN YOUNG SALPS. PEBBLES WHAT KNOWS, AND RATENTS WHAT KNOWS, ALSET.
NO--WHAT WE GOTS TO DO IS GET OUR #@$&IN' FRIEND OUT OF HERE BEFORE YOU GO TRYING TO CONVERT HIM TO THE CHURCH OF THE EGOMANIACAL RODENT--
THET GOOD RATENT'S ECO TAIN'T MEDIEVAL!
AND HE'S NO MURDERBLE--
FREEZE

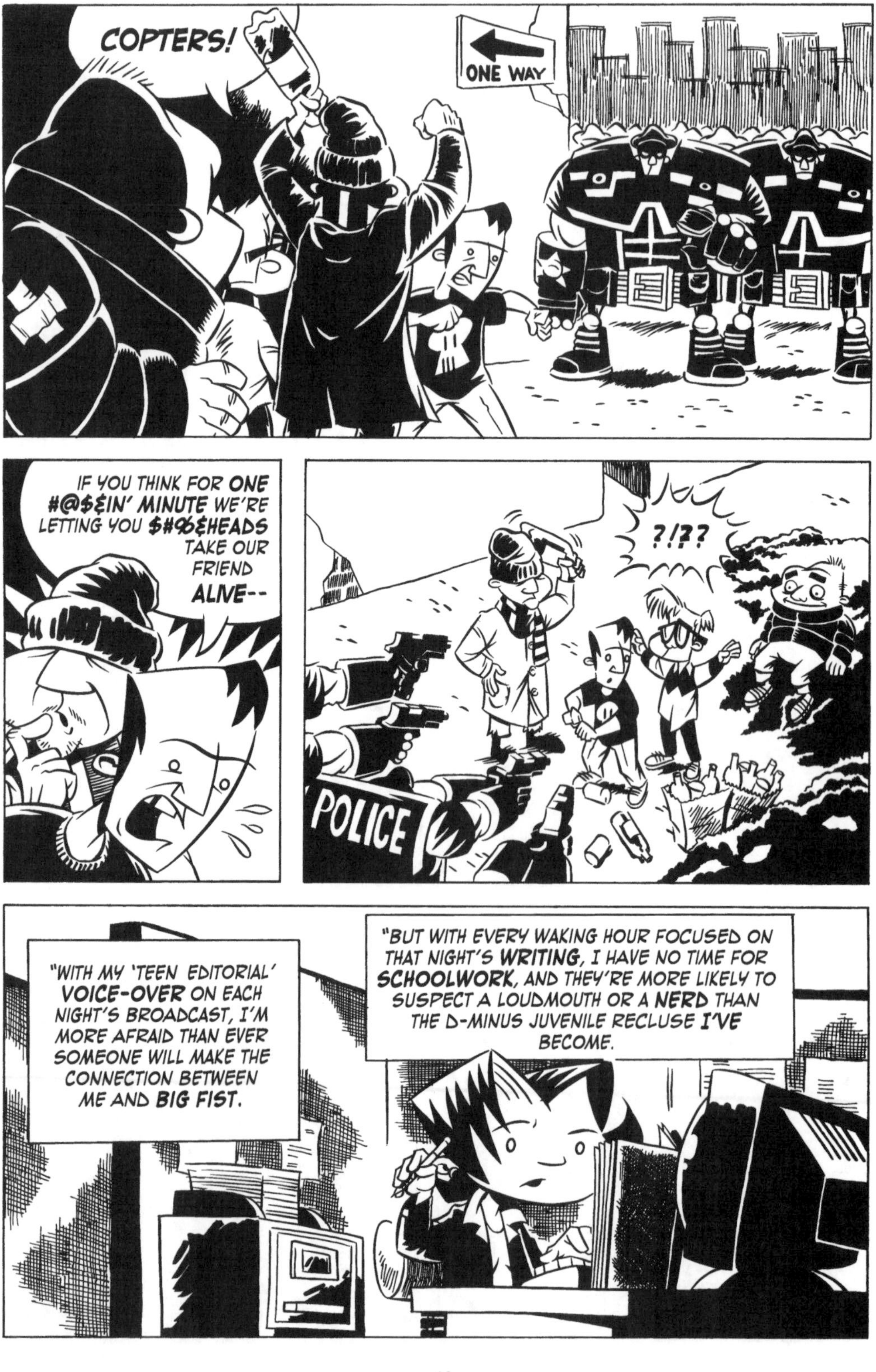
COPTERS!
ONE WAY
IF YOU THINK FOR ONE #@$&IN' MINUTE WE'RE LETTING YOU $#%&HEADS TAKE OUR FRIEND ALIVE--
?!??
POLICE
"WITH MY 'TEEN EDITORIAL' VOICE-OVER ON EACH NIGHT'S BROADCAST, I'M MORE AFRAID THAN EVER SOMEONE WILL MAKE THE CONNECTION BETWEEN ME AND BIG FIST.
"BUT WITH EVERY WAKING HOUR FOCUSED ON THAT NIGHT'S WRITING, I HAVE NO TIME FOR SCHOOLWORK, AND THEY'RE MORE LIKELY TO SUSPECT A LOUDMOUTH OR A NERD THAN THE D-MINUS JUVENILE RECLUSE I'VE BECOME.

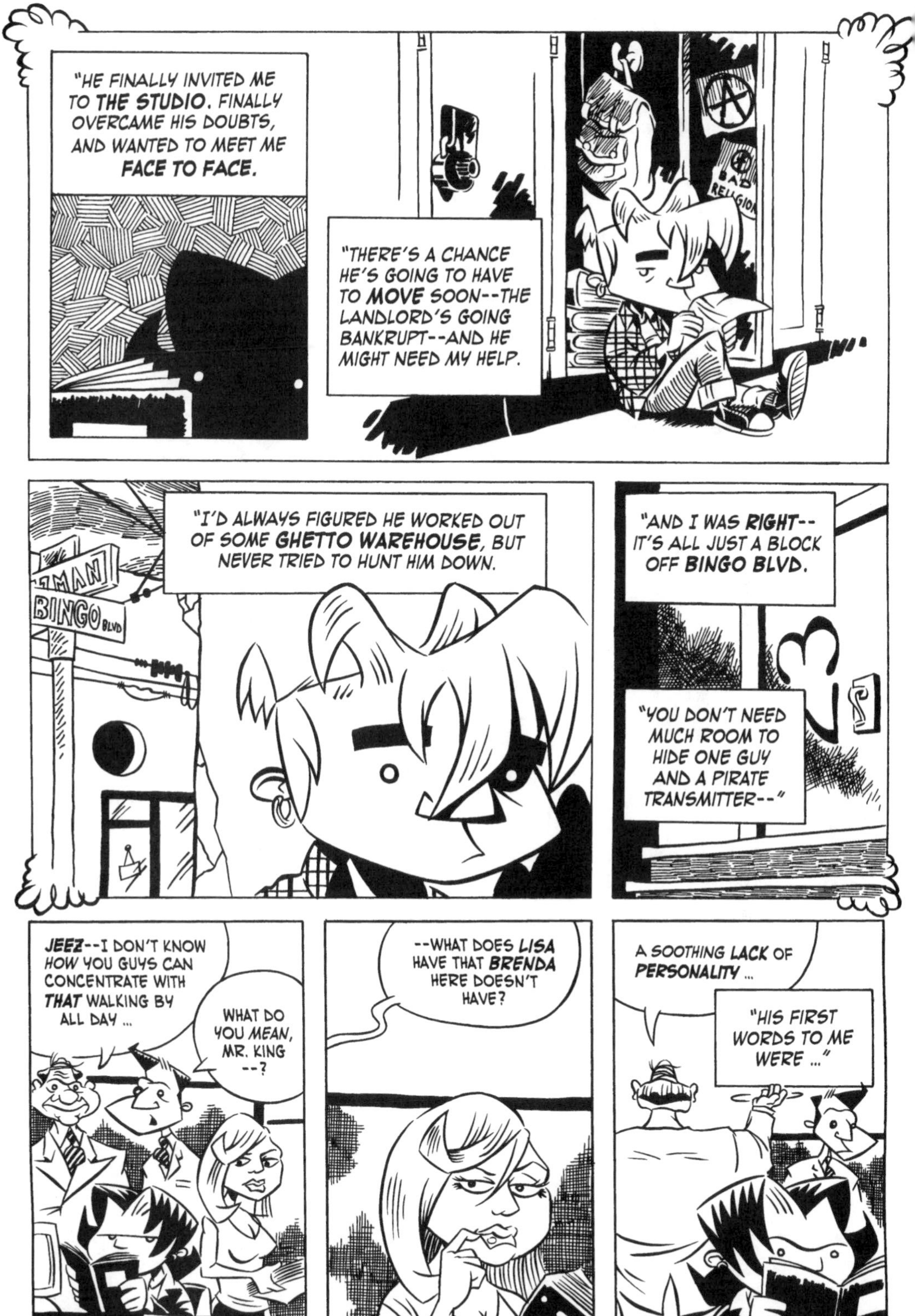
"HE FINALLY INVITED ME TO THE STUDIO. FINALLY OVERCAME HIS DOUBTS, AND WANTED TO MEET ME FACE TO FACE.
"THERE'S A CHANCE HE'S GOING TO HAVE TO MOVE SOON--THE LANDLORD'S GOING BANKRUPT--AND HE MIGHT NEED MY HELP.
BAD RELIGION
"I'D ALWAYS FIGURED HE WORKED OUT OF SOME GHETTO WAREHOUSE, BUT NEVER TRIED TO HUNT HIM DOWN.
BINGO BLVD
"AND I WAS RIGHT--IT'S ALL JUST A BLOCK OFF BINGO BLVD.
"YOU DON'T NEED MUCH ROOM TO HIDE ONE GUY AND A PIRATE TRANSMITTER--"
JEEZ--I DON'T KNOW HOW YOU GUYS CAN CONCENTRATE WITH THAT WALKING BY ALL DAY ...
WHAT DO YOU MEAN, MR. KING --?
--WHAT DOES LISA HAVE THAT BRENDA HERE DOESN'T HAVE?
A SOOTHING LACK OF PERSONALITY ...
"HIS FIRST WORDS TO ME WERE ..."

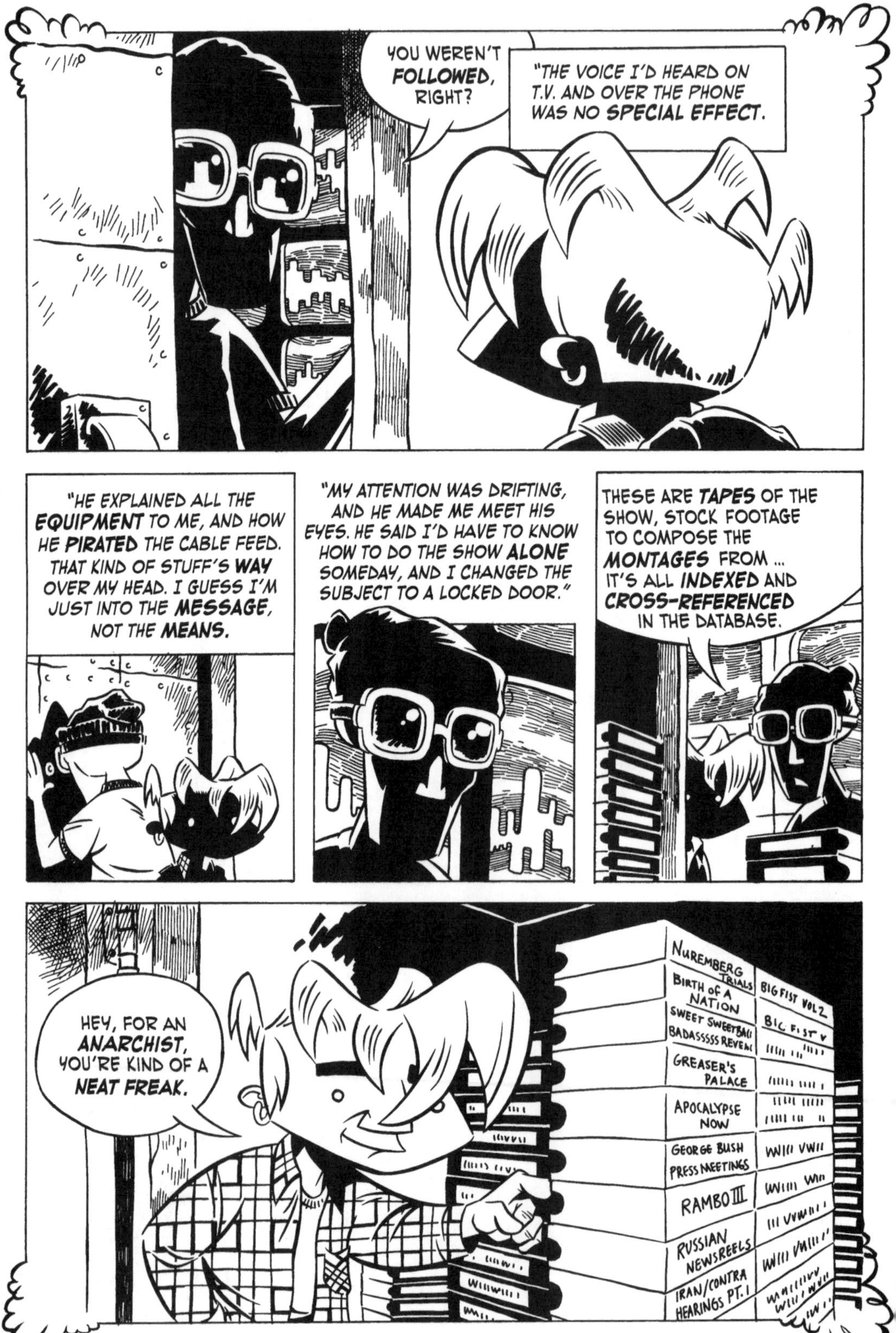
YOU WEREN'T **FOLLOWED**, RIGHT?
"THE VOICE I'D HEARD ON T.V. AND OVER THE PHONE WAS NO **SPECIAL EFFECT**.
"HE EXPLAINED ALL THE **EQUIPMENT** TO ME, AND HOW HE **PIRATED** THE CABLE FEED. THAT KIND OF STUFF'S **WAY** OVER MY HEAD. I GUESS I'M JUST INTO THE **MESSAGE**, NOT THE **MEANS**.
"MY ATTENTION WAS DRIFTING, AND HE MADE ME MEET HIS EYES. HE SAID I'D HAVE TO KNOW HOW TO DO THE SHOW **ALONE** SOMEDAY, AND I CHANGED THE SUBJECT TO A LOCKED DOOR."
THESE ARE **TAPES** OF THE SHOW, STOCK FOOTAGE TO COMPOSE THE **MONTAGES** FROM ... IT'S ALL **INDEXED** AND **CROSS-REFERENCED** IN THE DATABASE.
HEY, FOR AN **ANARCHIST**, YOU'RE KIND OF A **NEAT FREAK**.
NUREMBERG TRIALS
BIRTH OF A NATION
GREASER'S PALACE
APOCALYPSE NOW
GEORGE BUSH PRESS MEETINGS
RAMBO III
RUSSIAN NEWSREELS
IRAN/CONTRA HEARINGS PT. 1
BIG FIST VOL 2

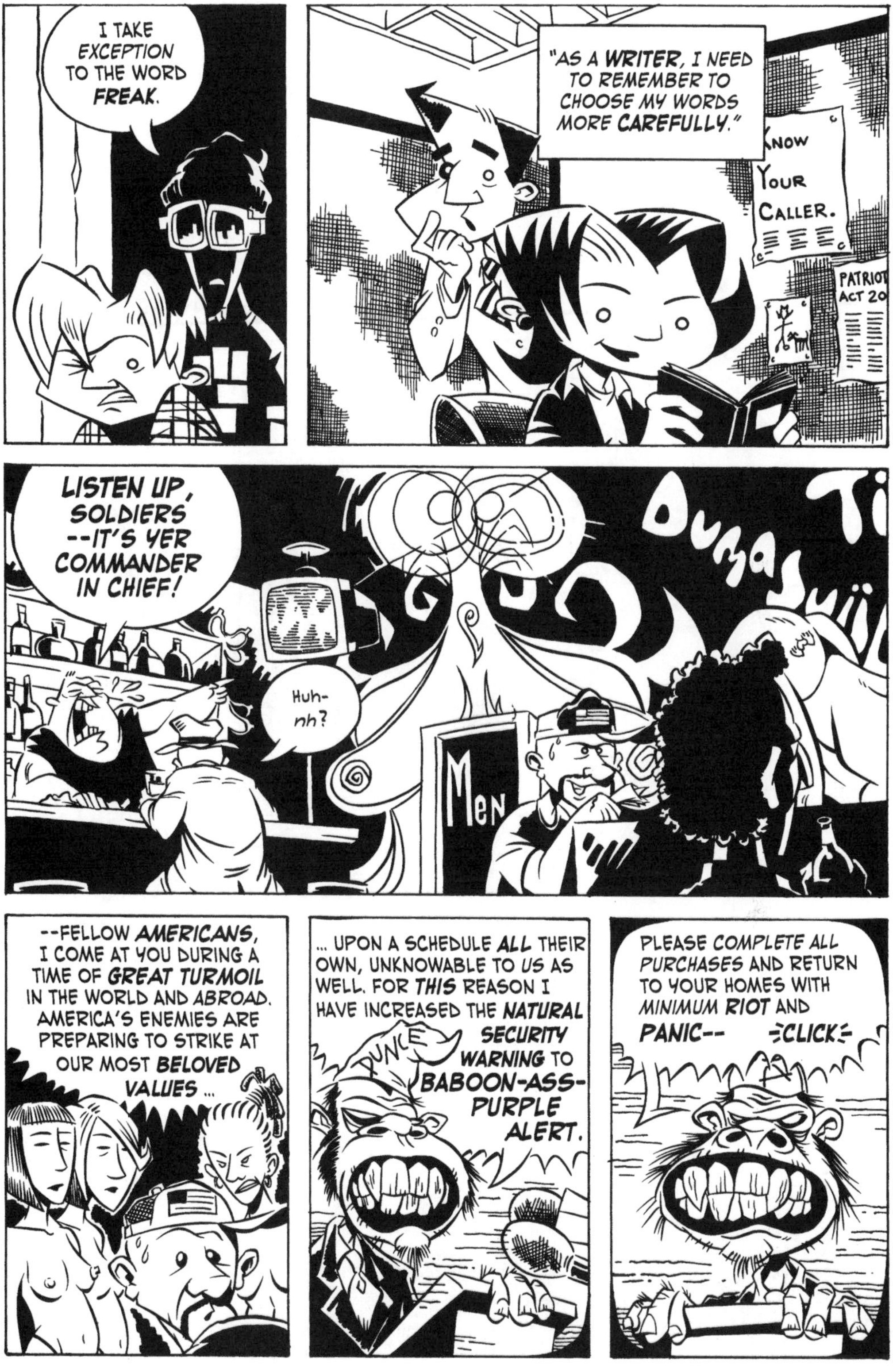
I TAKE EXCEPTION TO THE WORD FREAK.
"AS A WRITER, I NEED TO REMEMBER TO CHOOSE MY WORDS MORE CAREFULLY."
KNOW YOUR CALLER.
LISTEN UP, SOLDIERS --IT'S YER COMMANDER IN CHIEF!
Huh-nh?
Men
--FELLOW AMERICANS, I COME AT YOU DURING A TIME OF GREAT TURMOIL IN THE WORLD AND ABROAD. AMERICA'S ENEMIES ARE PREPARING TO STRIKE AT OUR MOST BELOVED VALUES ...
... UPON A SCHEDULE ALL THEIR OWN, UNKNOWABLE TO US AS WELL. FOR THIS REASON I HAVE INCREASED THE NATURAL SECURITY WARNING TO BABOON-ASS-PURPLE ALERT.
PLEASE COMPLETE ALL PURCHASES AND RETURN TO YOUR HOMES WITH MINIMUM RIOT AND PANIC--
CLICK

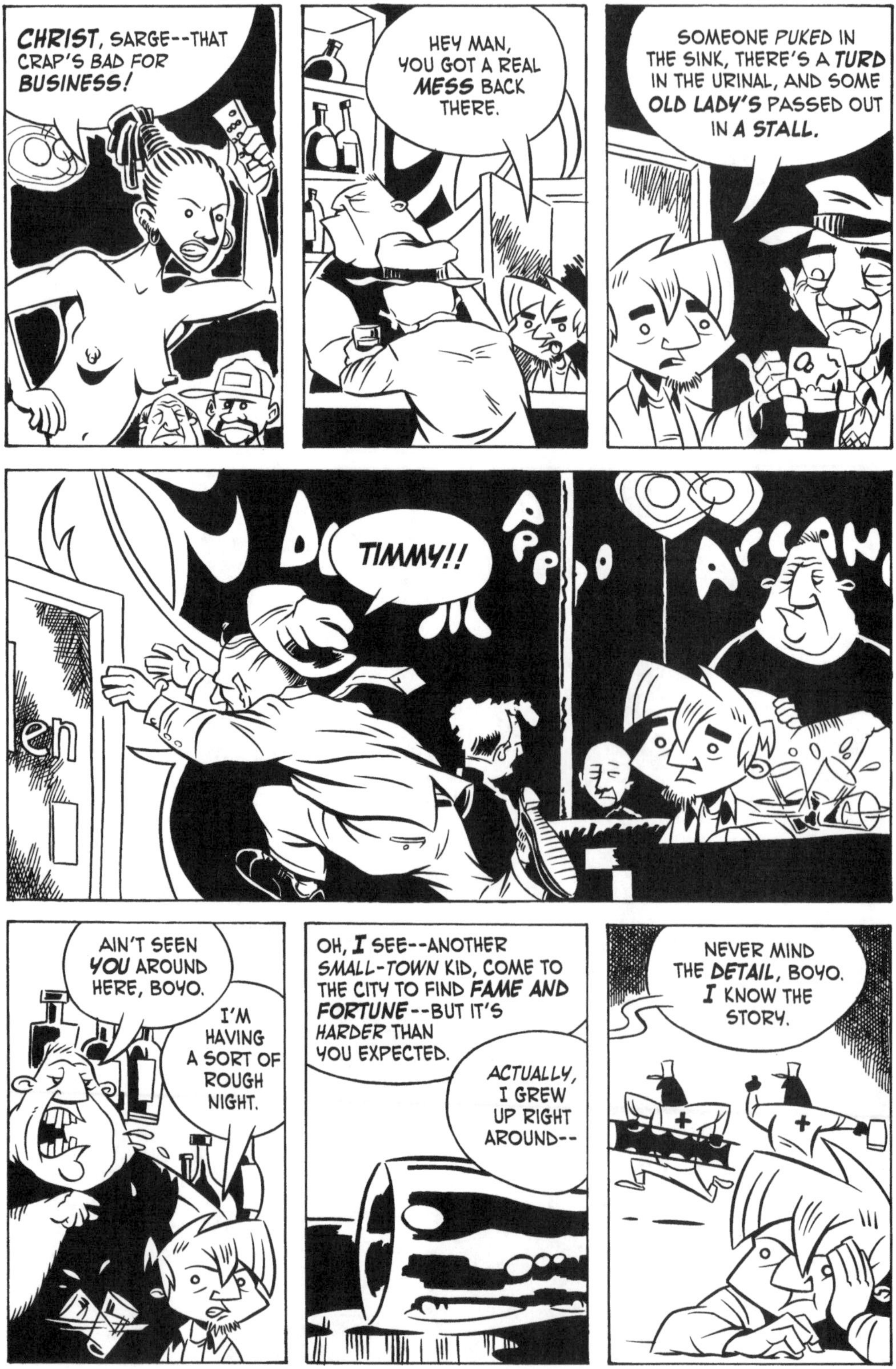
CHRIST, SARGE--THAT CRAP'S BAD FOR BUSINESS!
HEY MAN, YOU GOT A REAL MESS BACK THERE.
SOMEONE PUKED IN THE SINK, THERE'S A TURD IN THE URINAL, AND SOME OLD LADY'S PASSED OUT IN A STALL.
TIMMY!!
AIN'T SEEN YOU AROUND HERE, BOYO.
I'M HAVING A SORT OF ROUGH NIGHT.
OH, I SEE--ANOTHER SMALL-TOWN KID, COME TO THE CITY TO FIND FAME AND FORTUNE--BUT IT'S HARDER THAN YOU EXPECTED.
ACTUALLY, I GREW UP RIGHT AROUND--
NEVER MIND THE DETAIL, BOYO. I KNOW THE STORY.

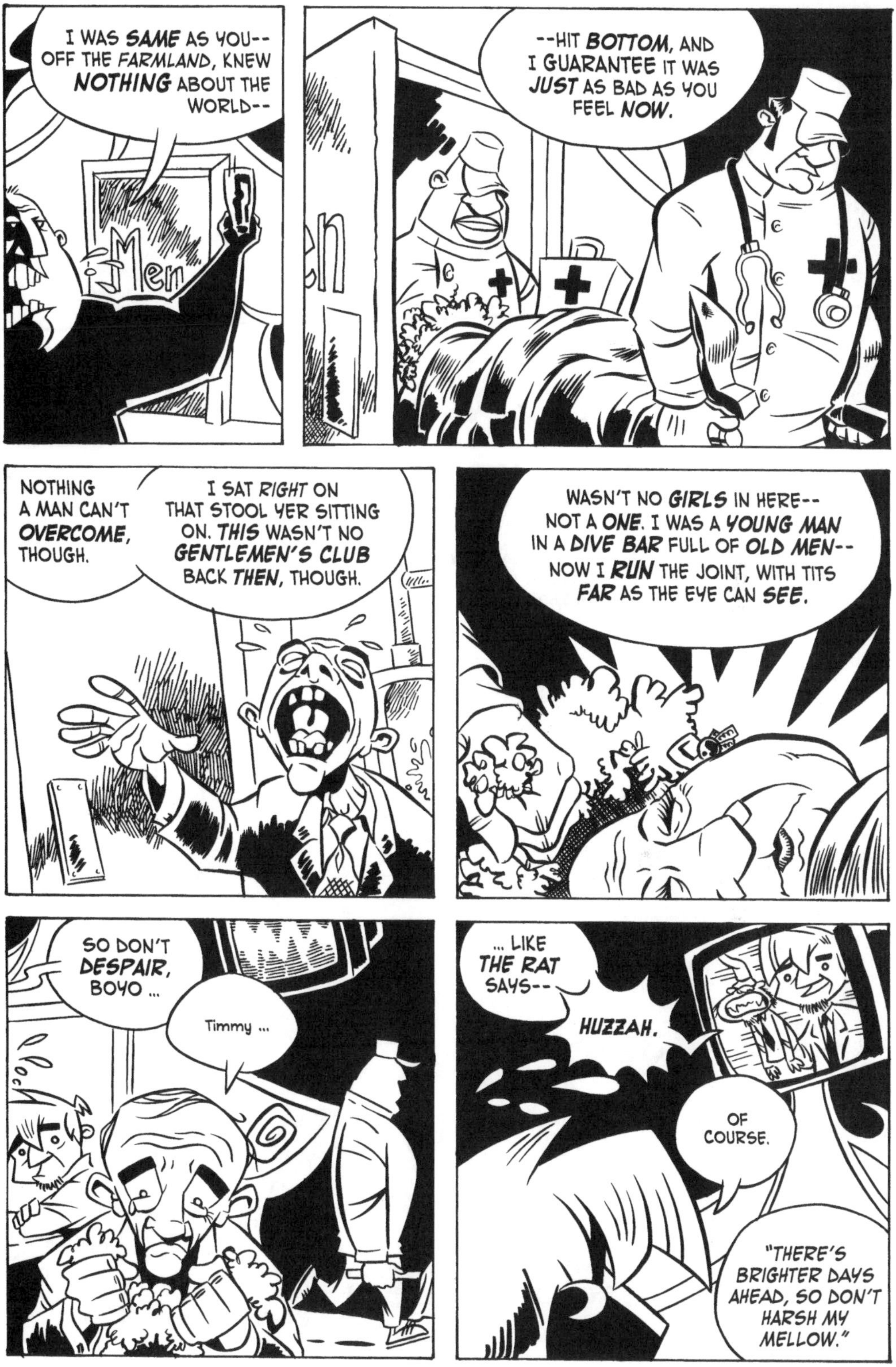
I WAS SAME AS YOU-- OFF THE FARMLAND, KNEW NOTHING ABOUT THE WORLD--
Men
--HIT BOTTOM, AND I GUARANTEE IT WAS JUST AS BAD AS YOU FEEL NOW.
NOTHING A MAN CAN'T OVERCOME, THOUGH.
I SAT RIGHT ON THAT STOOL YER SITTING ON. THIS WASN'T NO GENTLEMEN'S CLUB BACK THEN, THOUGH.
WASN'T NO GIRLS IN HERE-- NOT A ONE. I WAS A YOUNG MAN IN A DIVE BAR FULL OF OLD MEN-- NOW I RUN THE JOINT, WITH TITS FAR AS THE EYE CAN SEE.
SO DON'T DESPAIR, BOYO ...
Timmy ...
... LIKE THE RAT SAYS--
HUZZAH.
OF COURSE.
"THERE'S BRIGHTER DAYS AHEAD, SO DON'T HARSH MY MELLOW."

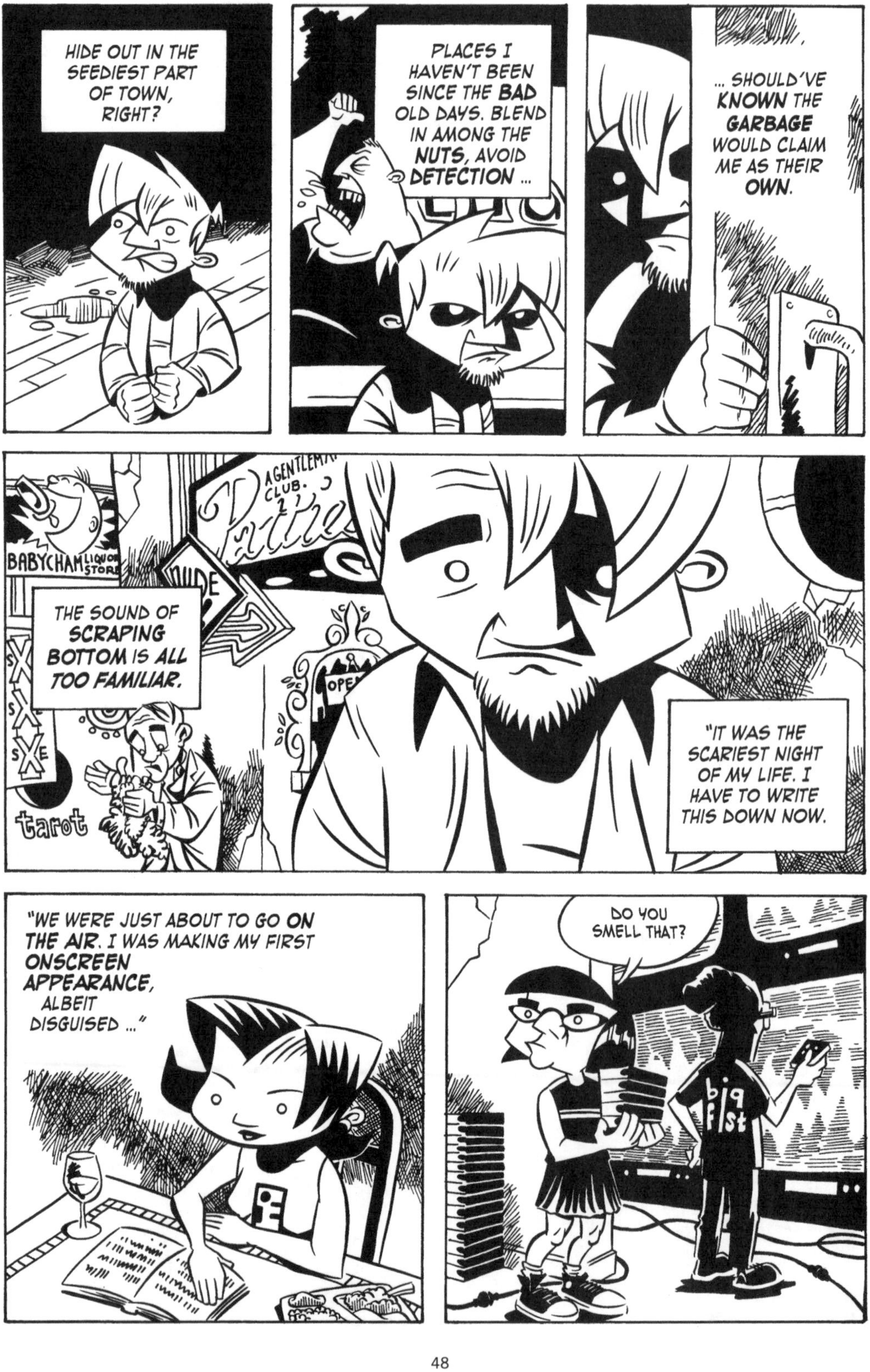
HIDE OUT IN THE SEEDIEST PART OF TOWN, RIGHT?
PLACES I HAVEN'T BEEN SINCE THE BAD OLD DAYS. BLEND IN AMONG THE NUTS, AVOID DETECTION ...
... SHOULD'VE KNOWN THE GARBAGE WOULD CLAIM ME AS THEIR OWN.
A GENTLEMAN CLUB.
BABYCHAM LIQUOR STORE
tarot
THE SOUND OF SCRAPING BOTTOM IS ALL TOO FAMILIAR.
"IT WAS THE SCARIEST NIGHT OF MY LIFE. I HAVE TO WRITE THIS DOWN NOW.
"WE WERE JUST ABOUT TO GO ON THE AIR. I WAS MAKING MY FIRST ONSCREEN APPEARANCE, ALBEIT DISGUISED ..."
DO YOU SMELL THAT?
big fist

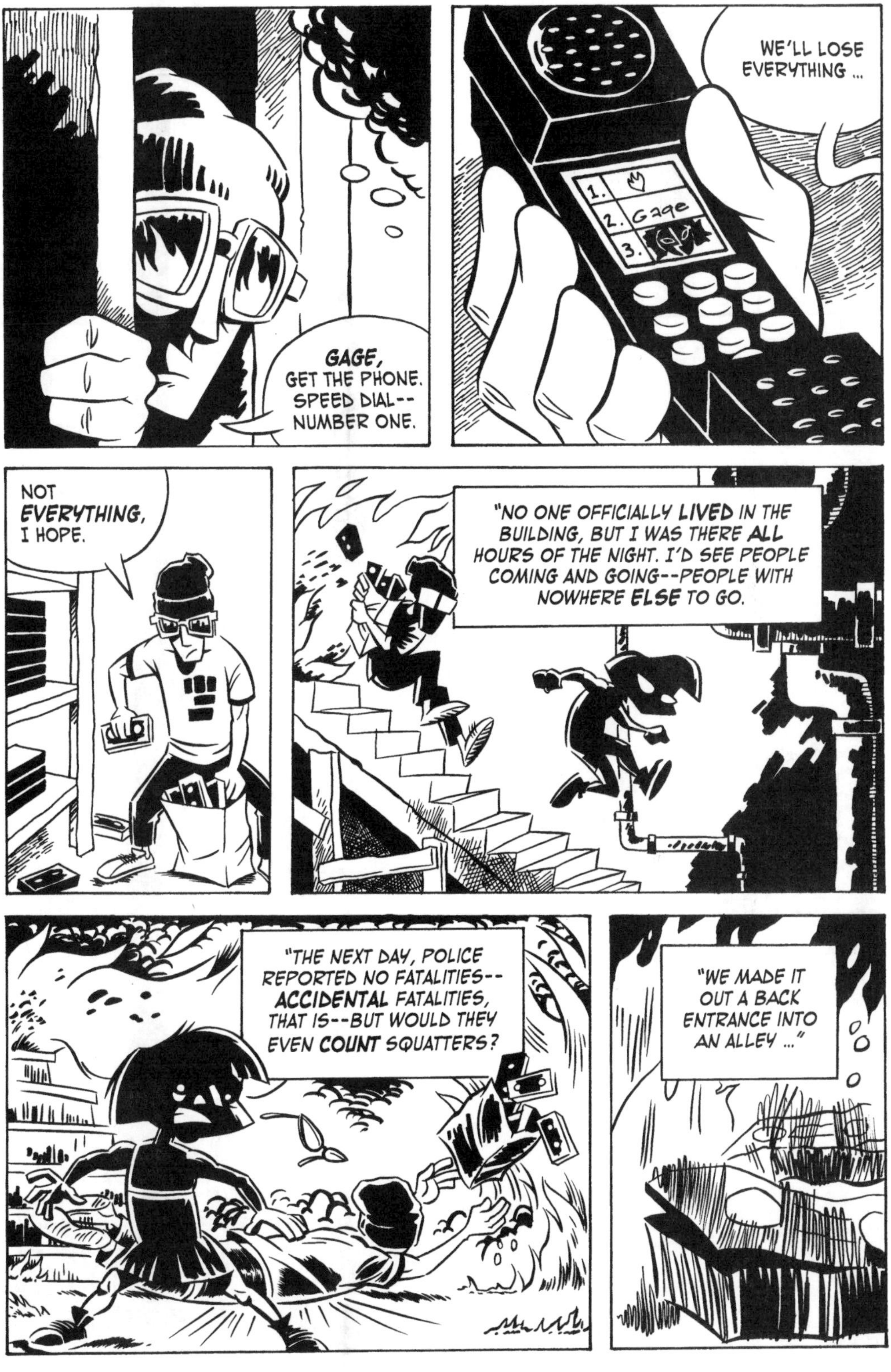
GAGE, GET THE PHONE. SPEED DIAL-- NUMBER ONE.
WE'LL LOSE EVERYTHING ...
1.
2. Gage
3.
NOT EVERYTHING, I HOPE.
"NO ONE OFFICIALLY LIVED IN THE BUILDING, BUT I WAS THERE ALL HOURS OF THE NIGHT. I'D SEE PEOPLE COMING AND GOING--PEOPLE WITH NOWHERE ELSE TO GO.
"THE NEXT DAY, POLICE REPORTED NO FATALITIES-- ACCIDENTAL FATALITIES, THAT IS--BUT WOULD THEY EVEN COUNT SQUATTERS?
"WE MADE IT OUT A BACK ENTRANCE INTO AN ALLEY ..."

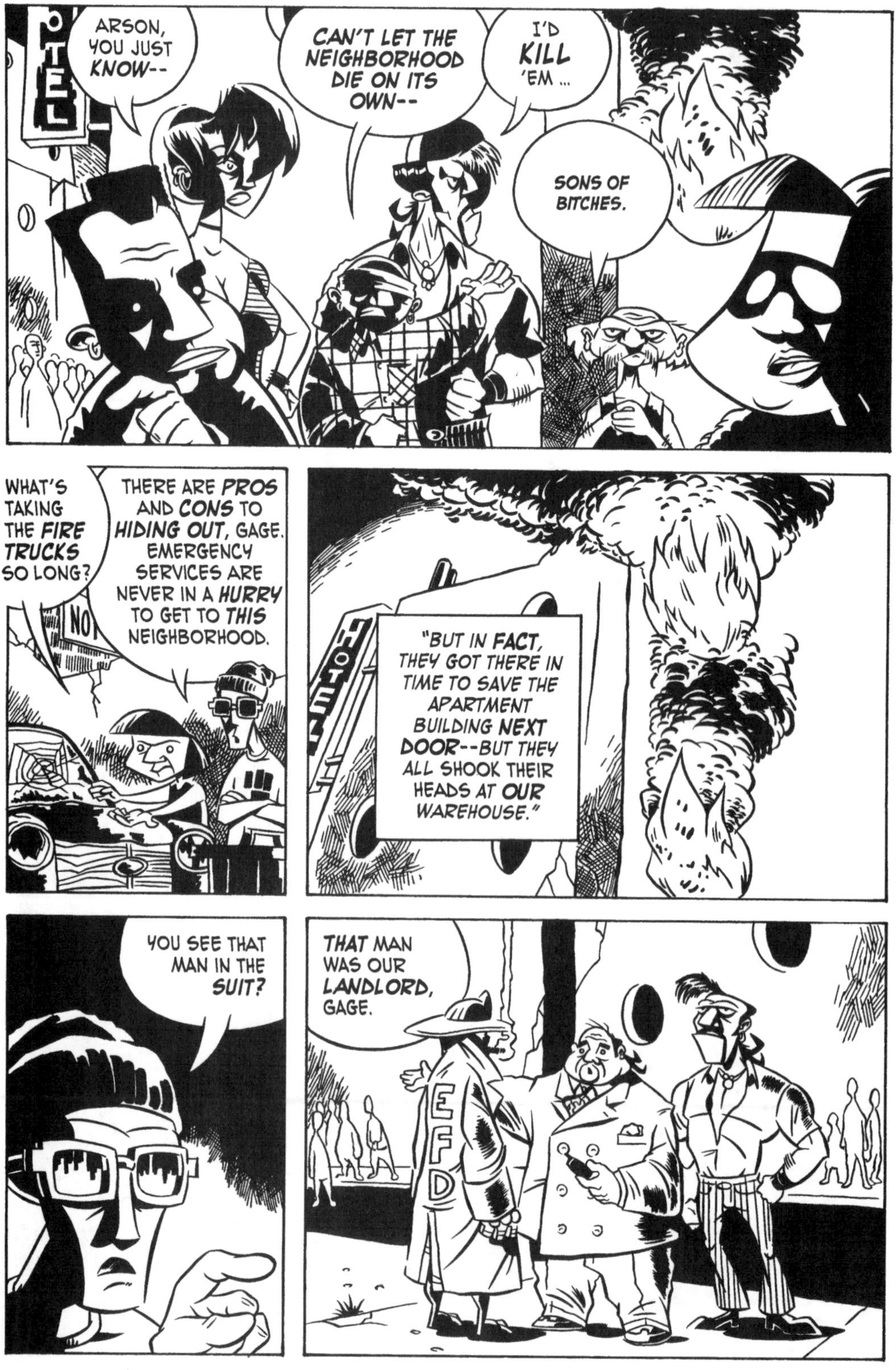
OTEL
ARSON, YOU JUST KNOW--
CAN'T LET THE NEIGHBORHOOD DIE ON ITS OWN--
I'D KILL 'EM ...
SONS OF BITCHES.
WHAT'S TAKING THE FIRE TRUCKS SO LONG?
THERE ARE PROS AND CONS TO HIDING OUT, GAGE. EMERGENCY SERVICES ARE NEVER IN A HURRY TO GET TO THIS NEIGHBORHOOD.
HOTEL
"BUT IN FACT, THEY GOT THERE IN TIME TO SAVE THE APARTMENT BUILDING NEXT DOOR--BUT THEY ALL SHOOK THEIR HEADS AT OUR WAREHOUSE."
YOU SEE THAT MAN IN THE SUIT?
THAT MAN WAS OUR LANDLORD, GAGE.
EFD

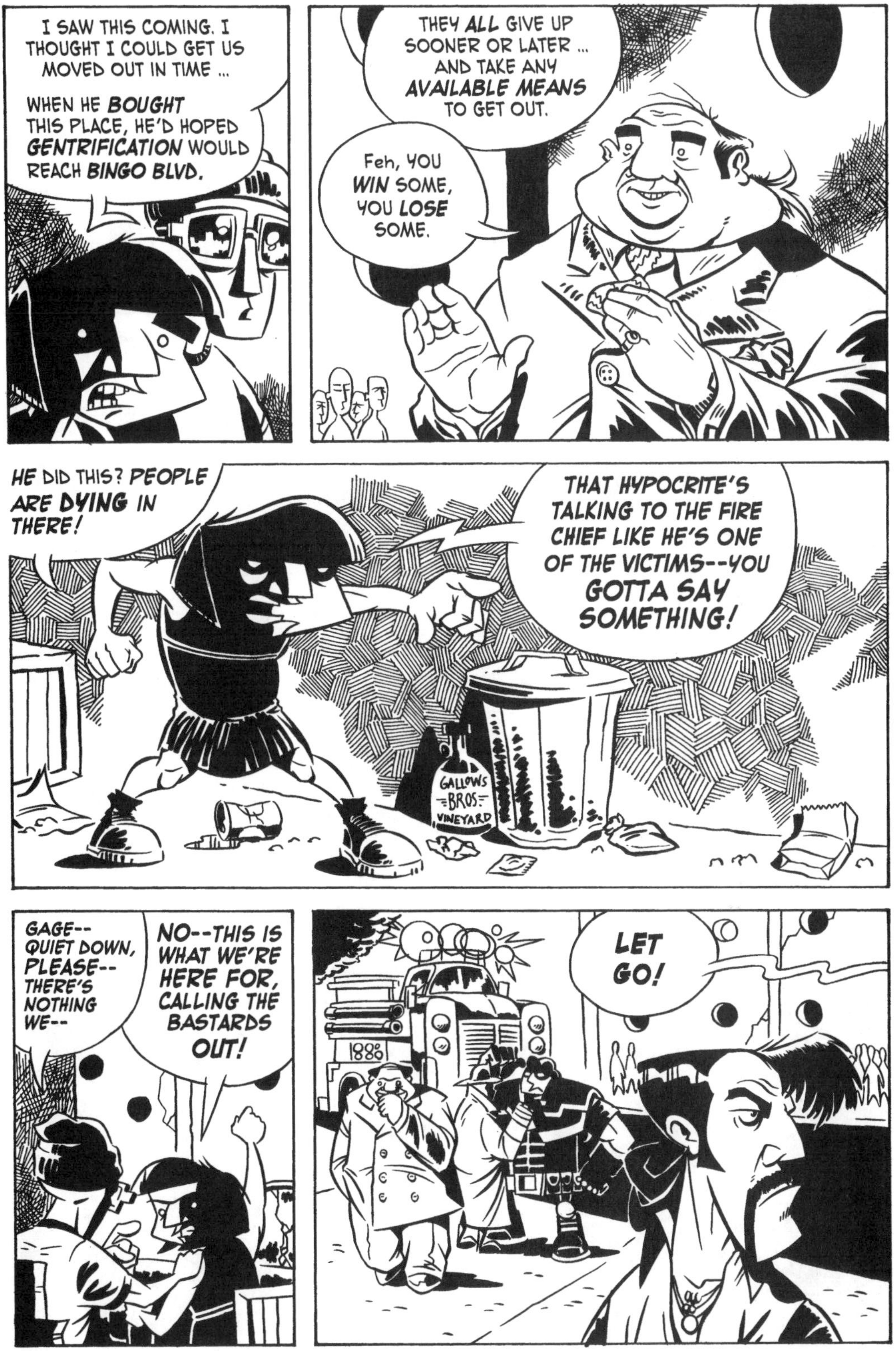
I SAW THIS COMING. I THOUGHT I COULD GET US MOVED OUT IN TIME ...
WHEN HE BOUGHT THIS PLACE, HE'D HOPED GENTRIFICATION WOULD REACH BINGO BLVD.
THEY ALL GIVE UP SOONER OR LATER ... AND TAKE ANY AVAILABLE MEANS TO GET OUT.
Feh, YOU WIN SOME, YOU LOSE SOME.
HE DID THIS? PEOPLE ARE DYING IN THERE!
THAT HYPOCRITE'S TALKING TO THE FIRE CHIEF LIKE HE'S ONE OF THE VICTIMS--YOU GOTTA SAY SOMETHING!
GALLOWS BROS. VINEYARD
GAGE--QUIET DOWN, PLEASE--THERE'S NOTHING WE--
NO--THIS IS WHAT WE'RE HERE FOR, CALLING THE BASTARDS OUT!
1889
LET GO!

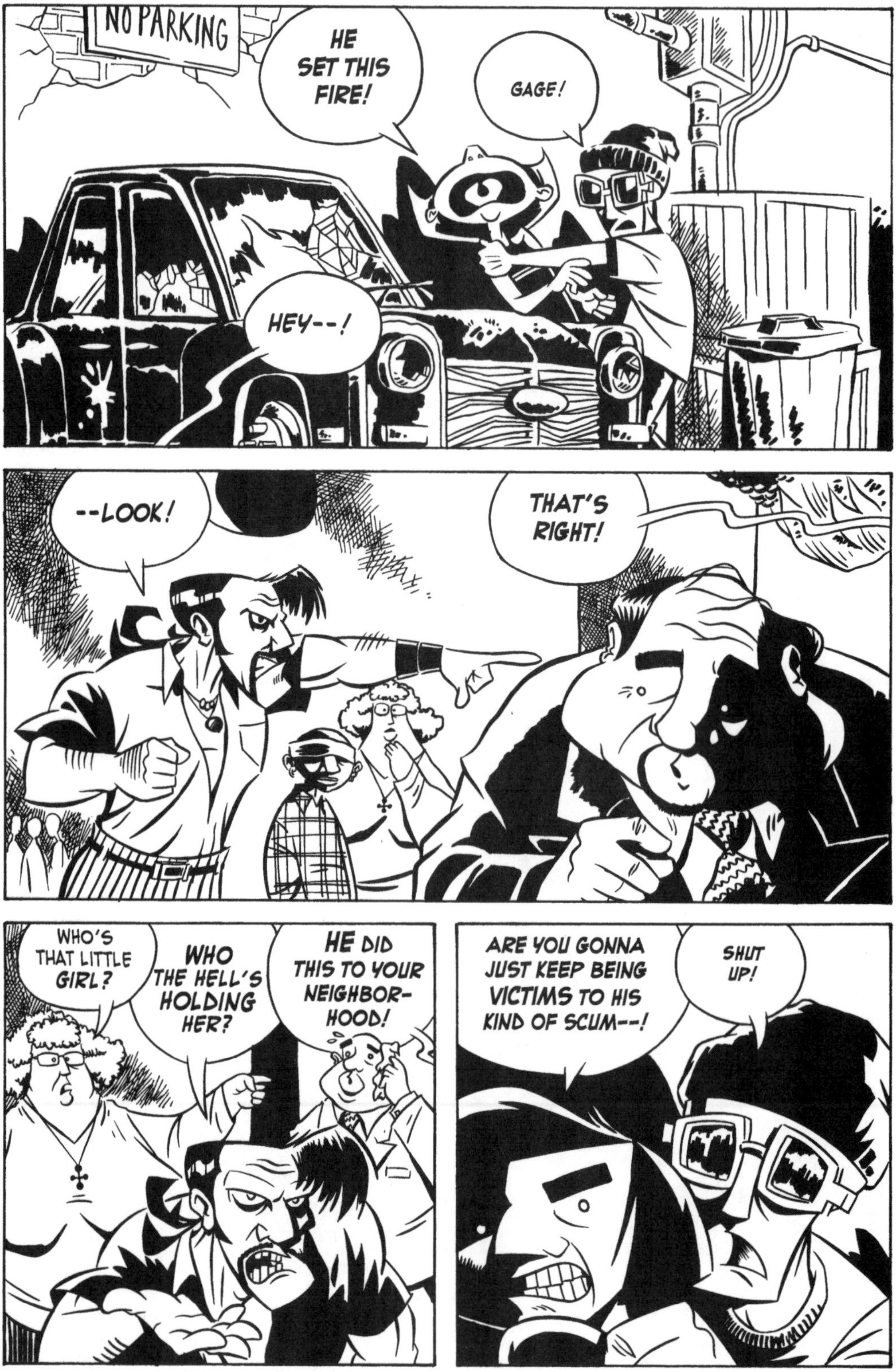
NO PARKING
HE SET THIS FIRE!
GAGE!
HEY--!
--LOOK!
THAT'S RIGHT!
WHO'S THAT LITTLE GIRL?
WHO THE HELL'S HOLDING HER?
HE DID THIS TO YOUR NEIGHBOR-HOOD!
ARE YOU GONNA JUST KEEP BEING VICTIMS TO HIS KIND OF SCUM--!
SHUT UP!

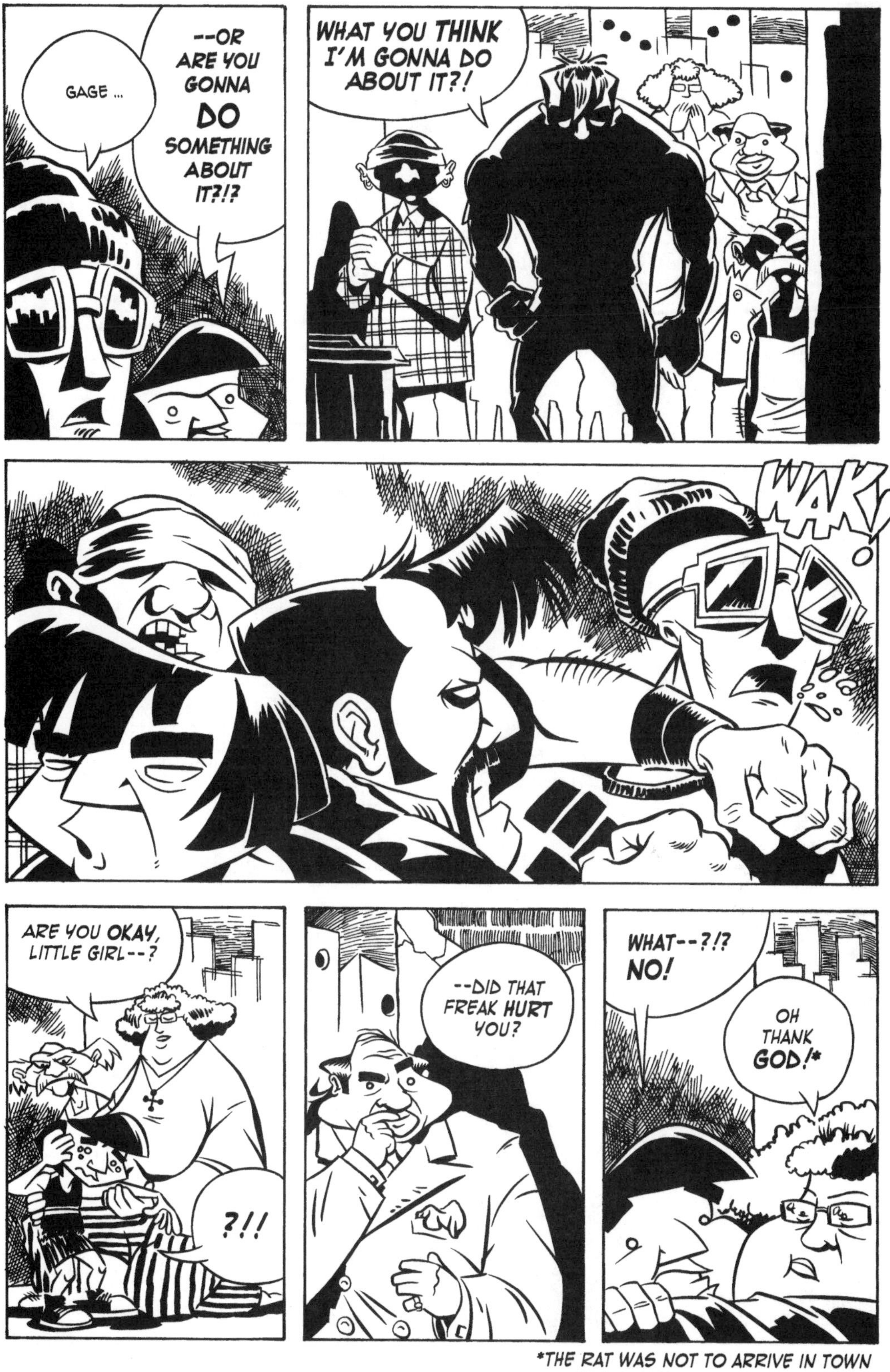
GAGE ...
--OR ARE YOU GONNA DO SOMETHING ABOUT IT?!?
WHAT YOU THINK I'M GONNA DO ABOUT IT?!
WAK!
ARE YOU OKAY, LITTLE GIRL--?
?!!
--DID THAT FREAK HURT YOU?
WHAT--?!? NO!
OH THANK GOD!*

*THE RAT WAS NOT TO ARRIVE IN TOWN FOR A FEW MORE YEARS--EDITOR

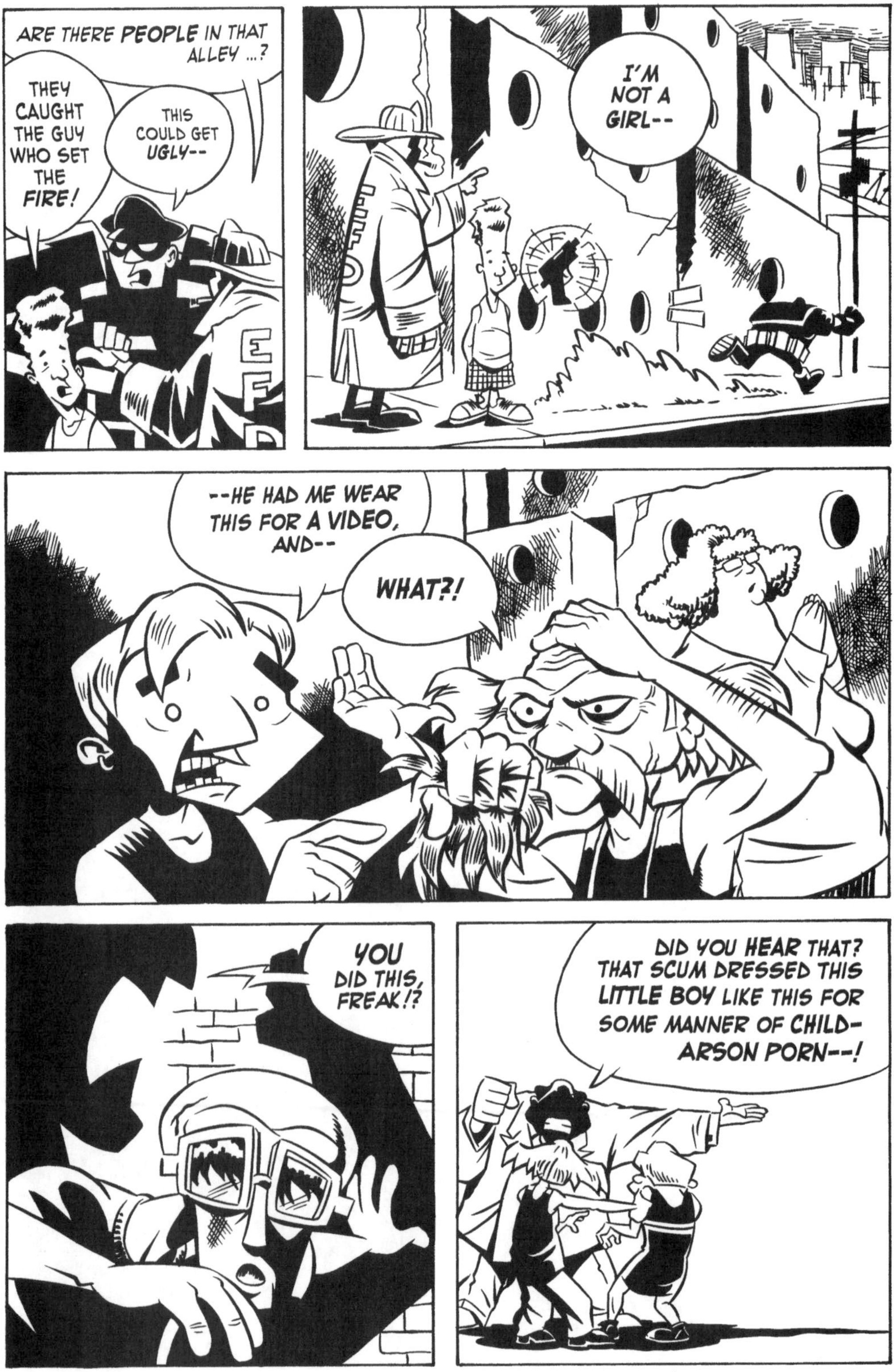
ARE THERE PEOPLE IN THAT ALLEY ...?
THEY CAUGHT THE GUY WHO SET THE FIRE!
THIS COULD GET UGLY--
I'M NOT A GIRL--
--HE HAD ME WEAR THIS FOR A VIDEO, AND--
WHAT?!
YOU DID THIS, FREAK!?
DID YOU HEAR THAT? THAT SCUM DRESSED THIS LITTLE BOY LIKE THIS FOR SOME MANNER OF CHILD-ARSON PORN--!

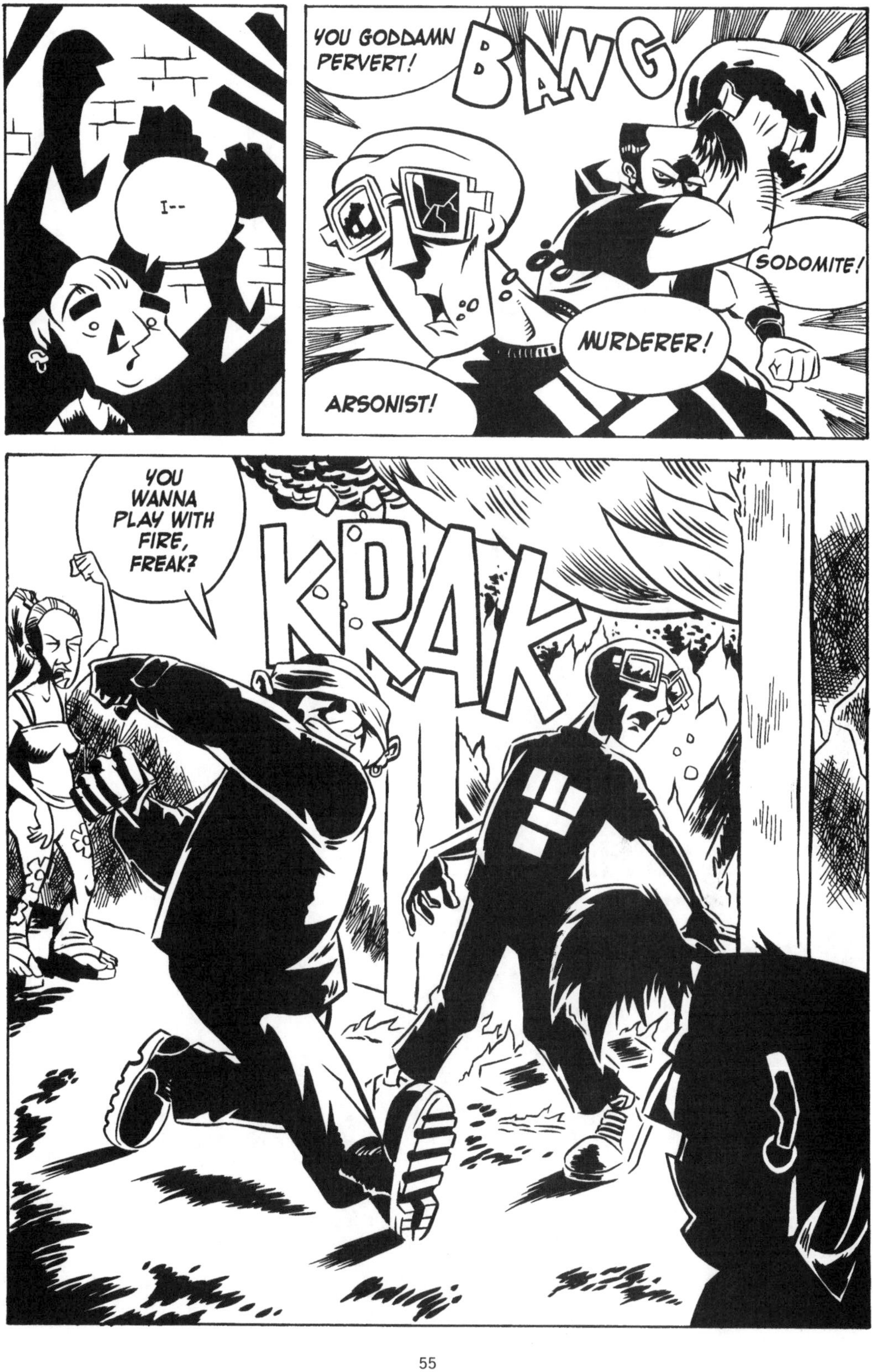
I--
YOU GODDAMN PERVERT!
BANG
SODOMITE!
MURDERER!
ARSONIST!
YOU WANNA PLAY WITH FIRE, FREAK?
KRAK

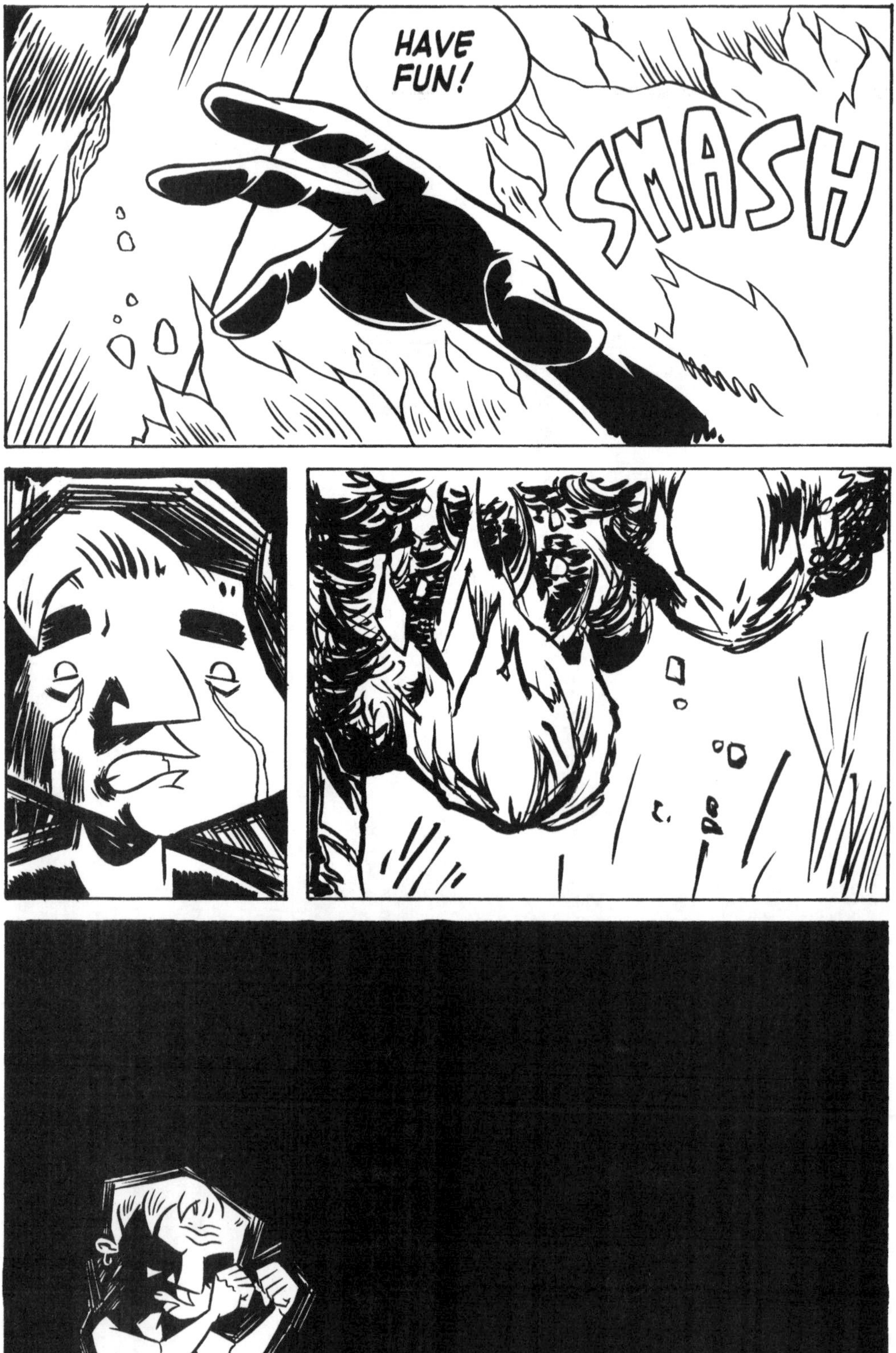
HAVE FUN!
SMASH

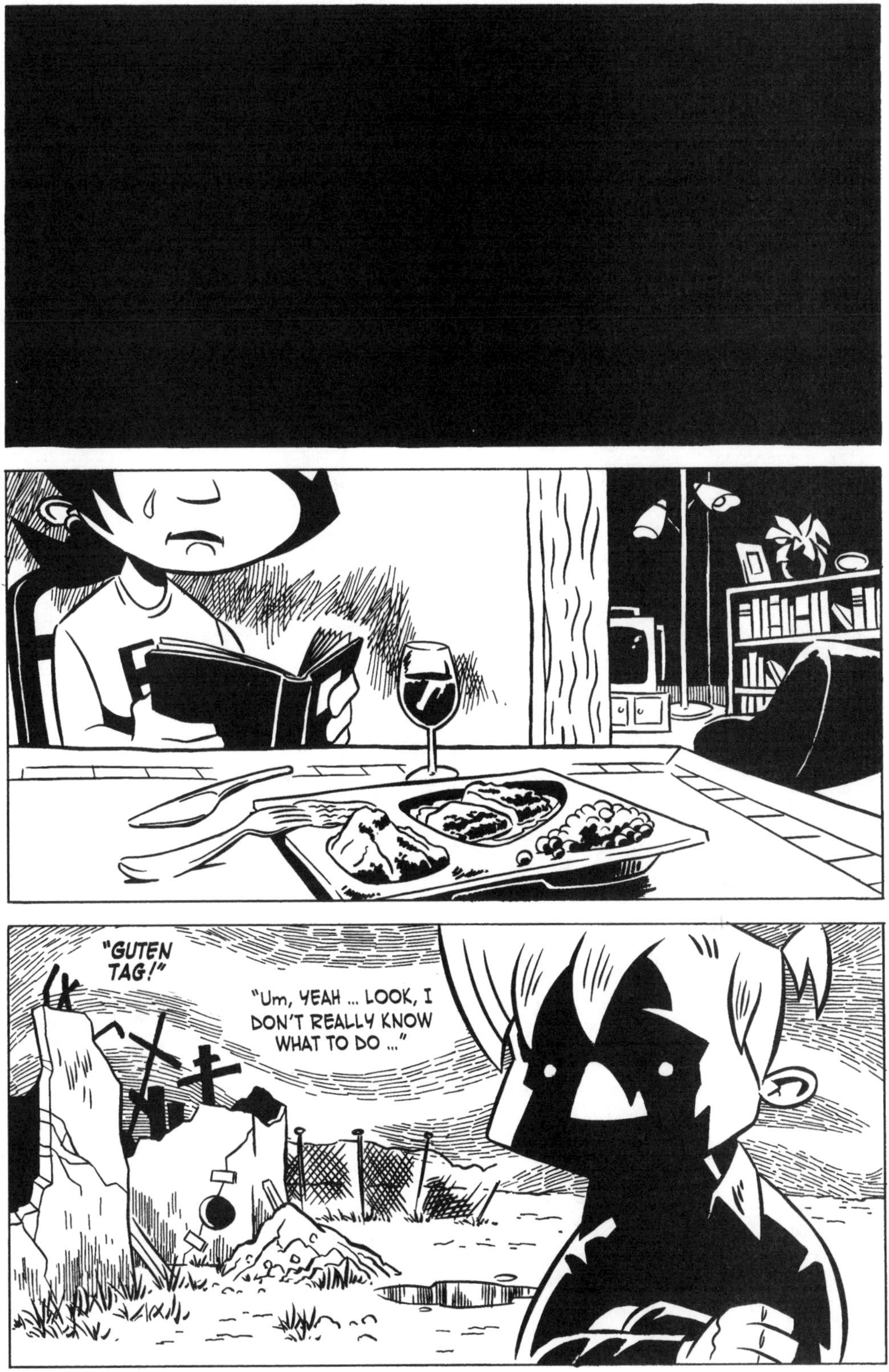
"GUTEN TAG!"
"Um, YEAH ... LOOK, I DON'T REALLY KNOW WHAT TO DO ..."

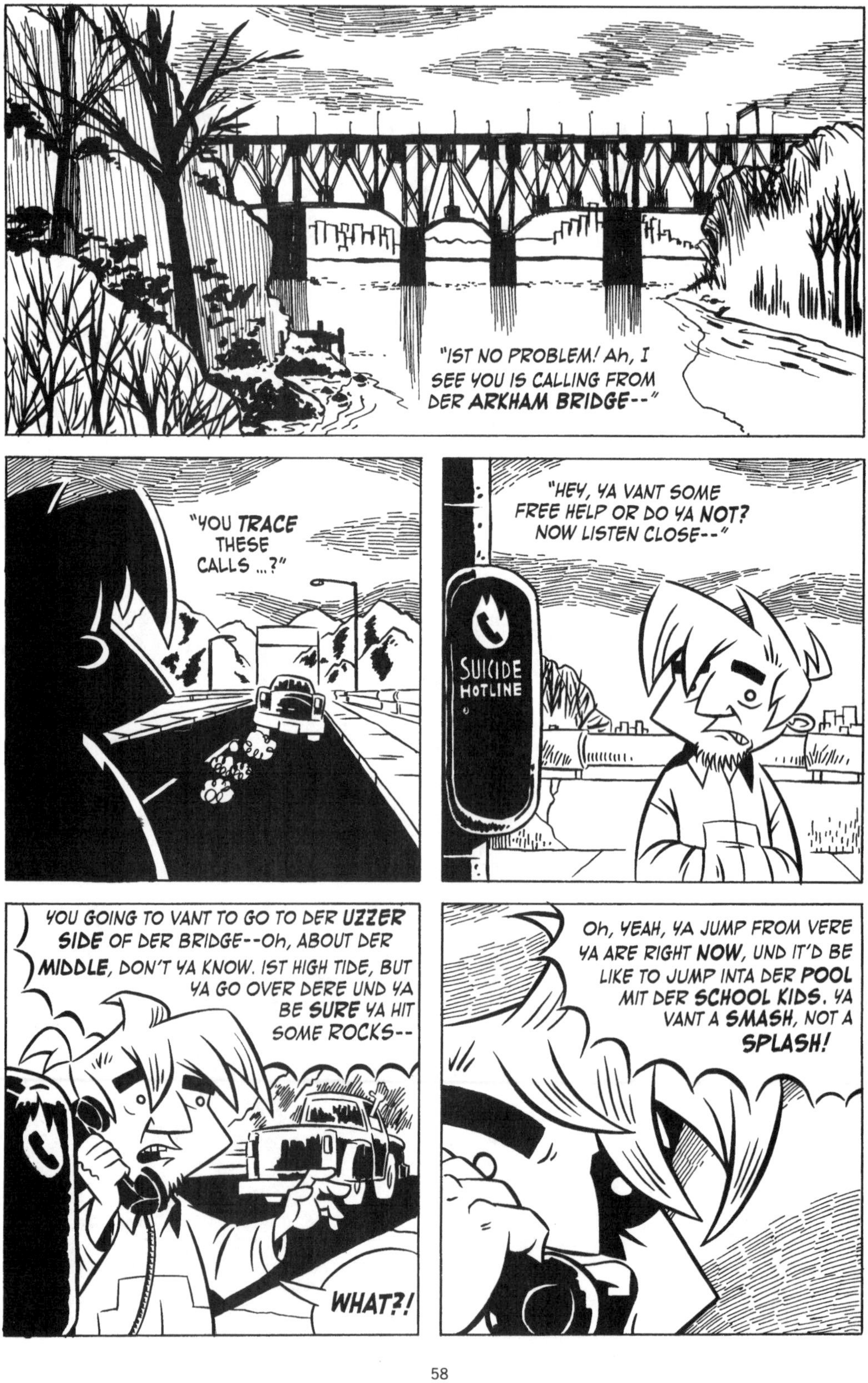
"IST NO PROBLEM! Ah, I SEE YOU IS CALLING FROM DER ARKHAM BRIDGE--"
"YOU TRACE THESE CALLS ...?"
"HEY, YA VANT SOME FREE HELP OR DO YA NOT? NOW LISTEN CLOSE--"
SUICIDE HOTLINE
YOU GOING TO VANT TO GO TO DER UZZER SIDE OF DER BRIDGE--Oh, ABOUT DER MIDDLE, DON'T YA KNOW. IST HIGH TIDE, BUT YA GO OVER DERE UND YA BE SURE YA HIT SOME ROCKS--
WHAT?!
Oh, YEAH, YA JUMP FROM VERE YA ARE RIGHT NOW, UND IT'D BE LIKE TO JUMP INTA DER POOL MIT DER SCHOOL KIDS. YA VANT A SMASH, NOT A SPLASH!

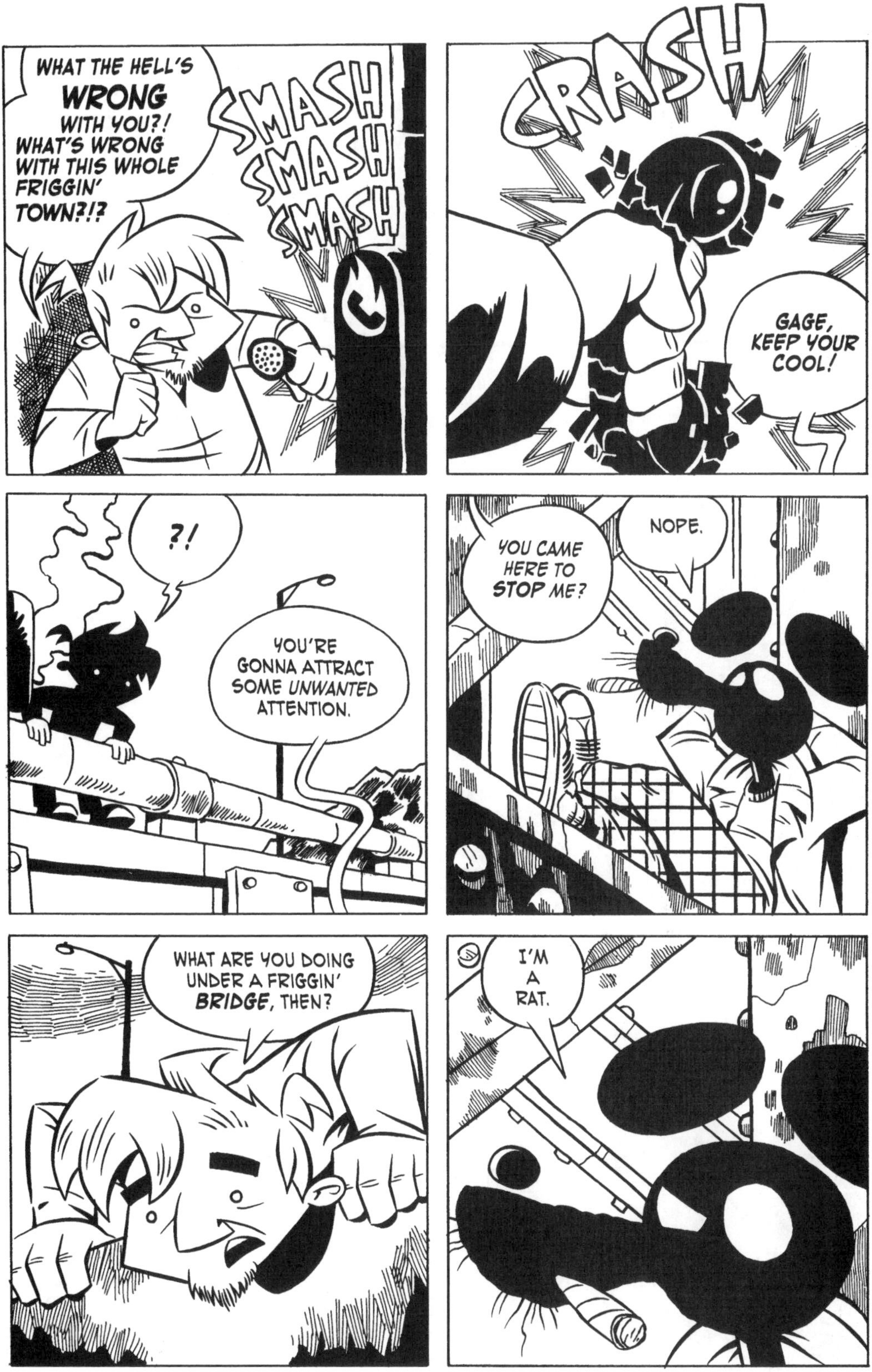
WHAT THE HELL'S WRONG WITH YOU?! WHAT'S WRONG WITH THIS WHOLE FRIGGIN' TOWN?!?
SMASH SMASH SMASH
CRASH
GAGE, KEEP YOUR COOL!
?!
YOU'RE GONNA ATTRACT SOME UNWANTED ATTENTION.
YOU CAME HERE TO STOP ME?
NOPE.
WHAT ARE YOU DOING UNDER A FRIGGIN' BRIDGE, THEN?
I'M A RAT.

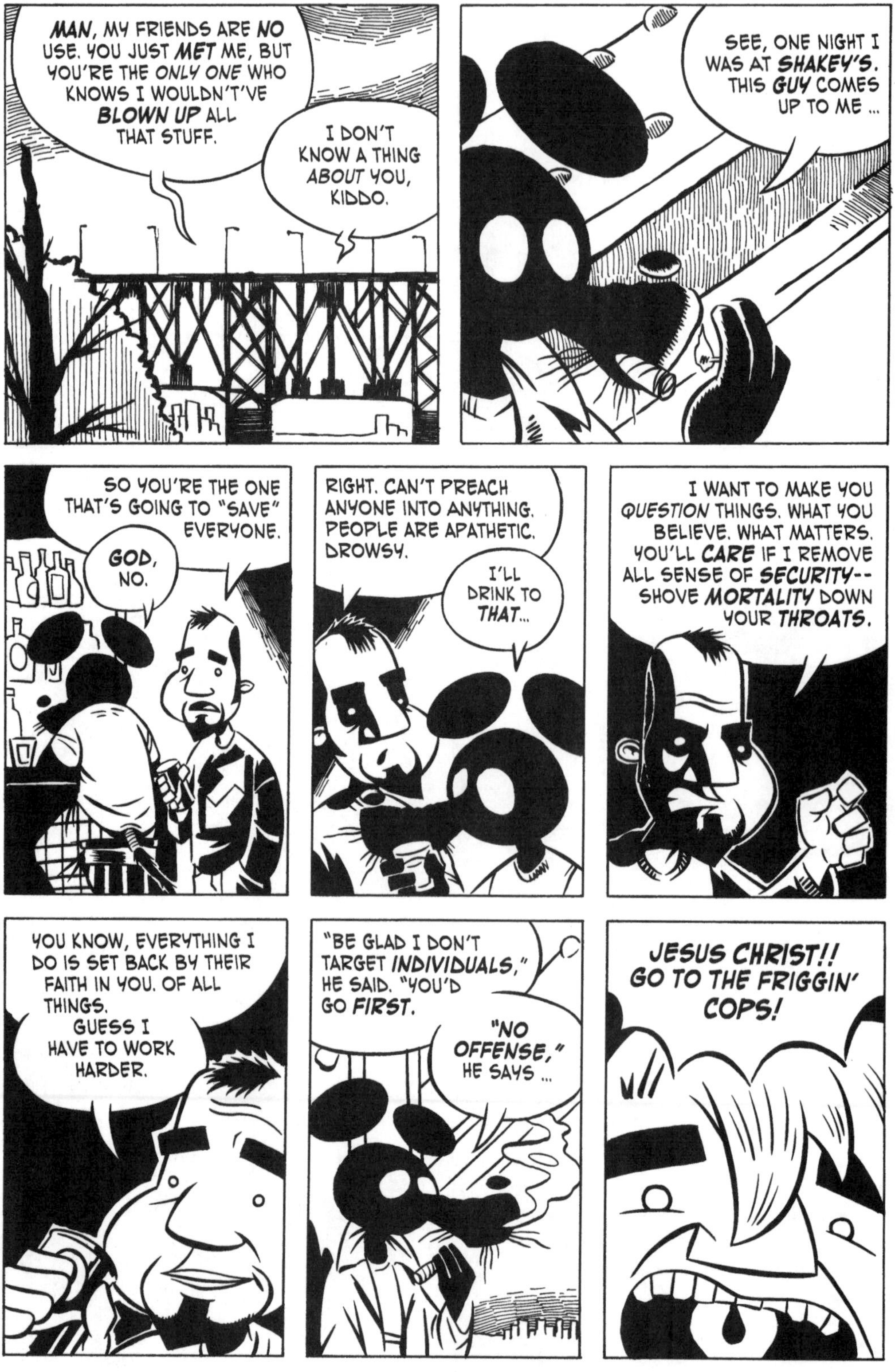
MAN, MY FRIENDS ARE NO USE. YOU JUST MET ME, BUT YOU'RE THE ONLY ONE WHO KNOWS I WOULDN'T'VE BLOWN UP ALL THAT STUFF.
I DON'T KNOW A THING ABOUT YOU, KIDDO.
SEE, ONE NIGHT I WAS AT SHAKEY'S. THIS GUY COMES UP TO ME ...
SO YOU'RE THE ONE THAT'S GOING TO "SAVE" EVERYONE.
GOD, NO.
RIGHT. CAN'T PREACH ANYONE INTO ANYTHING. PEOPLE ARE APATHETIC. DROWSY.
I'LL DRINK TO THAT...
I WANT TO MAKE YOU QUESTION THINGS. WHAT YOU BELIEVE. WHAT MATTERS. YOU'LL CARE IF I REMOVE ALL SENSE OF SECURITY-- SHOVE MORTALITY DOWN YOUR THROATS.
YOU KNOW, EVERYTHING I DO IS SET BACK BY THEIR FAITH IN YOU. OF ALL THINGS.
GUESS I HAVE TO WORK HARDER.
"BE GLAD I DON'T TARGET INDIVIDUALS," HE SAID. "YOU'D GO FIRST.
"NO OFFENSE," HE SAYS ...
JESUS CHRIST!! GO TO THE FRIGGIN' COPS!

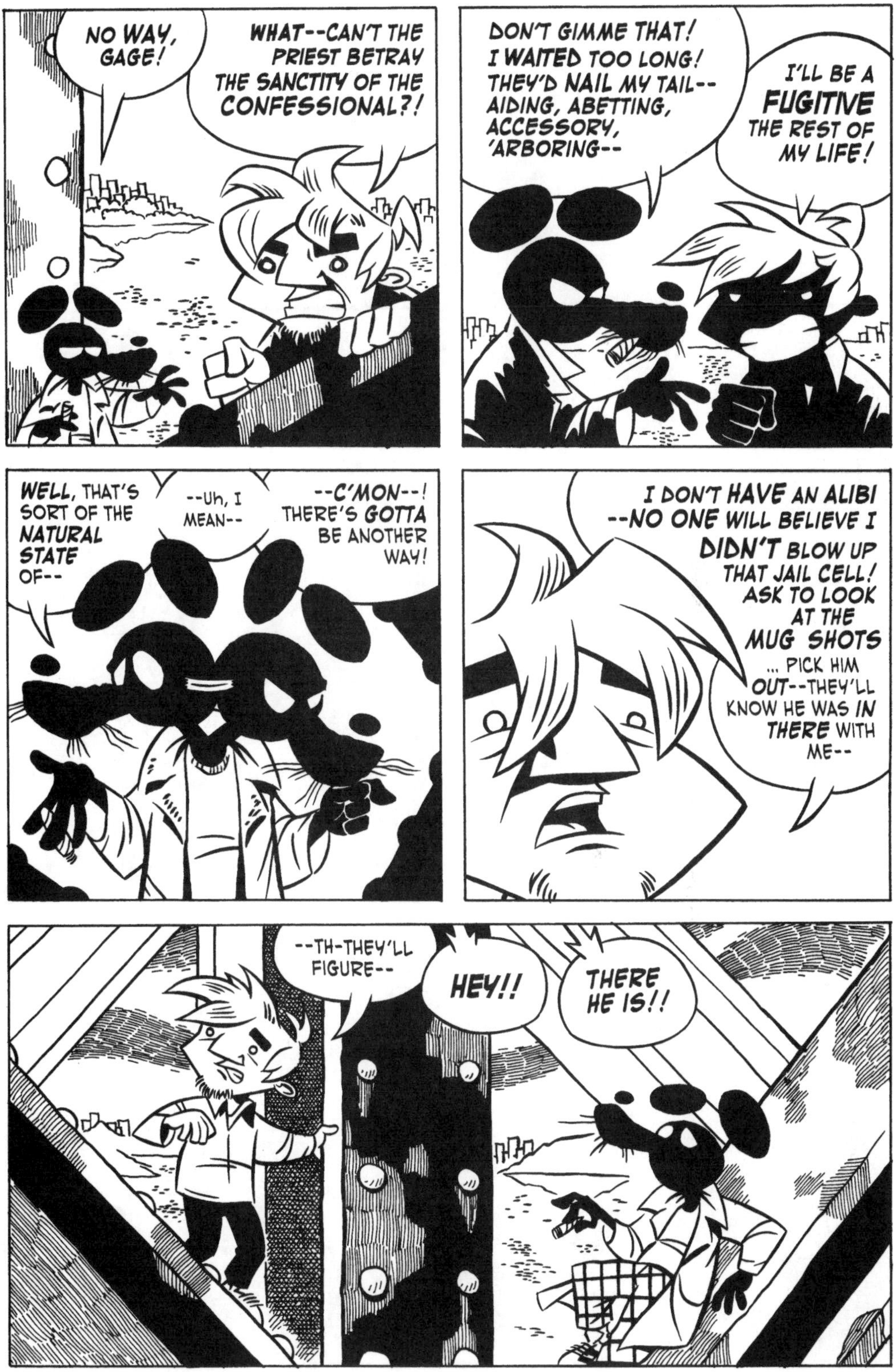
NO WAY, GAGE!
WHAT--CAN'T THE PRIEST BETRAY THE SANCTITY OF THE CONFESSIONAL?!
DON'T GIMME THAT! I WAITED TOO LONG! THEY'D NAIL MY TAIL--AIDING, ABETTING, ACCESSORY, 'ARBORING--
I'LL BE A FUGITIVE THE REST OF MY LIFE!
WELL, THAT'S SORT OF THE NATURAL STATE OF--
--Uh, I MEAN--
--C'MON--! THERE'S GOTTA BE ANOTHER WAY!
I DON'T HAVE AN ALIBI --NO ONE WILL BELIEVE I DIDN'T BLOW UP THAT JAIL CELL! ASK TO LOOK AT THE MUG SHOTS ... PICK HIM OUT--THEY'LL KNOW HE WAS IN THERE WITH ME--
--TH-THEY'LL FIGURE--
HEY!!
THERE HE IS!!

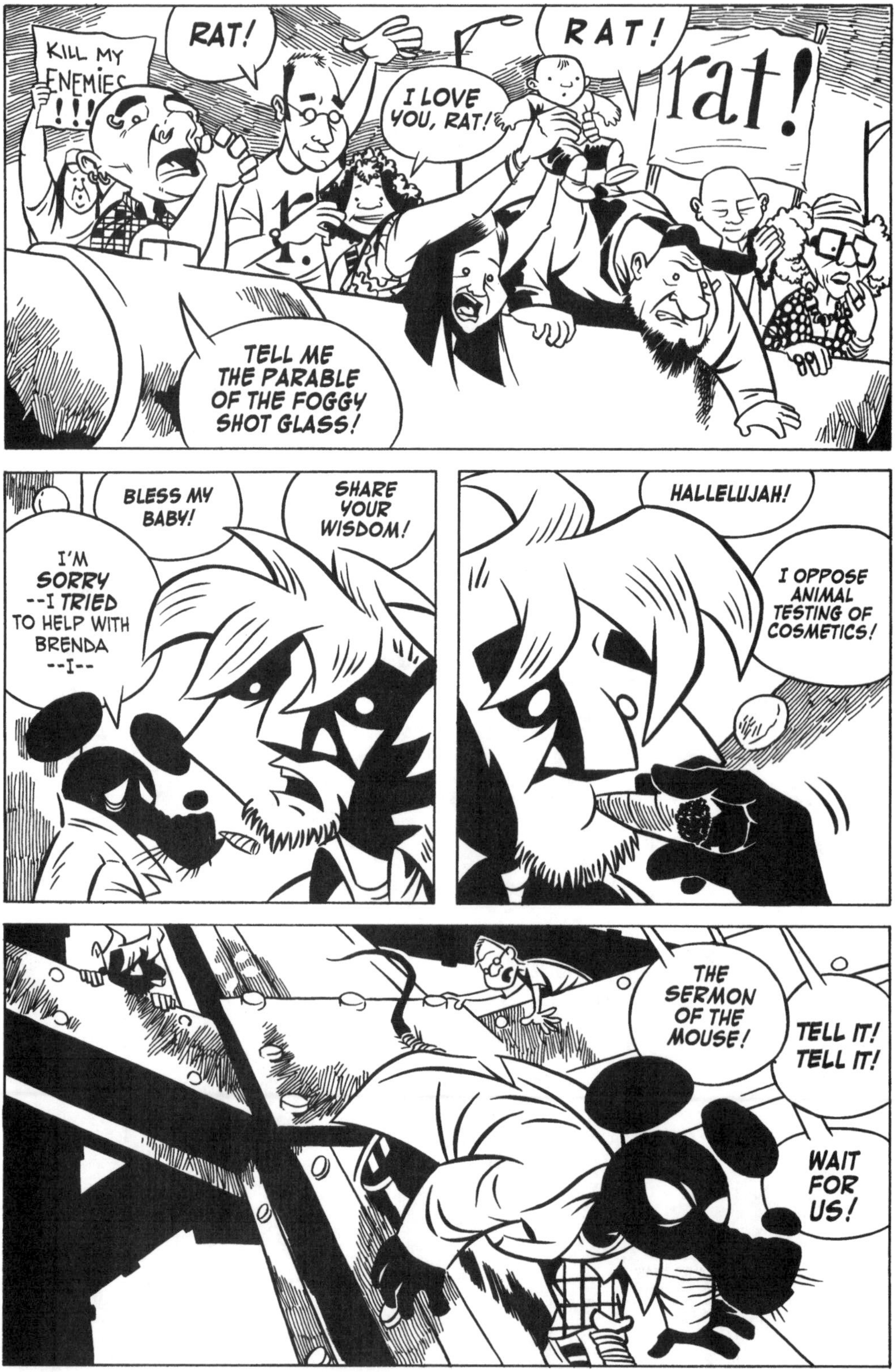
KILL MY ENEMIES !!!
RAT!
RAT!
rat!
I LOVE YOU, RAT!
TELL ME THE PARABLE OF THE FOGGY SHOT GLASS!
BLESS MY BABY!
SHARE YOUR WISDOM!
I'M SORRY --I TRIED TO HELP WITH BRENDA --I--
HALLELUJAH!
I OPPOSE ANIMAL TESTING OF COSMETICS!
THE SERMON OF THE MOUSE!
TELL IT! TELL IT!
WAIT FOR US!

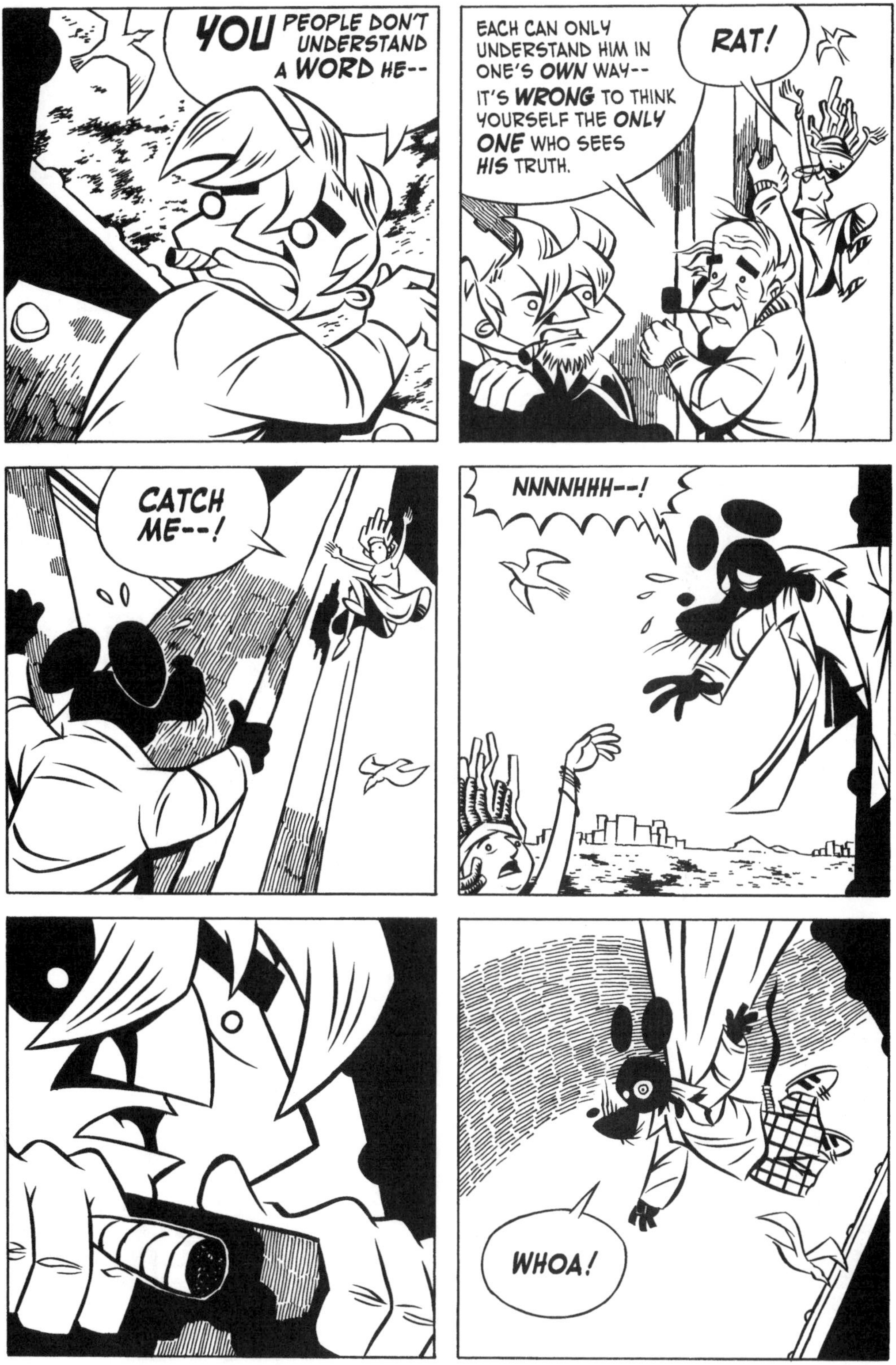
YOU PEOPLE DON'T UNDERSTAND A WORD HE--
EACH CAN ONLY UNDERSTAND HIM IN ONE'S OWN WAY-- IT'S WRONG TO THINK YOURSELF THE ONLY ONE WHO SEES HIS TRUTH.
RAT!
CATCH ME--!
NNNNHHH--!
WHOA!

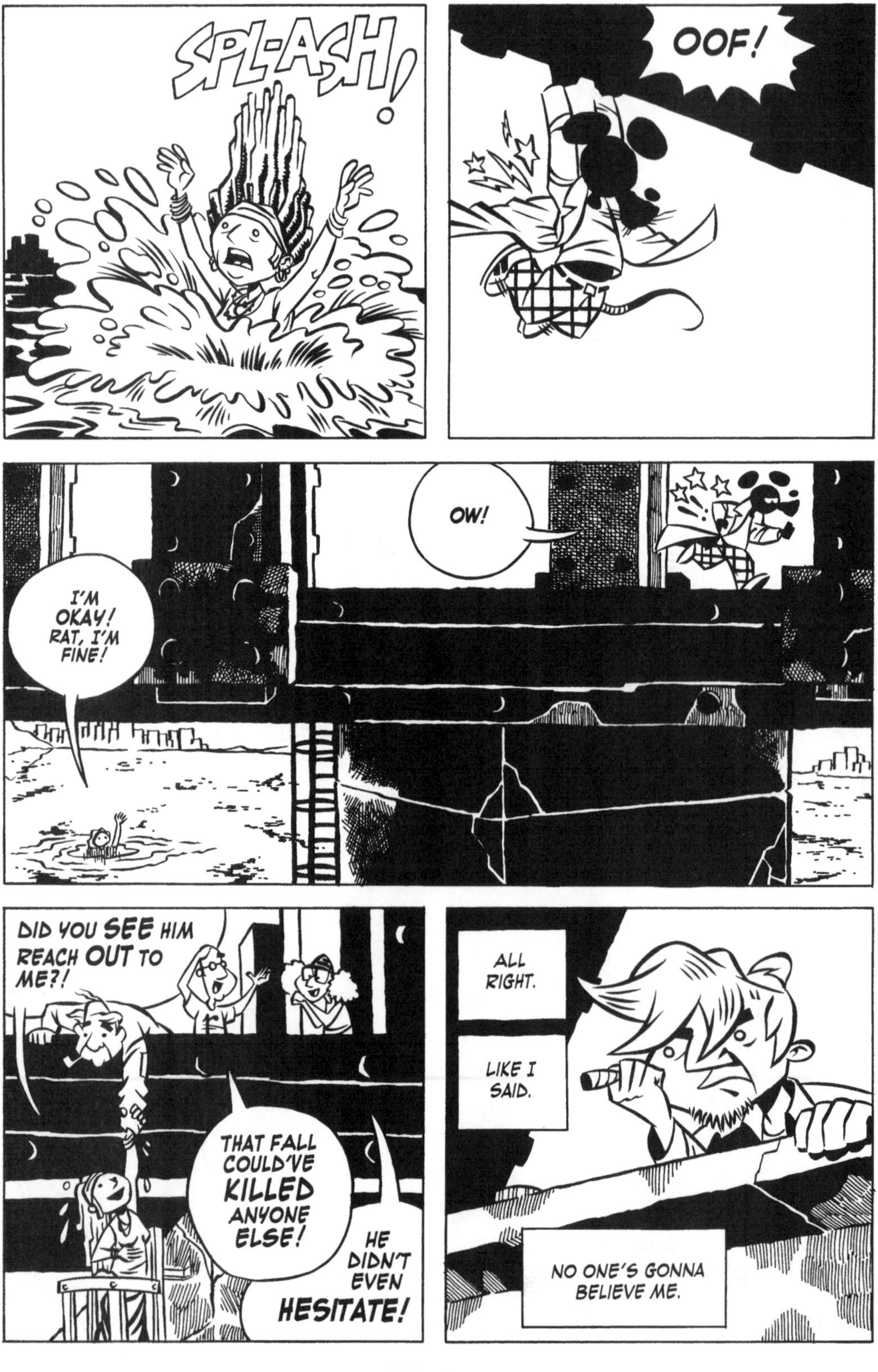
SPL-ASH!
OOF!
OW!
I'M OKAY! RAT, I'M FINE!
DID YOU SEE HIM REACH OUT TO ME?!
THAT FALL COULD'VE KILLED ANYONE ELSE!
HE DIDN'T EVEN HESITATE!
ALL RIGHT.
LIKE I SAID.
NO ONE'S GONNA BELIEVE ME.

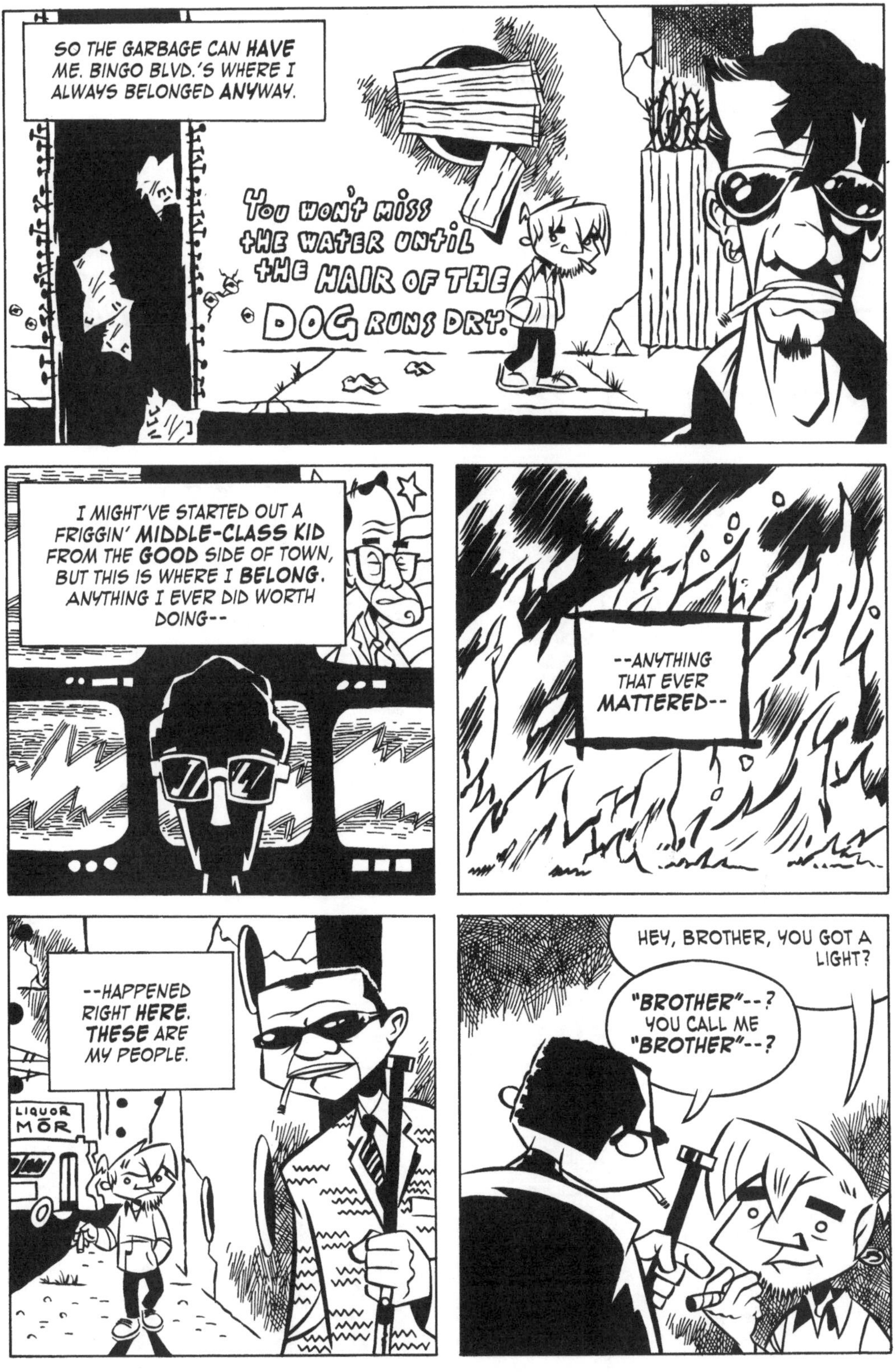
SO THE GARBAGE CAN HAVE ME. BINGO BLVD.'S WHERE I ALWAYS BELONGED ANYWAY.
YOU WON'T MISS THE WATER UNTIL THE HAIR OF THE DOG RUNS DRY.
I MIGHT'VE STARTED OUT A FRIGGIN' MIDDLE-CLASS KID FROM THE GOOD SIDE OF TOWN, BUT THIS IS WHERE I BELONG. ANYTHING I EVER DID WORTH DOING--
--ANYTHING THAT EVER MATTERED--
--HAPPENED RIGHT HERE. THESE ARE MY PEOPLE.
LIQUOR
MŌR
HEY, BROTHER, YOU GOT A LIGHT?
"BROTHER"--? YOU CALL ME "BROTHER"--?

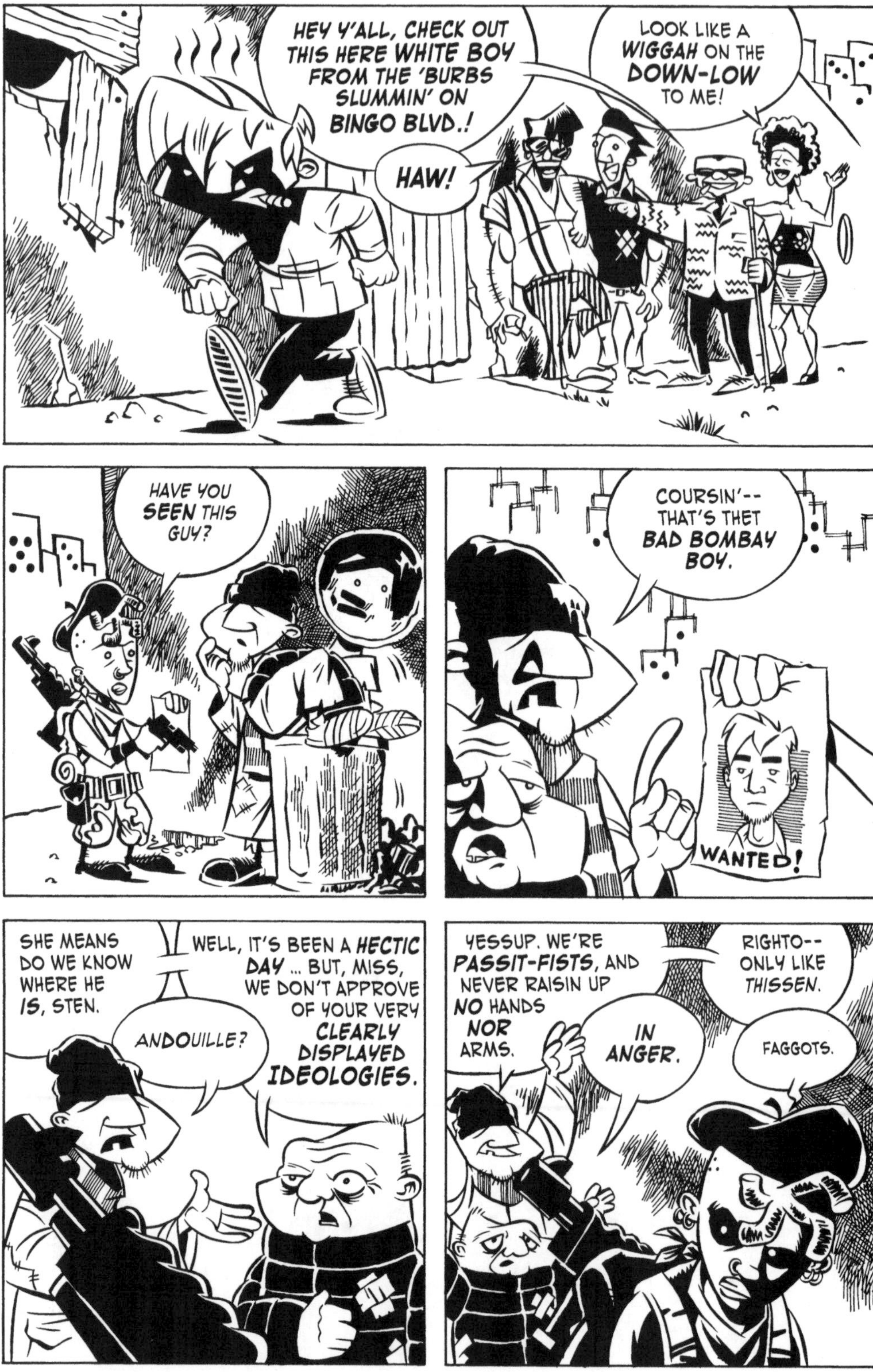
HEY Y'ALL, CHECK OUT THIS HERE WHITE BOY FROM THE 'BURBS SLUMMIN' ON BINGO BLVD.!
LOOK LIKE A WIGGAH ON THE DOWN-LOW TO ME!
HAW!
HAVE YOU SEEN THIS GUY?
COURSIN'-- THAT'S THET BAD BOMBAY BOY.
WANTED!
SHE MEANS DO WE KNOW WHERE HE IS, STEN.
WELL, IT'S BEEN A HECTIC DAY ... BUT, MISS, WE DON'T APPROVE OF YOUR VERY CLEARLY DISPLAYED IDEOLOGIES.
ANDOUILLE?
YESSUP. WE'RE PASSIT-FISTS, AND NEVER RAISIN UP NO HANDS NOR ARMS.
IN ANGER.
RIGHTO-- ONLY LIKE THISSEN.
FAGGOTS.

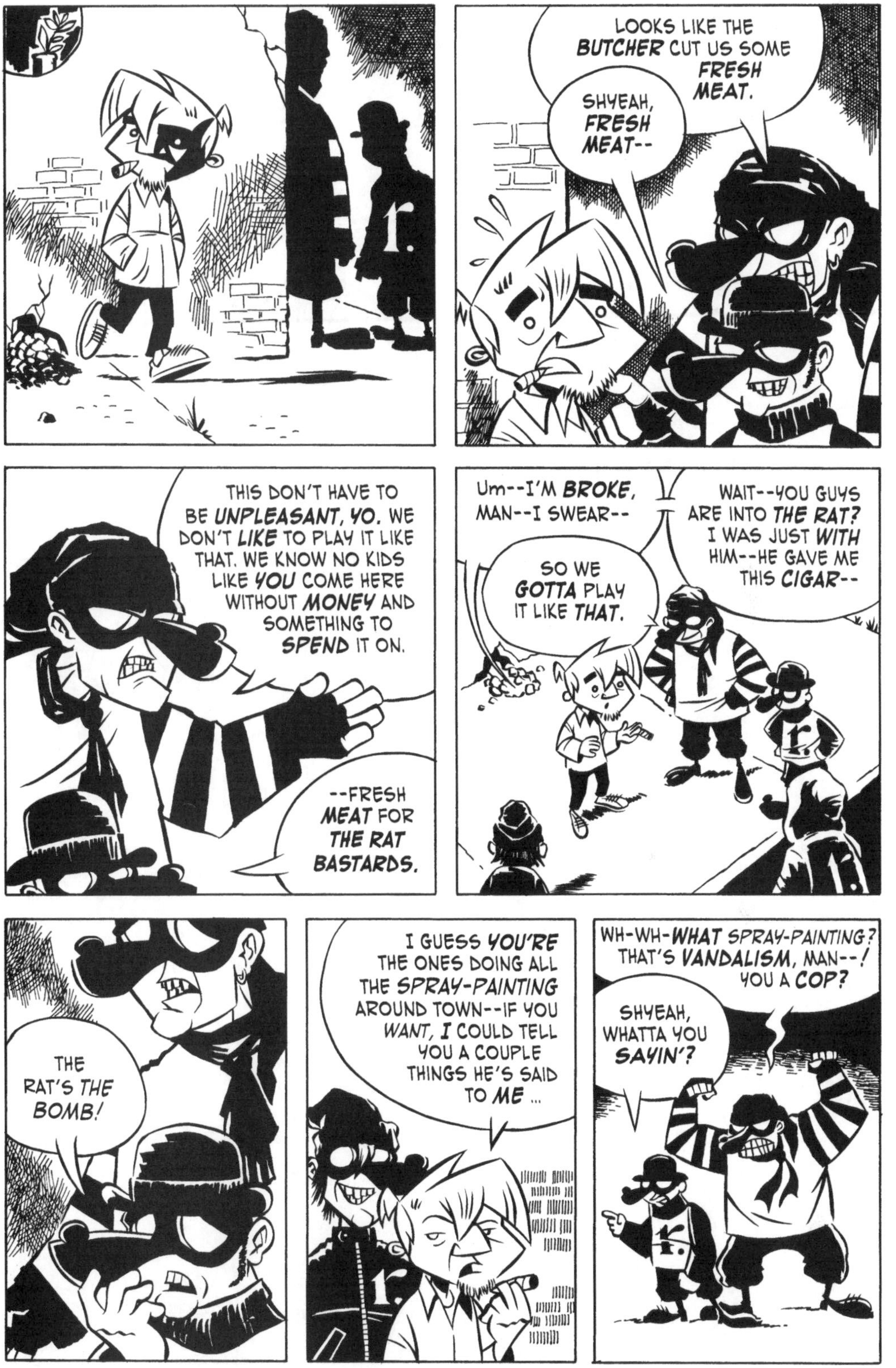
LOOKS LIKE THE BUTCHER CUT US SOME FRESH MEAT.
SHYEAH, FRESH MEAT--
THIS DON'T HAVE TO BE UNPLEASANT, YO. WE DON'T LIKE TO PLAY IT LIKE THAT. WE KNOW NO KIDS LIKE YOU COME HERE WITHOUT MONEY AND SOMETHING TO SPEND IT ON.
--FRESH MEAT FOR THE RAT BASTARDS.
Um--I'M BROKE, MAN--I SWEAR--
SO WE GOTTA PLAY IT LIKE THAT.
WAIT--YOU GUYS ARE INTO THE RAT? I WAS JUST WITH HIM--HE GAVE ME THIS CIGAR--
THE RAT'S THE BOMB!
I GUESS YOU'RE THE ONES DOING ALL THE SPRAY-PAINTING AROUND TOWN--IF YOU WANT, I COULD TELL YOU A COUPLE THINGS HE'S SAID TO ME ...
WH-WH-WHAT SPRAY-PAINTING? THAT'S VANDALISM, MAN--! YOU A COP?
SHYEAH, WHATTA YOU SAYIN'?

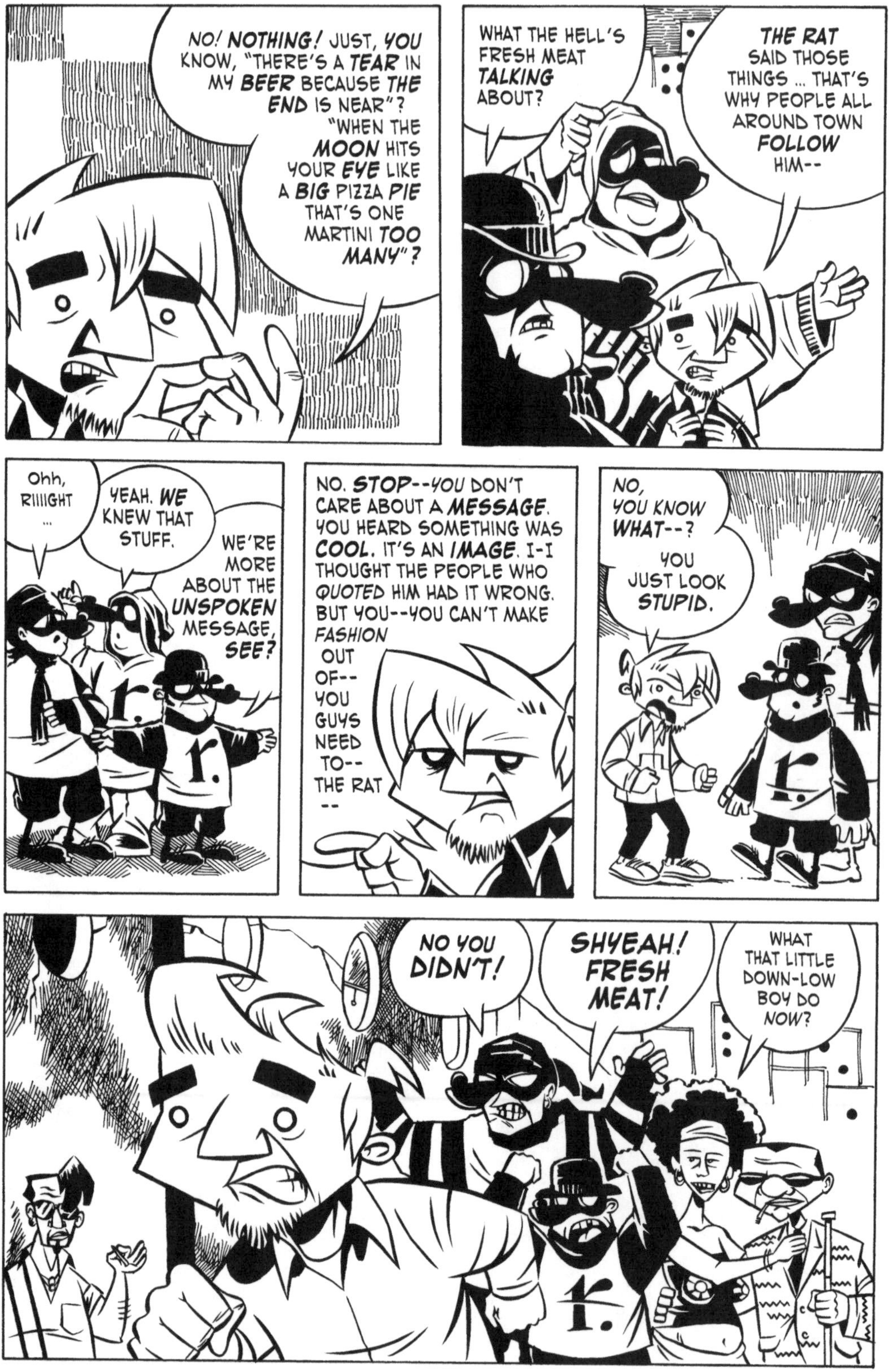
NO! NOTHING! JUST, YOU KNOW, "THERE'S A TEAR IN MY BEER BECAUSE THE END IS NEAR"? "WHEN THE MOON HITS YOUR EYE LIKE A BIG PIZZA PIE THAT'S ONE MARTINI TOO MANY"?
WHAT THE HELL'S FRESH MEAT TALKING ABOUT?
THE RAT SAID THOSE THINGS ... THAT'S WHY PEOPLE ALL AROUND TOWN FOLLOW HIM--
Ohh, RIIIIGHT ...
YEAH. WE KNEW THAT STUFF.
WE'RE MORE ABOUT THE UNSPOKEN MESSAGE, SEE?
NO. STOP--YOU DON'T CARE ABOUT A MESSAGE. YOU HEARD SOMETHING WAS COOL. IT'S AN IMAGE. I-I THOUGHT THE PEOPLE WHO QUOTED HIM HAD IT WRONG. BUT YOU--YOU CAN'T MAKE FASHION OUT OF-- YOU GUYS NEED TO-- THE RAT --
NO, YOU KNOW WHAT--?
YOU JUST LOOK STUPID.
NO YOU DIDN'T!
SHYEAH! FRESH MEAT!
WHAT THAT LITTLE DOWN-LOW BOY DO NOW?

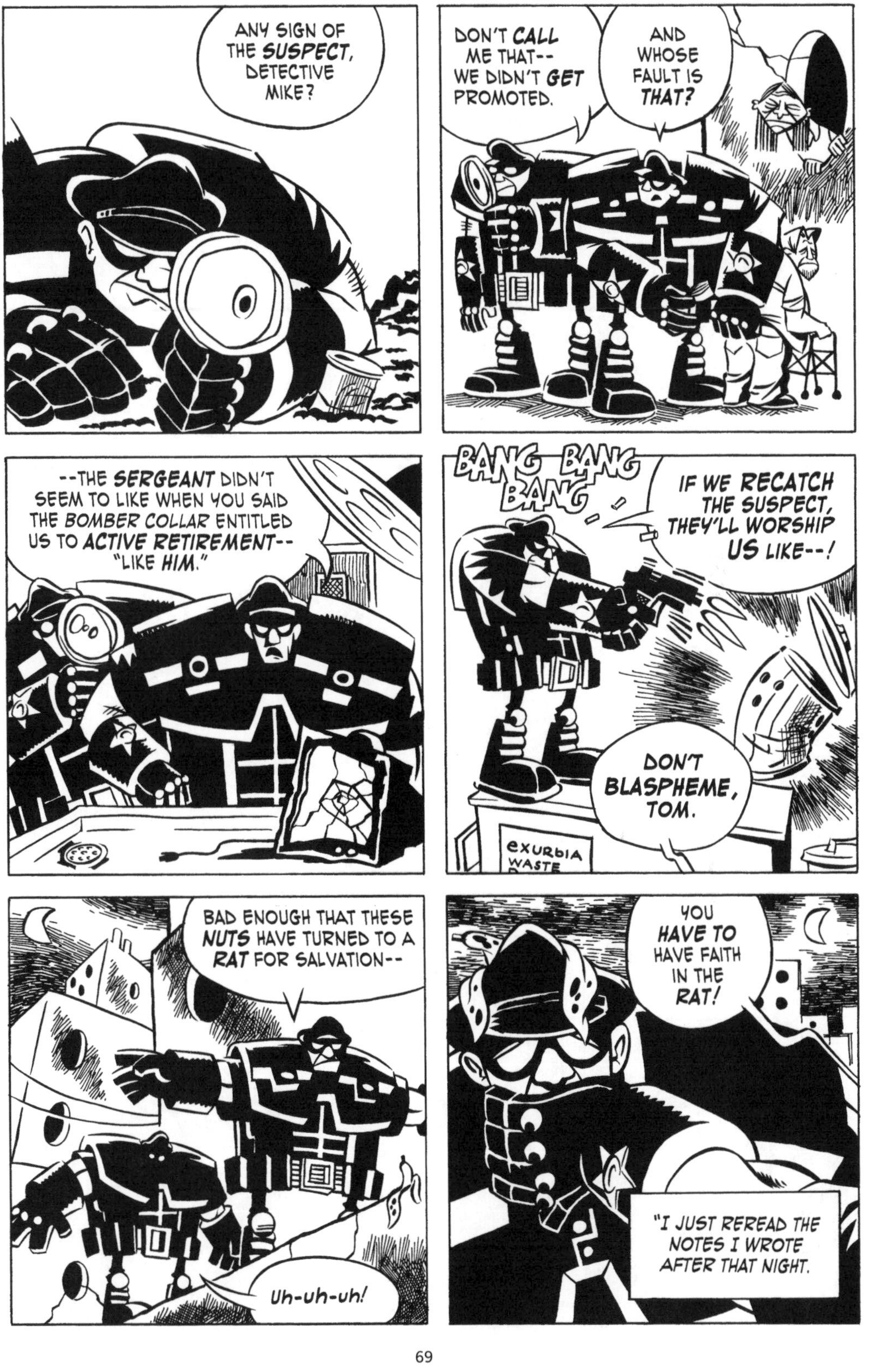
ANY SIGN OF THE SUSPECT, DETECTIVE MIKE?
DON'T CALL ME THAT-- WE DIDN'T GET PROMOTED.
AND WHOSE FAULT IS THAT?
--THE SERGEANT DIDN'T SEEM TO LIKE WHEN YOU SAID THE BOMBER COLLAR ENTITLED US TO ACTIVE RETIREMENT-- "LIKE HIM."
BANG BANG BANG
IF WE RECATCH THE SUSPECT, THEY'LL WORSHIP US LIKE--!
DON'T BLASPHEME, TOM.
EXURBIA WASTE
BAD ENOUGH THAT THESE NUTS HAVE TURNED TO A RAT FOR SALVATION--
Uh-uh-uh!
YOU HAVE TO HAVE FAITH IN THE RAT!
"I JUST REREAD THE NOTES I WROTE AFTER THAT NIGHT.

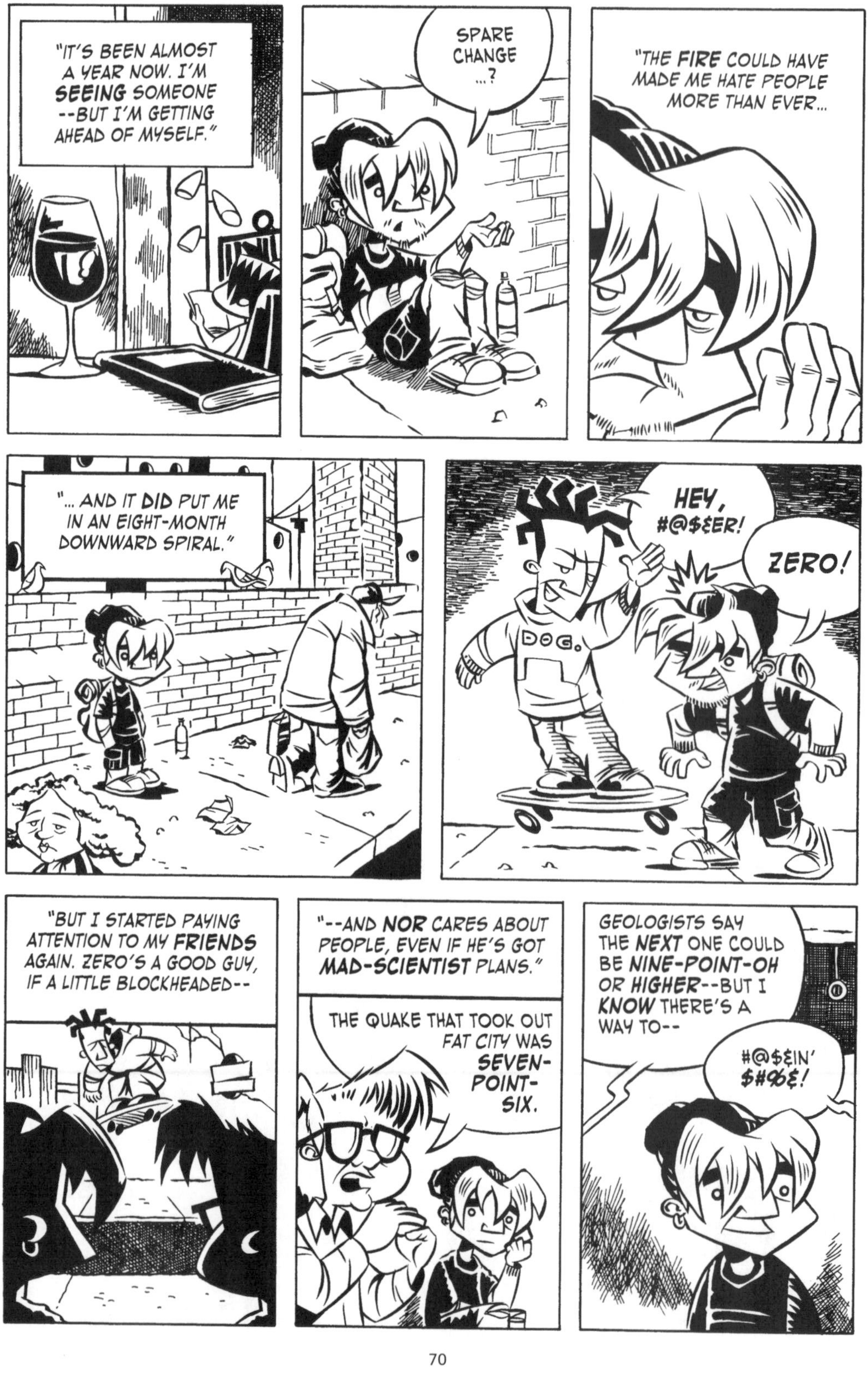
"IT'S BEEN ALMOST A YEAR NOW. I'M SEEING SOMEONE --BUT I'M GETTING AHEAD OF MYSELF."
SPARE CHANGE ...?
"THE FIRE COULD HAVE MADE ME HATE PEOPLE MORE THAN EVER...
"... AND IT DID PUT ME IN AN EIGHT-MONTH DOWNWARD SPIRAL."
HEY, #@$£ER!
ZERO!
DOG.
"BUT I STARTED PAYING ATTENTION TO MY FRIENDS AGAIN. ZERO'S A GOOD GUY, IF A LITTLE BLOCKHEADED--
"--AND NOR CARES ABOUT PEOPLE, EVEN IF HE'S GOT MAD-SCIENTIST PLANS."
THE QUAKE THAT TOOK OUT FAT CITY WAS SEVEN-POINT-SIX.
GEOLOGISTS SAY THE NEXT ONE COULD BE NINE-POINT-OH OR HIGHER--BUT I KNOW THERE'S A WAY TO--
#@$£IN' $#%£!

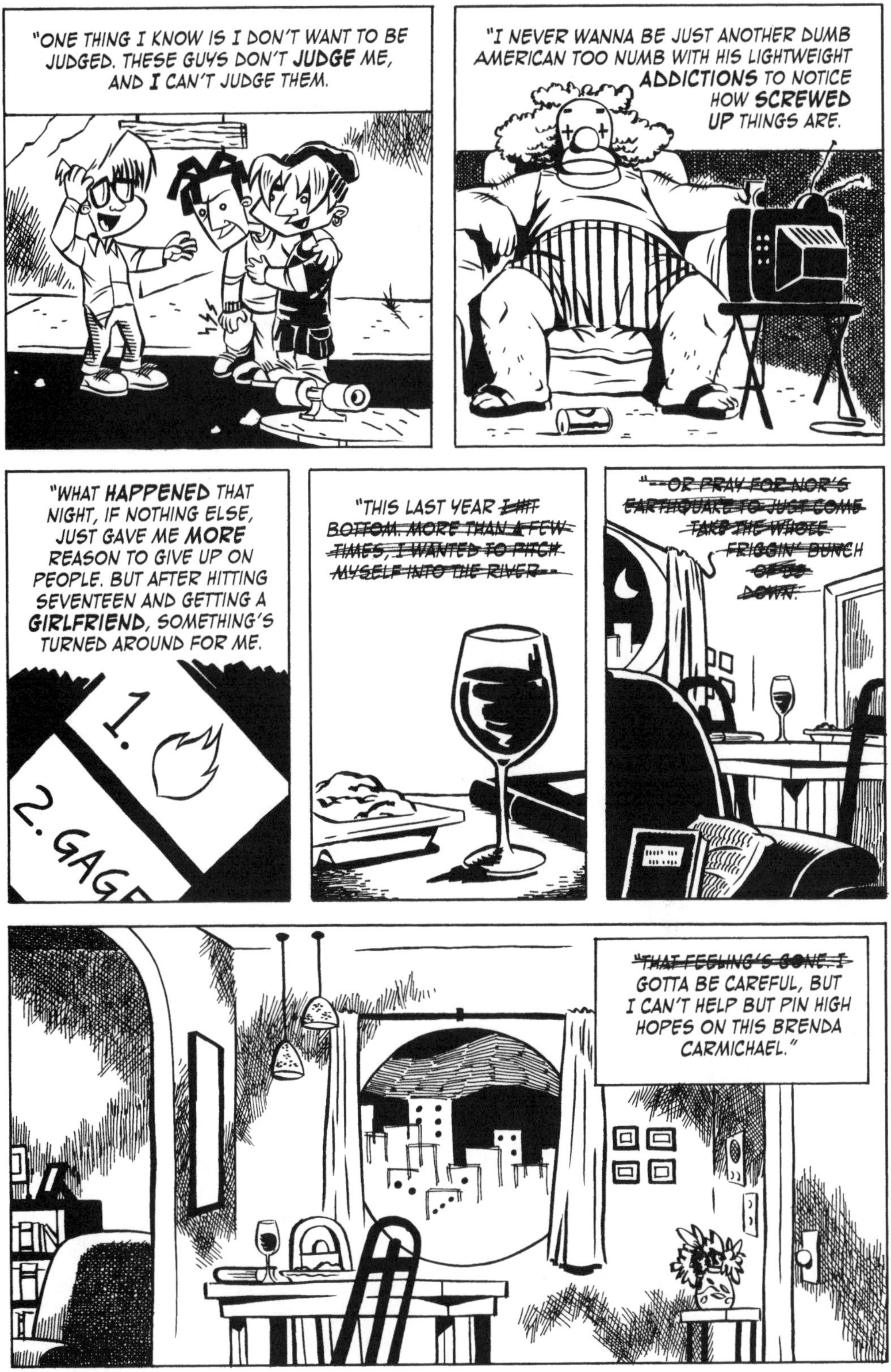
"ONE THING I KNOW IS I DON'T WANT TO BE JUDGED. THESE GUYS DON'T JUDGE ME, AND I CAN'T JUDGE THEM.
"I NEVER WANNA BE JUST ANOTHER DUMB AMERICAN TOO NUMB WITH HIS LIGHTWEIGHT ADDICTIONS TO NOTICE HOW SCREWED UP THINGS ARE.
"WHAT HAPPENED THAT NIGHT, IF NOTHING ELSE, JUST GAVE ME MORE REASON TO GIVE UP ON PEOPLE. BUT AFTER HITTING SEVENTEEN AND GETTING A GIRLFRIEND, SOMETHING'S TURNED AROUND FOR ME.
"THIS LAST YEAR ~~I HIT BOTTOM. MORE THAN A FEW TIMES, I WANTED TO PITCH MYSELF INTO THE RIVER--~~
~~"--OR PRAY FOR NOR'S EARTHQUAKE TO JUST COME TAKE THE WHOLE~~ FRIGGIN' BUNCH ~~OF US DOWN.~~
~~"THAT FEELING'S GONE. I~~ GOTTA BE CAREFUL, BUT I CAN'T HELP BUT PIN HIGH HOPES ON THIS BRENDA CARMICHAEL."

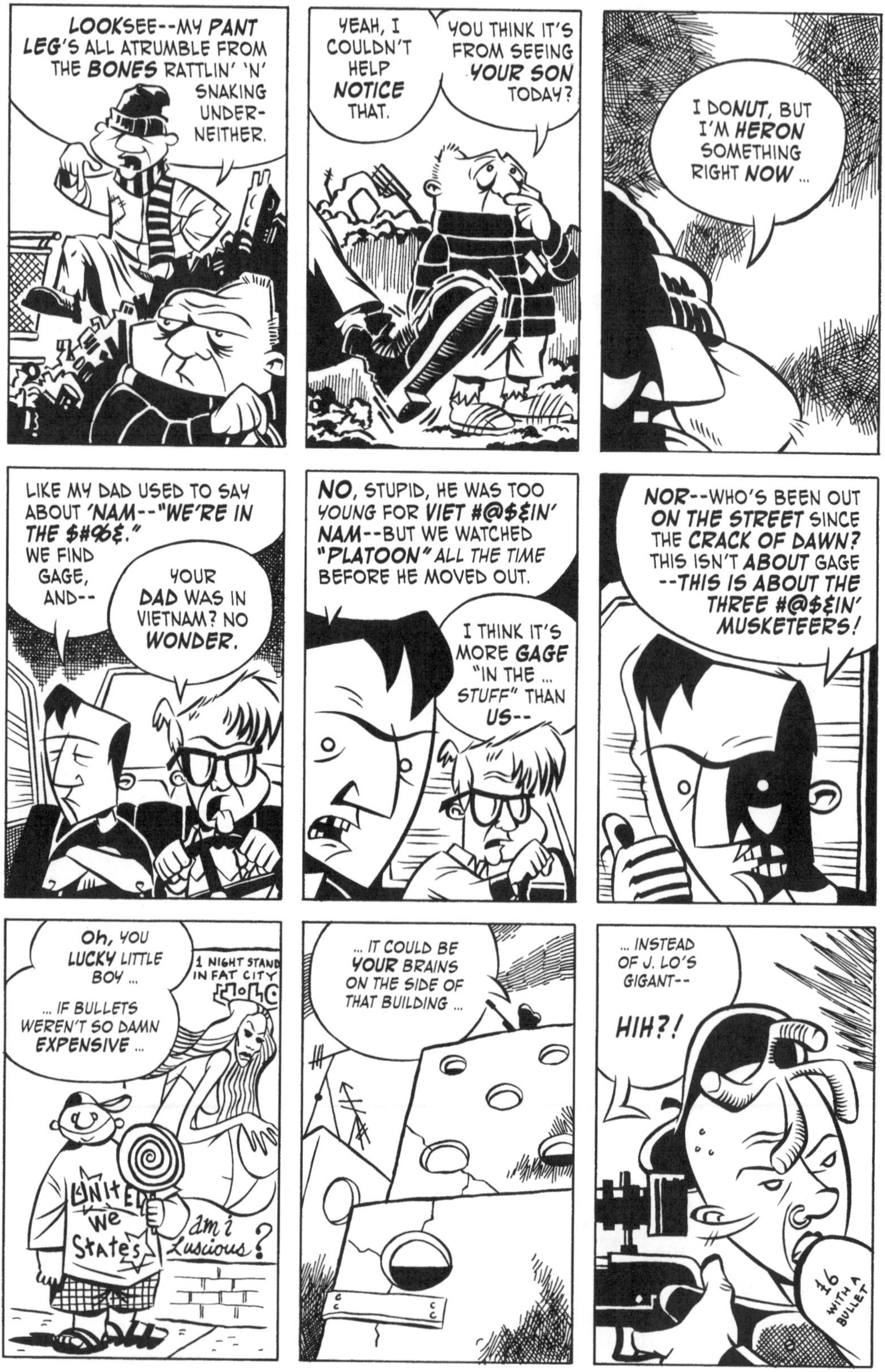
LOOKSEE--MY PANT LEG'S ALL ATRUMBLE FROM THE BONES RATTLIN' 'N' SNAKING UNDER-NEITHER.
YEAH, I COULDN'T HELP NOTICE THAT.
YOU THINK IT'S FROM SEEING YOUR SON TODAY?
I DONUT, BUT I'M HERON SOMETHING RIGHT NOW ...
LIKE MY DAD USED TO SAY ABOUT 'NAM--"WE'RE IN THE $#%&." WE FIND GAGE, AND--
YOUR DAD WAS IN VIETNAM? NO WONDER.
NO, STUPID, HE WAS TOO YOUNG FOR VIET #@$&IN' NAM--BUT WE WATCHED "PLATOON" ALL THE TIME BEFORE HE MOVED OUT.
I THINK IT'S MORE GAGE "IN THE ... STUFF" THAN US--
NOR--WHO'S BEEN OUT ON THE STREET SINCE THE CRACK OF DAWN? THIS ISN'T ABOUT GAGE --THIS IS ABOUT THE THREE #@$&IN' MUSKETEERS!
Oh, YOU LUCKY LITTLE BOY ...
... IF BULLETS WEREN'T SO DAMN EXPENSIVE ...
1 NIGHT STAND IN FAT CITY
UNITED We States
am i Luscious?
... IT COULD BE YOUR BRAINS ON THE SIDE OF THAT BUILDING ...
... INSTEAD OF J. LO'S GIGANT--
HIH?!
16 WITH A BULLET

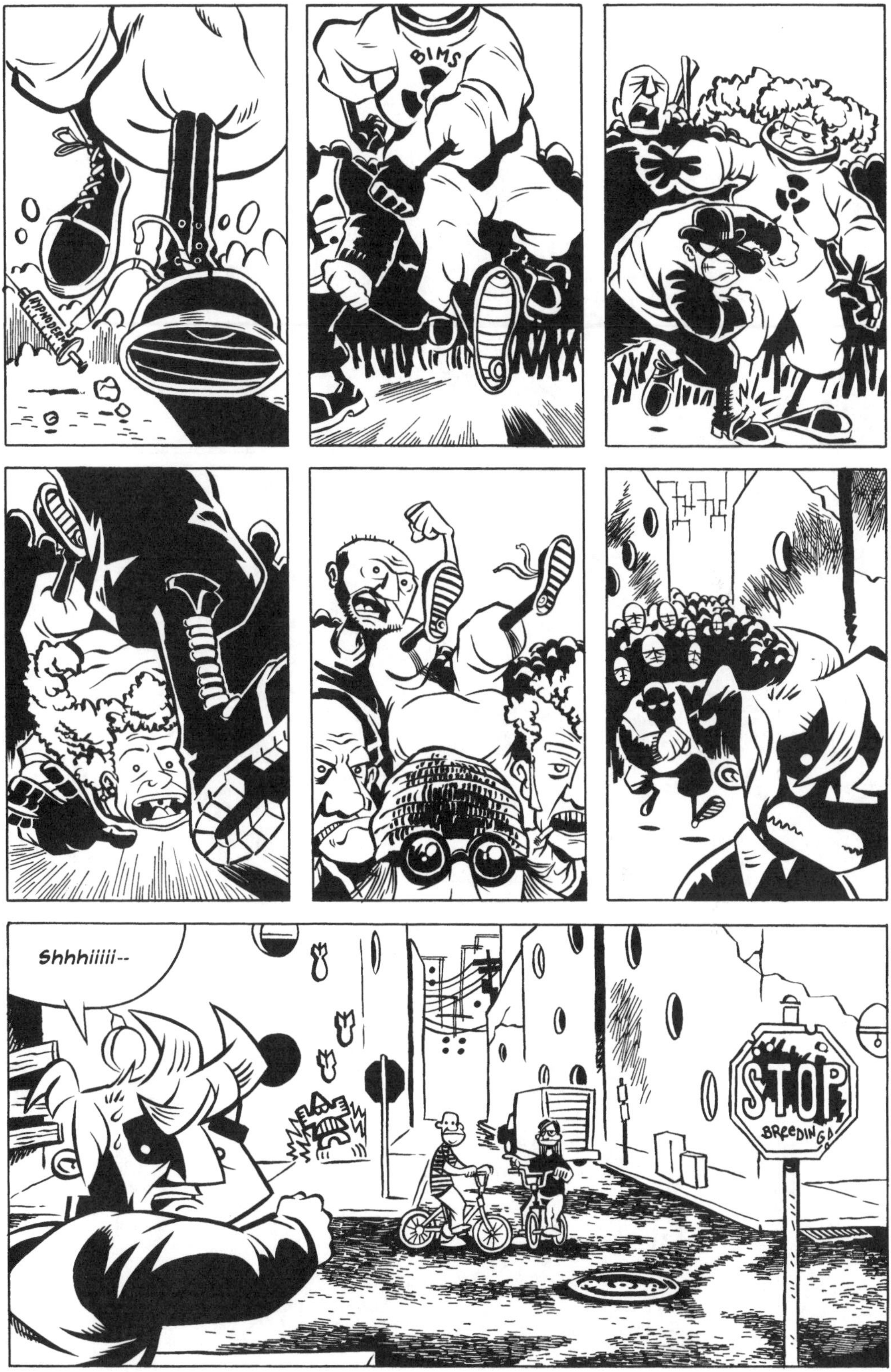
HYPNODERM
BIMS
Shhhiiiii--
STOP
BREEDING

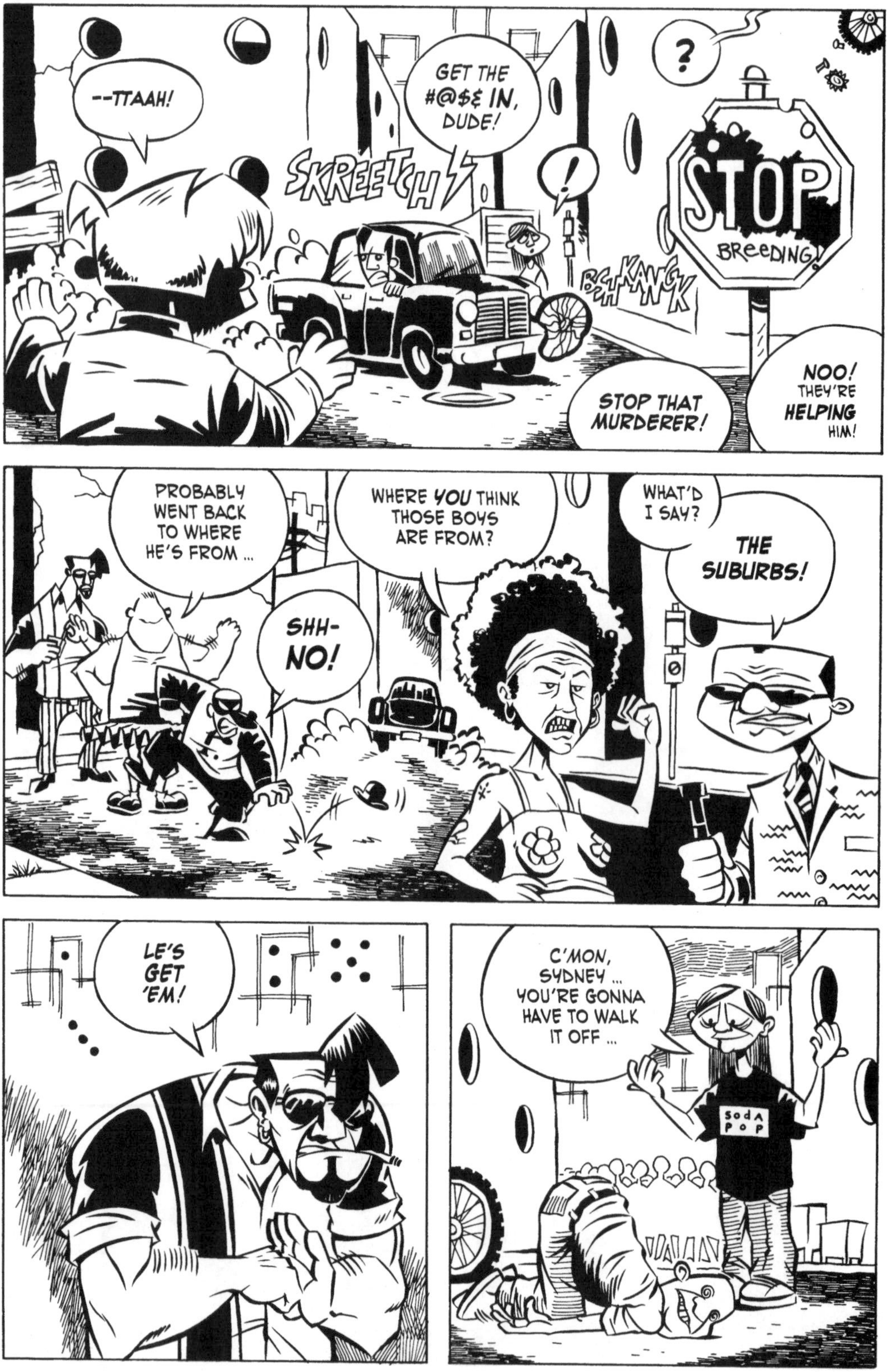
--TTAAH!
GET THE #@$& IN, DUDE!
SKREETCH
?
!
STOP
BREEDING!
BCHKANGK
STOP THAT MURDERER!
NOO! THEY'RE HELPING HIM!
PROBABLY WENT BACK TO WHERE HE'S FROM ...
SHH- NO!
WHERE YOU THINK THOSE BOYS ARE FROM?
WHAT'D I SAY?
THE SUBURBS!
LE'S GET 'EM!
C'MON, SYDNEY ... YOU'RE GONNA HAVE TO WALK IT OFF ...
sodA POP

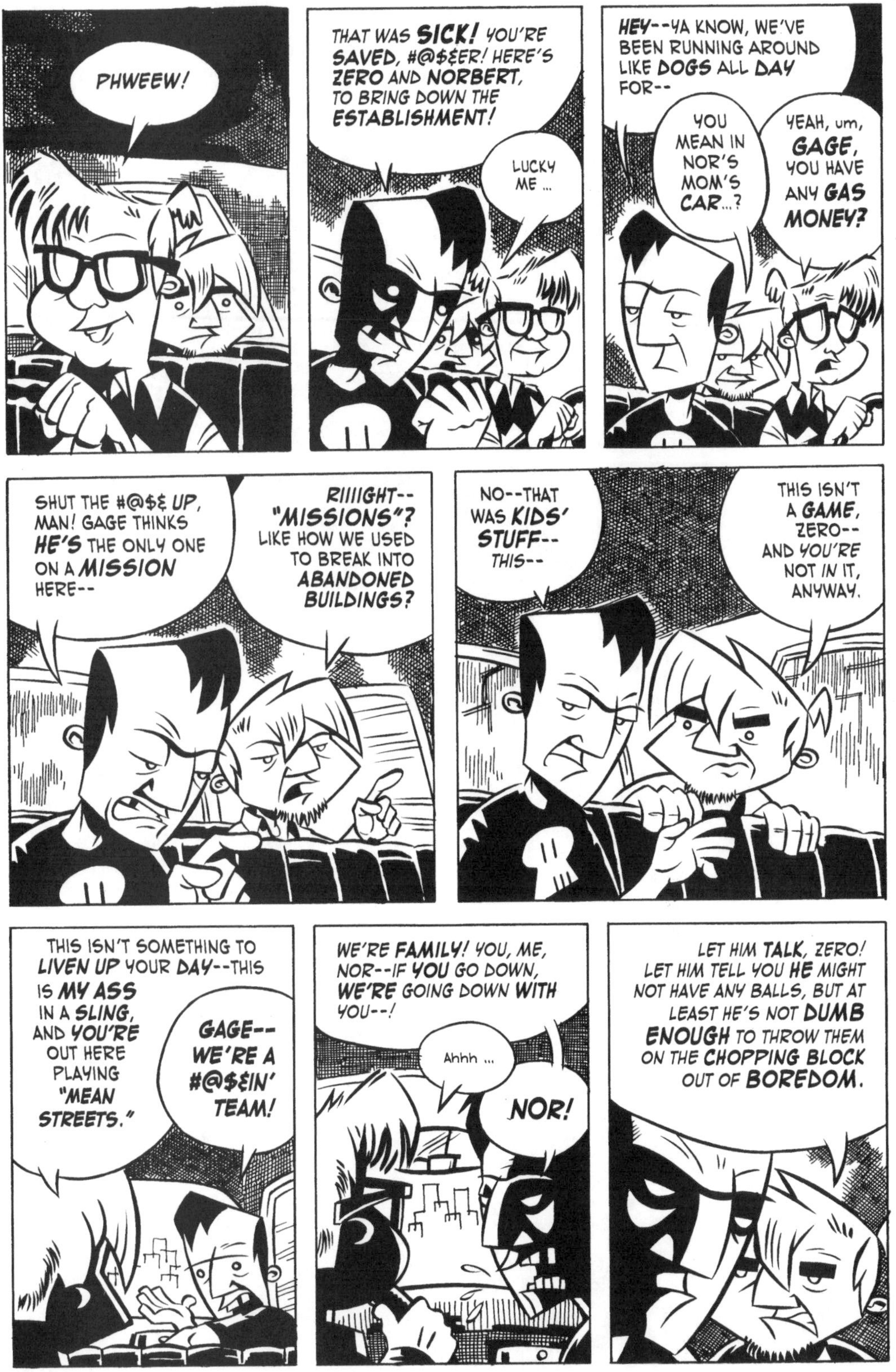
PHWEEW!
THAT WAS SICK! YOU'RE SAVED, #@$&ER! HERE'S ZERO AND NORBERT, TO BRING DOWN THE ESTABLISHMENT!
LUCKY ME ...
HEY--YA KNOW, WE'VE BEEN RUNNING AROUND LIKE DOGS ALL DAY FOR--
YOU MEAN IN NOR'S MOM'S CAR...?
YEAH, um, GAGE, YOU HAVE ANY GAS MONEY?
SHUT THE #@$& UP, MAN! GAGE THINKS HE'S THE ONLY ONE ON A MISSION HERE--
RIIIIGHT-- "MISSIONS"? LIKE HOW WE USED TO BREAK INTO ABANDONED BUILDINGS?
NO--THAT WAS KIDS' STUFF-- THIS--
THIS ISN'T A GAME, ZERO-- AND YOU'RE NOT IN IT, ANYWAY.
THIS ISN'T SOMETHING TO LIVEN UP YOUR DAY--THIS IS MY ASS IN A SLING, AND YOU'RE OUT HERE PLAYING "MEAN STREETS."
GAGE-- WE'RE A #@$&IN' TEAM!
WE'RE FAMILY! YOU, ME, NOR--IF YOU GO DOWN, WE'RE GOING DOWN WITH YOU--!
Ahhh ...
NOR!
LET HIM TALK, ZERO! LET HIM TELL YOU HE MIGHT NOT HAVE ANY BALLS, BUT AT LEAST HE'S NOT DUMB ENOUGH TO THROW THEM ON THE CHOPPING BLOCK OUT OF BOREDOM.

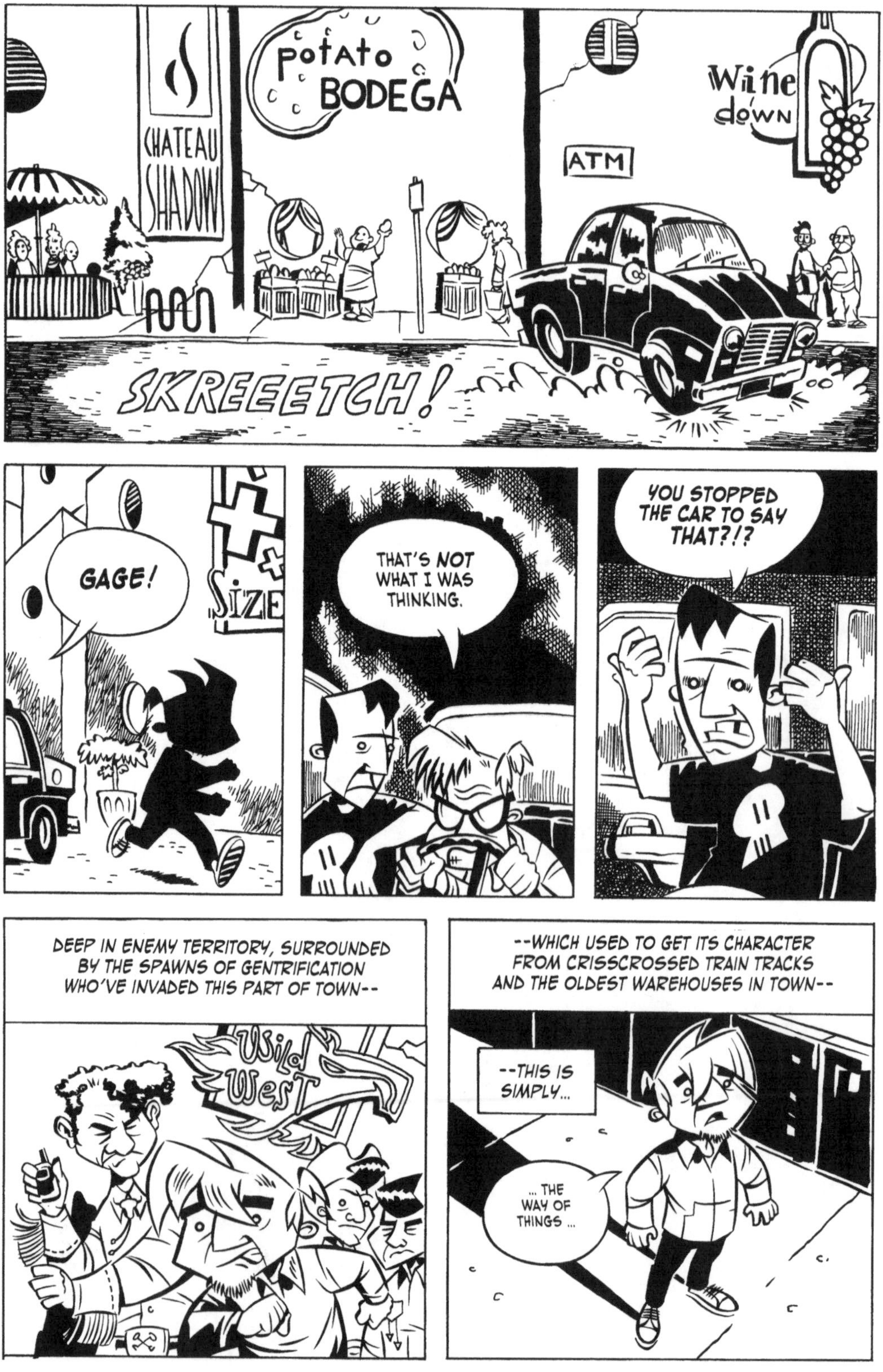
CHATEAU SHADOW
potato BODEGA
ATM
Wine down
SKREEETCH!
GAGE!
SIZE
THAT'S NOT WHAT I WAS THINKING.
YOU STOPPED THE CAR TO SAY THAT?!?
DEEP IN ENEMY TERRITORY, SURROUNDED BY THE SPAWNS OF GENTRIFICATION WHO'VE INVADED THIS PART OF TOWN--
Wild West
--WHICH USED TO GET ITS CHARACTER FROM CRISSCROSSED TRAIN TRACKS AND THE OLDEST WAREHOUSES IN TOWN--
--THIS IS SIMPLY...
... THE WAY OF THINGS ...

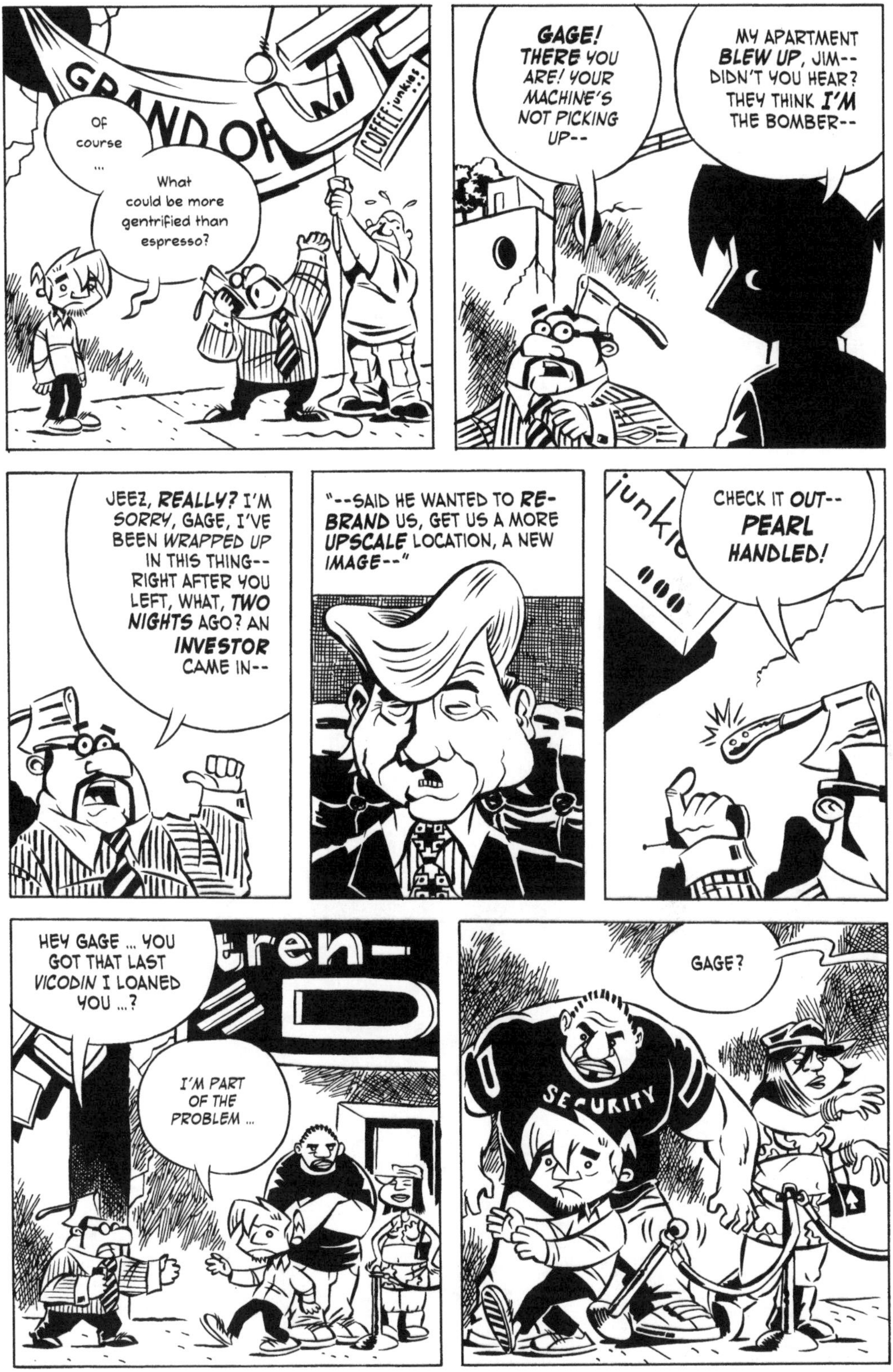
GRAND OP
COFFE junkie!
Of course ...
What could be more gentrified than espresso?
GAGE! THERE YOU ARE! YOUR MACHINE'S NOT PICKING UP--
MY APARTMENT BLEW UP, JIM-- DIDN'T YOU HEAR? THEY THINK I'M THE BOMBER--
JEEZ, REALLY? I'M SORRY, GAGE, I'VE BEEN WRAPPED UP IN THIS THING-- RIGHT AFTER YOU LEFT, WHAT, TWO NIGHTS AGO? AN INVESTOR CAME IN--
"--SAID HE WANTED TO RE-BRAND US, GET US A MORE UPSCALE LOCATION, A NEW IMAGE--"
CHECK IT OUT-- PEARL HANDLED!
HEY GAGE ... YOU GOT THAT LAST VICODIN I LOANED YOU ...?
tren-
I'M PART OF THE PROBLEM ...
GAGE?
SECURITY

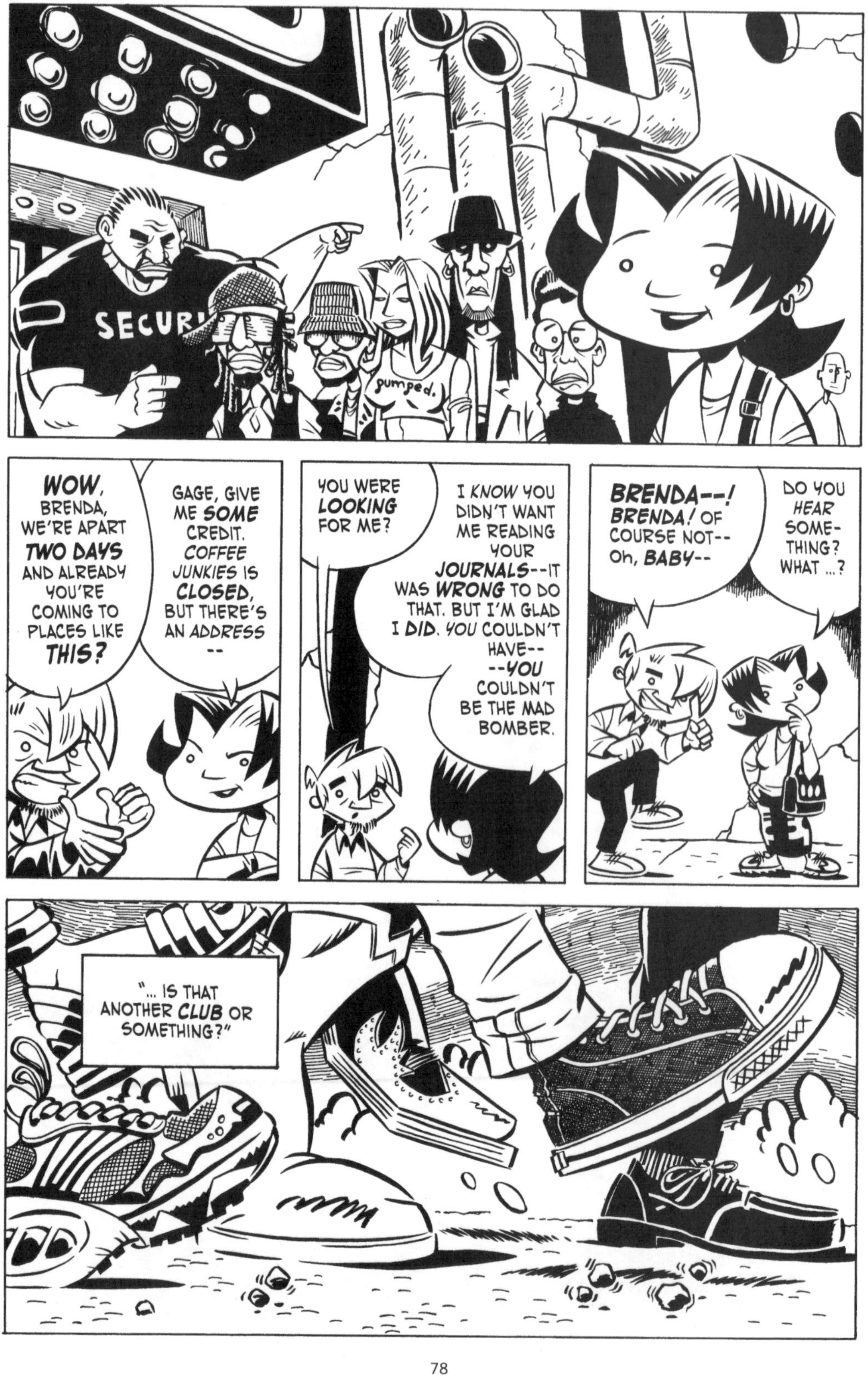
SECURI
pumped.
WOW, BRENDA, WE'RE APART TWO DAYS AND ALREADY YOU'RE COMING TO PLACES LIKE THIS?
GAGE, GIVE ME SOME CREDIT. COFFEE JUNKIES IS CLOSED, BUT THERE'S AN ADDRESS --
YOU WERE LOOKING FOR ME?
I KNOW YOU DIDN'T WANT ME READING YOUR JOURNALS--IT WAS WRONG TO DO THAT. BUT I'M GLAD I DID. YOU COULDN'T HAVE-- --YOU COULDN'T BE THE MAD BOMBER.
BRENDA--! BRENDA! OF COURSE NOT-- Oh, BABY--
DO YOU HEAR SOME-THING? WHAT ...?
"... IS THAT ANOTHER CLUB OR SOMETHING?"

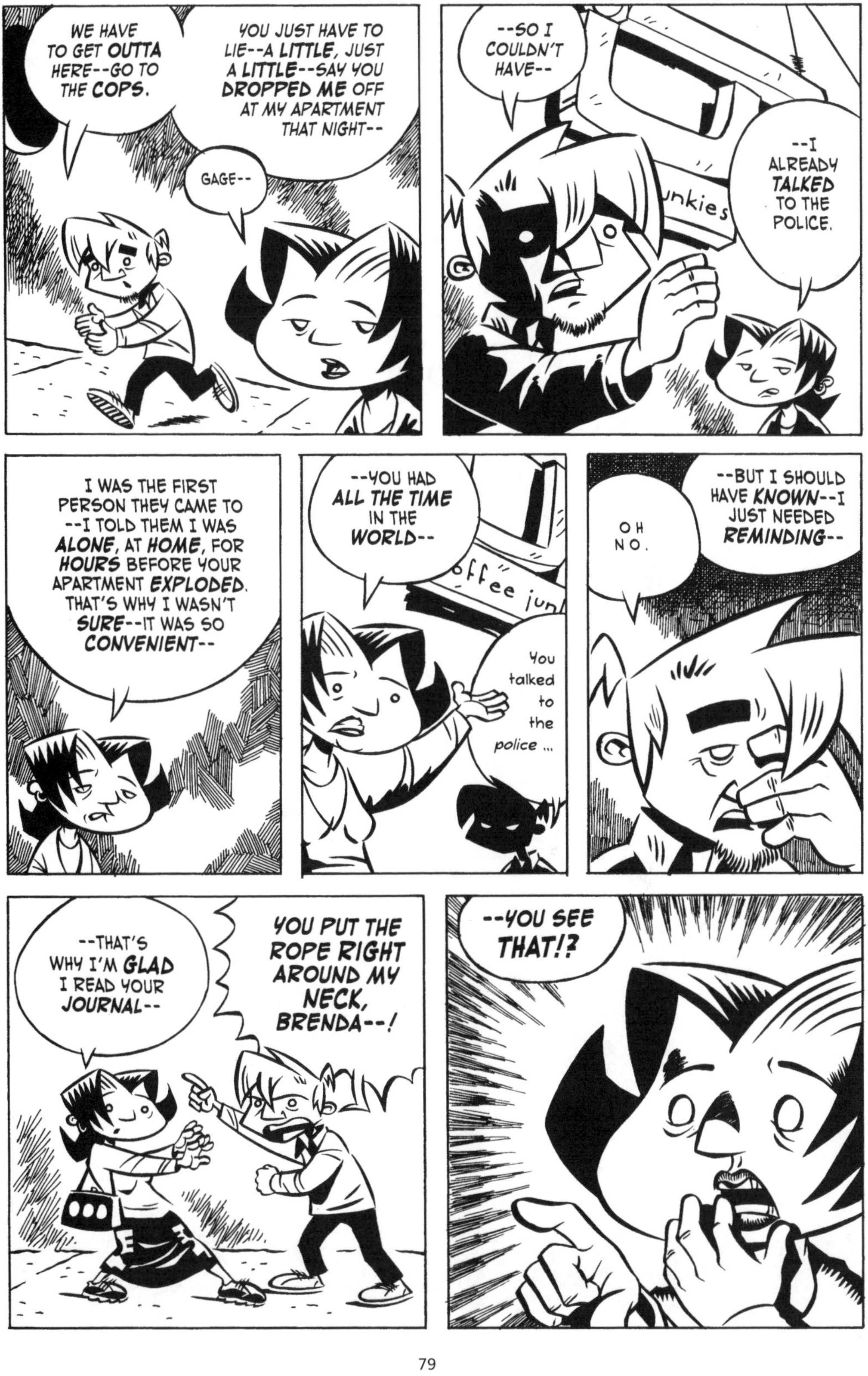

WE HAVE TO GET OUTTA HERE--GO TO THE COPS.
YOU JUST HAVE TO LIE--A LITTLE, JUST A LITTLE--SAY YOU DROPPED ME OFF AT MY APARTMENT THAT NIGHT--
GAGE--
--SO I COULDN'T HAVE--
--I ALREADY TALKED TO THE POLICE.
I WAS THE FIRST PERSON THEY CAME TO --I TOLD THEM I WAS ALONE, AT HOME, FOR HOURS BEFORE YOUR APARTMENT EXPLODED. THAT'S WHY I WASN'T SURE--IT WAS SO CONVENIENT--
--YOU HAD ALL THE TIME IN THE WORLD--
You talked to the police ...
OH NO.
--BUT I SHOULD HAVE KNOWN--I JUST NEEDED REMINDING--
--THAT'S WHY I'M GLAD I READ YOUR JOURNAL--
YOU PUT THE ROPE RIGHT AROUND MY NECK, BRENDA--!
--YOU SEE THAT!?

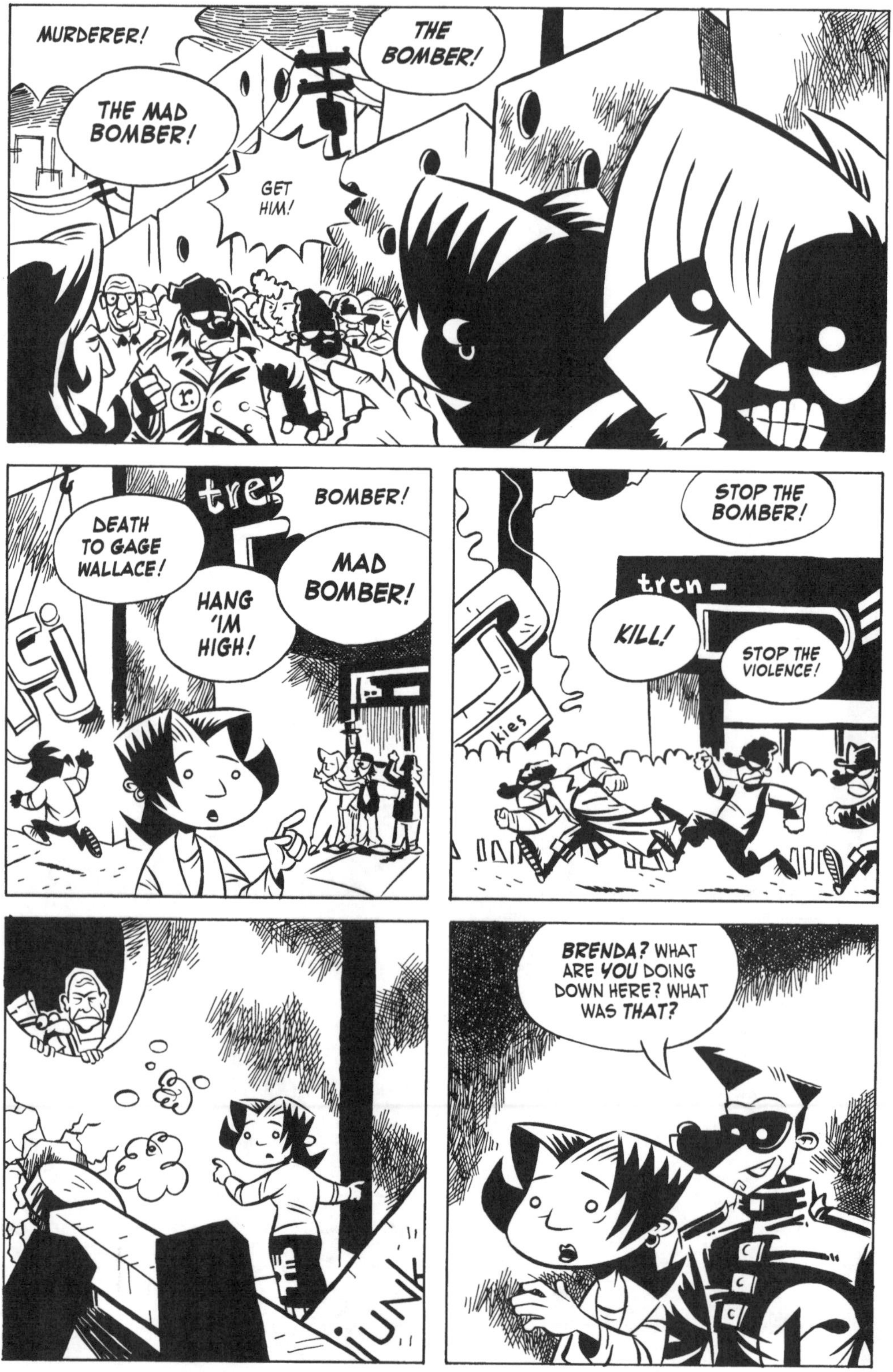
MURDERER!
THE MAD BOMBER!
THE BOMBER!
GET HIM!
DEATH TO GAGE WALLACE!
BOMBER!
HANG 'IM HIGH!
MAD BOMBER!
STOP THE BOMBER!
KILL!
STOP THE VIOLENCE!
BRENDA? WHAT ARE YOU DOING DOWN HERE? WHAT WAS THAT?

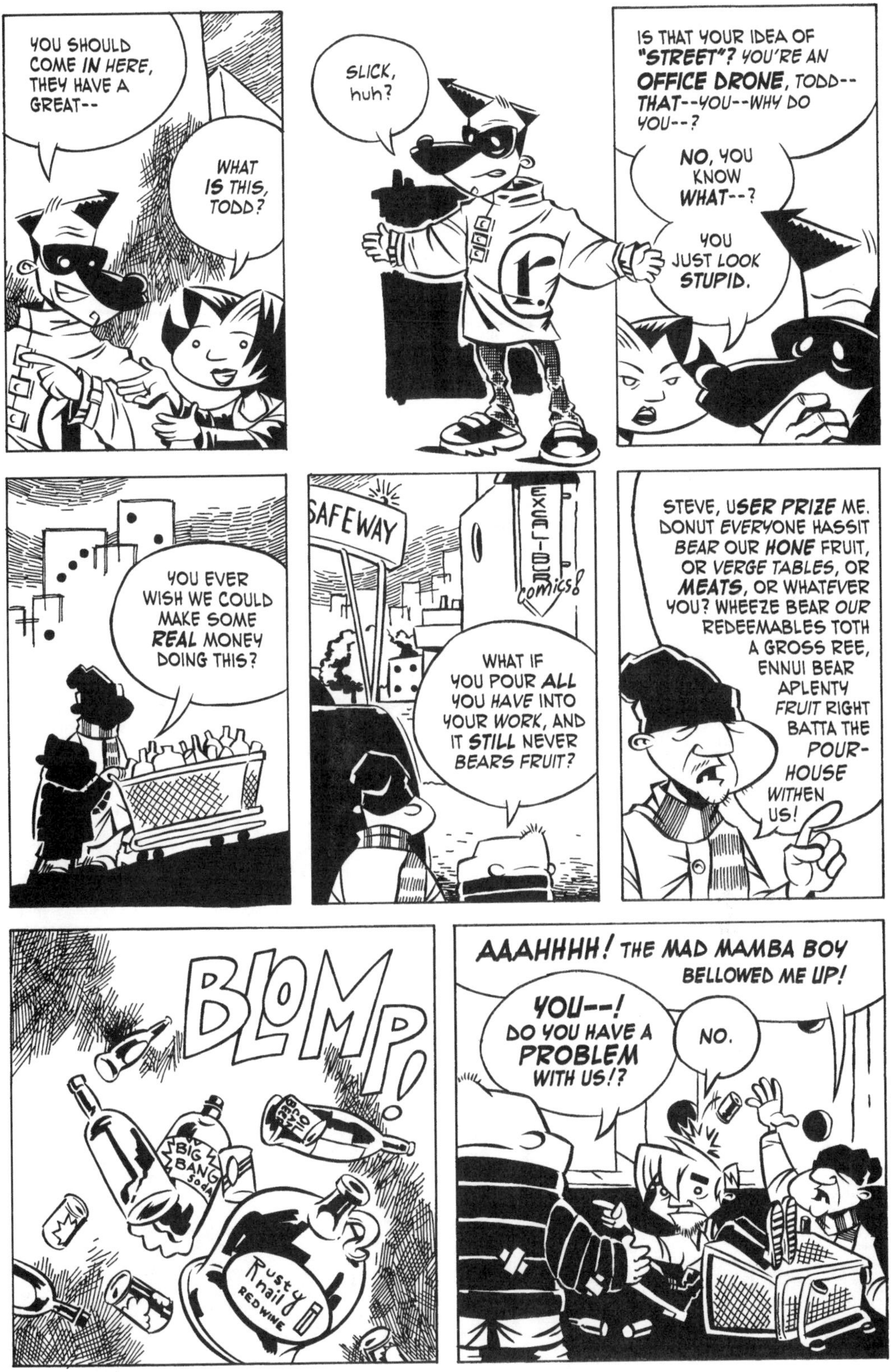
YOU SHOULD COME IN HERE, THEY HAVE A GREAT--
WHAT IS THIS, TODD?
SLICK, huh?
IS THAT YOUR IDEA OF "STREET"? YOU'RE AN OFFICE DRONE, TODD-- THAT--YOU--WHY DO YOU--?
NO, YOU KNOW WHAT--?
YOU JUST LOOK STUPID.
YOU EVER WISH WE COULD MAKE SOME REAL MONEY DOING THIS?
SAFEWAY
EXCALIBUR comics!
WHAT IF YOU POUR ALL YOU HAVE INTO YOUR WORK, AND IT STILL NEVER BEARS FRUIT?
STEVE, USER PRIZE ME. DONUT EVERYONE HASSIT BEAR OUR HONE FRUIT, OR VERGE TABLES, OR MEATS, OR WHATEVER YOU? WHEEZE BEAR OUR REDEEMABLES TOTH A GROSS REE, ENNUI BEAR APLENTY FRUIT RIGHT BATTA THE POUR-HOUSE WITHEN US!
BLOMP!
BIG BANG SODA
Rusty nail RED WINE
AAAHHHH! THE MAD MAMBA BOY BELLOWED ME UP!
YOU--! DO YOU HAVE A PROBLEM WITH US!?
NO.

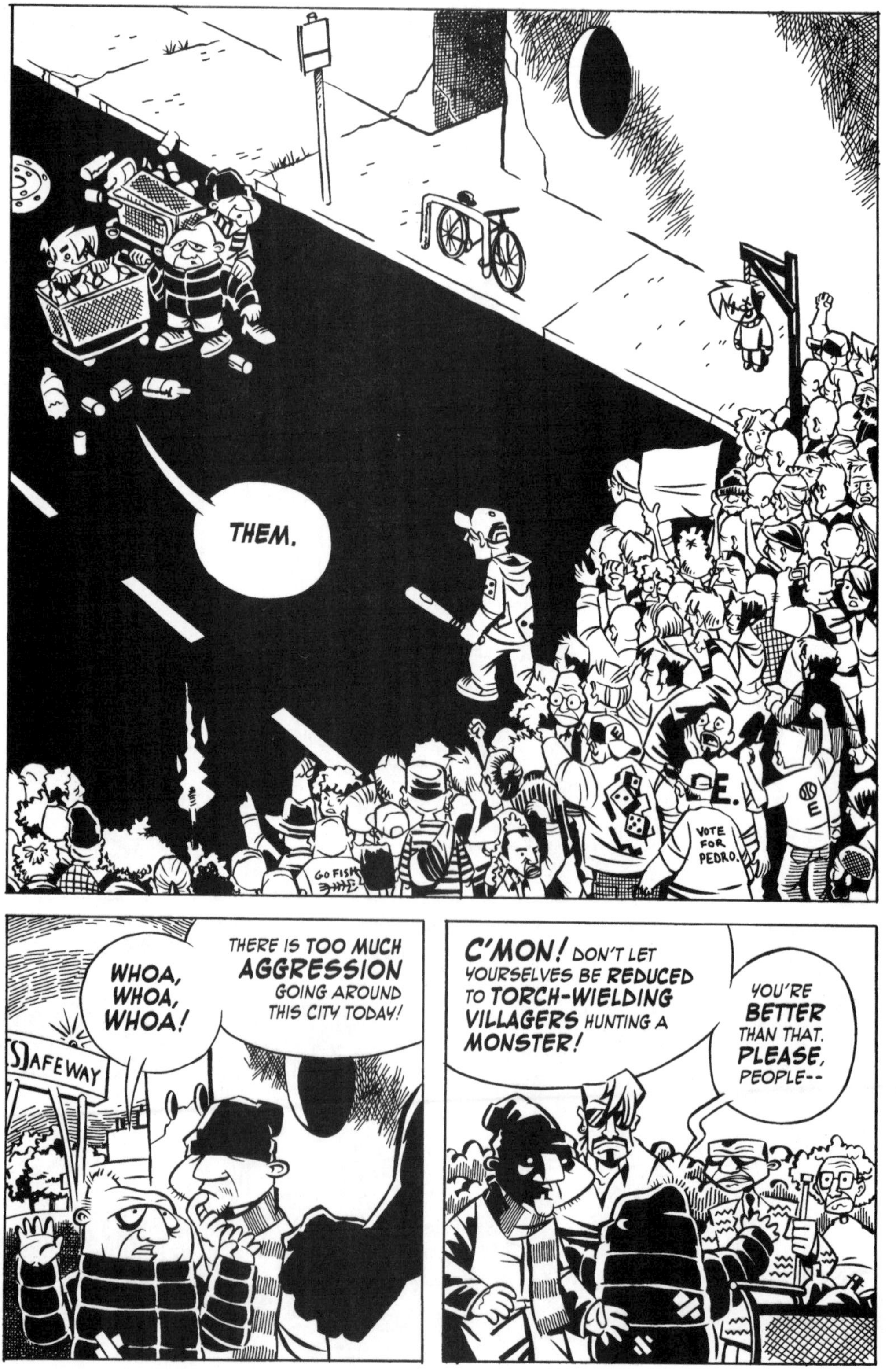
THEM.
GO FISH
VOTE FOR PEDRO.
WHOA, WHOA, WHOA!
THERE IS TOO MUCH AGGRESSION GOING AROUND THIS CITY TODAY!
SAFEWAY
C'MON! DON'T LET YOURSELVES BE REDUCED TO TORCH-WIELDING VILLAGERS HUNTING A MONSTER!
YOU'RE BETTER THAN THAT. PLEASE, PEOPLE--

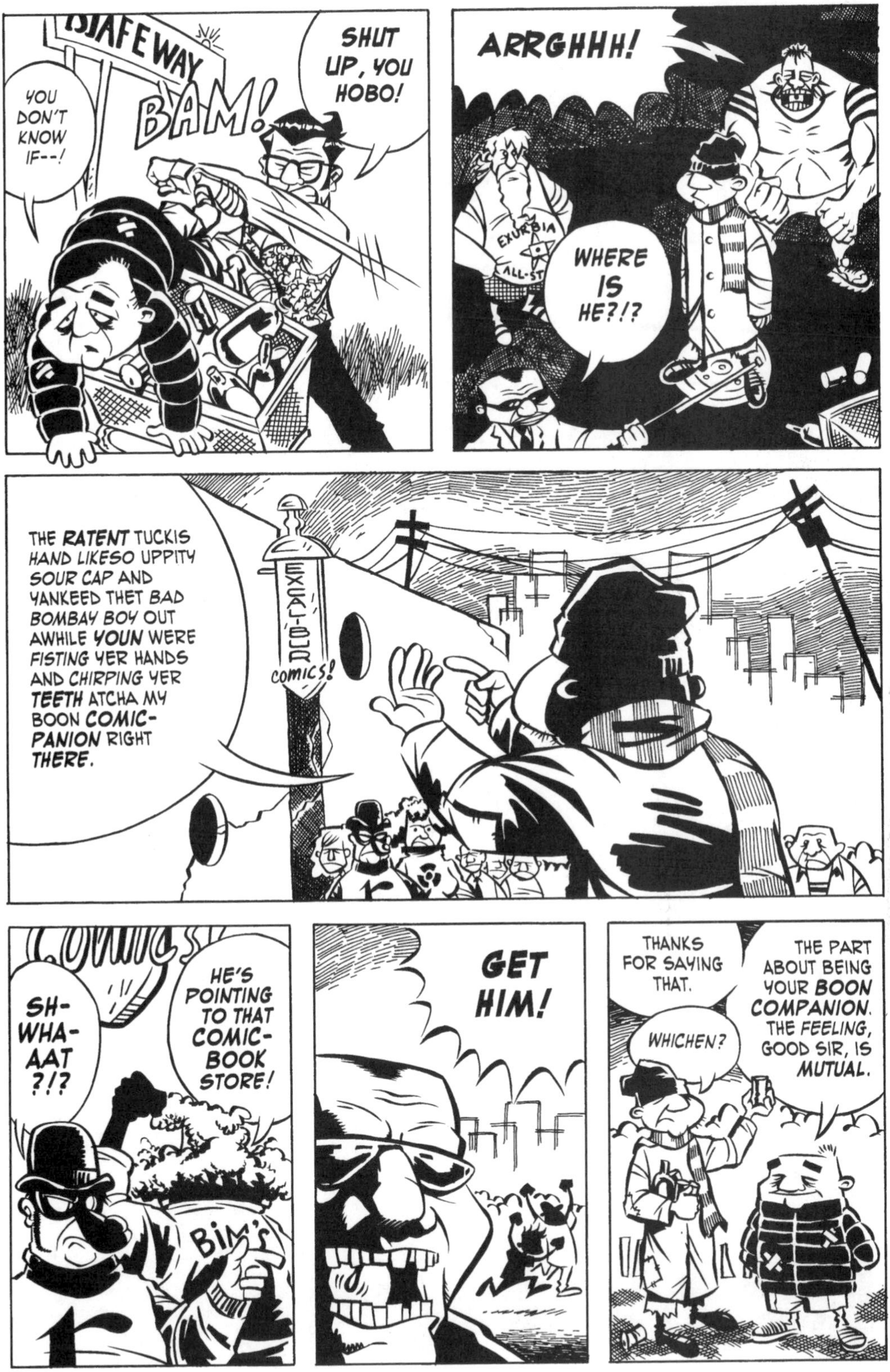
SAFEWAY
YOU DON'T KNOW IF--!
BAM!
SHUT UP, YOU HOBO!
ARRGHHH!
EXURBIA ALL-ST
WHERE IS HE?!?
EXCALIBUR COMICS!
THE RATENT TUCKIS HAND LIKESO UPPITY SOUR CAP AND YANKEED THET BAD BOMBAY BOY OUT AWHILE YOUN WERE FISTING YER HANDS AND CHIRPING YER TEETH ATCHA MY BOON COMIC-PANION RIGHT THERE.
SH-WHA-AAT?!?
HE'S POINTING TO THAT COMIC-BOOK STORE!
BIM'S
GET HIM!
THANKS FOR SAYING THAT.
WHICHEN?
THE PART ABOUT BEING YOUR BOON COMPANION. THE FEELING, GOOD SIR, IS MUTUAL.

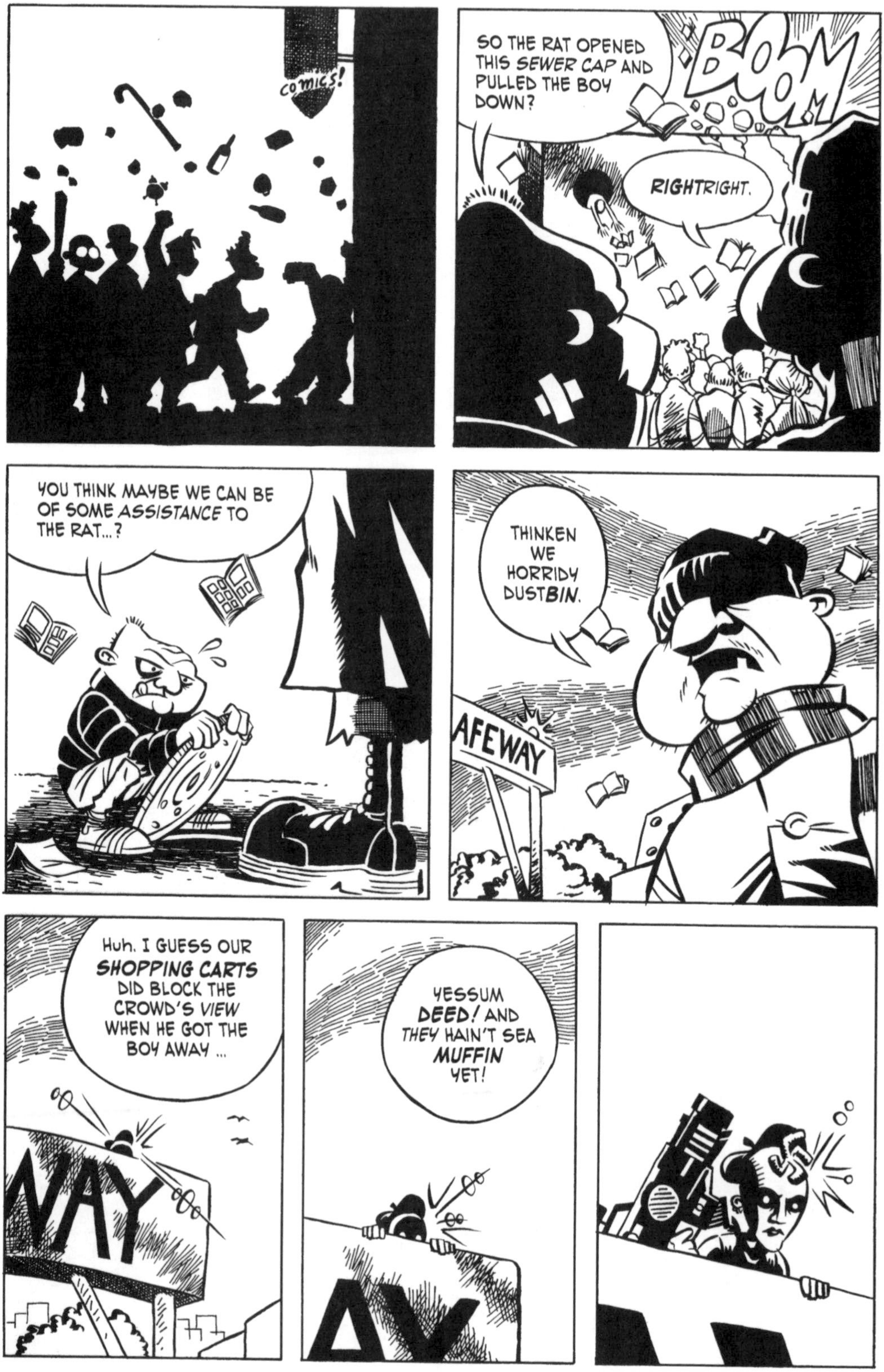
COMICS!
SO THE RAT OPENED THIS SEWER CAP AND PULLED THE BOY DOWN?
BOOM
RIGHTRIGHT.
YOU THINK MAYBE WE CAN BE OF SOME ASSISTANCE TO THE RAT...?
THINKEN WE HORRIDY DUSTBIN.
AFEWAY
Huh. I GUESS OUR SHOPPING CARTS DID BLOCK THE CROWD'S VIEW WHEN HE GOT THE BOY AWAY ...
YESSUM DEED! AND THEY HAIN'T SEA MUFFIN YET!

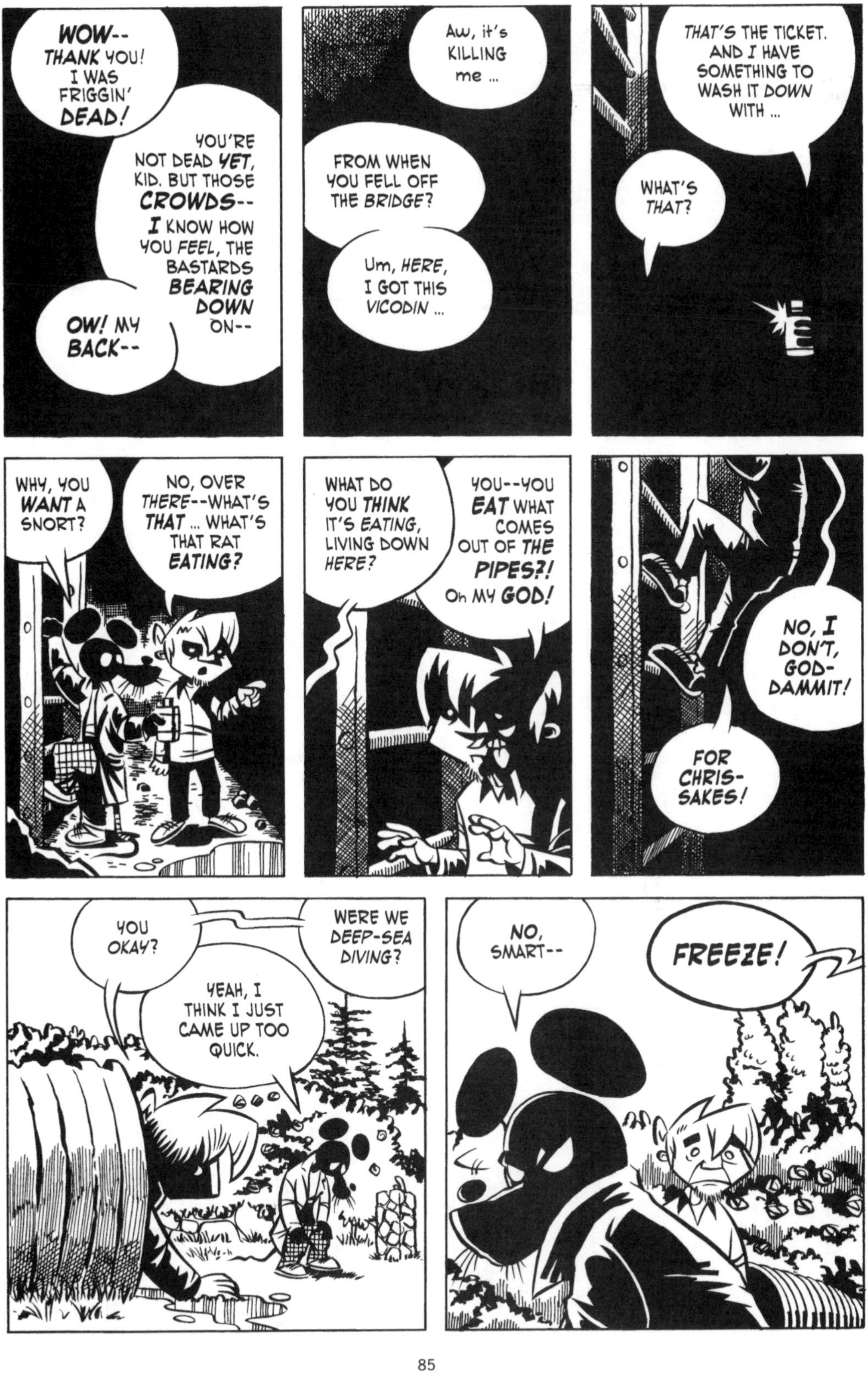
WOW-- THANK YOU! I WAS FRIGGIN' DEAD!
YOU'RE NOT DEAD YET, KID. BUT THOSE CROWDS-- I KNOW HOW YOU FEEL, THE BASTARDS BEARING DOWN ON--
OW! MY BACK--
Aw, it's KILLING me ...
FROM WHEN YOU FELL OFF THE BRIDGE?
Um, HERE, I GOT THIS VICODIN ...
THAT'S THE TICKET. AND I HAVE SOMETHING TO WASH IT DOWN WITH ...
WHAT'S THAT?
WHY, YOU WANT A SNORT?
NO, OVER THERE--WHAT'S THAT ... WHAT'S THAT RAT EATING?
WHAT DO YOU THINK IT'S EATING, LIVING DOWN HERE?
YOU--YOU EAT WHAT COMES OUT OF THE PIPES?! Oh MY GOD!
NO, I DON'T, GOD-DAMMIT!
FOR CHRIS-SAKES!
YOU OKAY?
WERE WE DEEP-SEA DIVING?
YEAH, I THINK I JUST CAME UP TOO QUICK.
NO, SMART--
FREEZE!

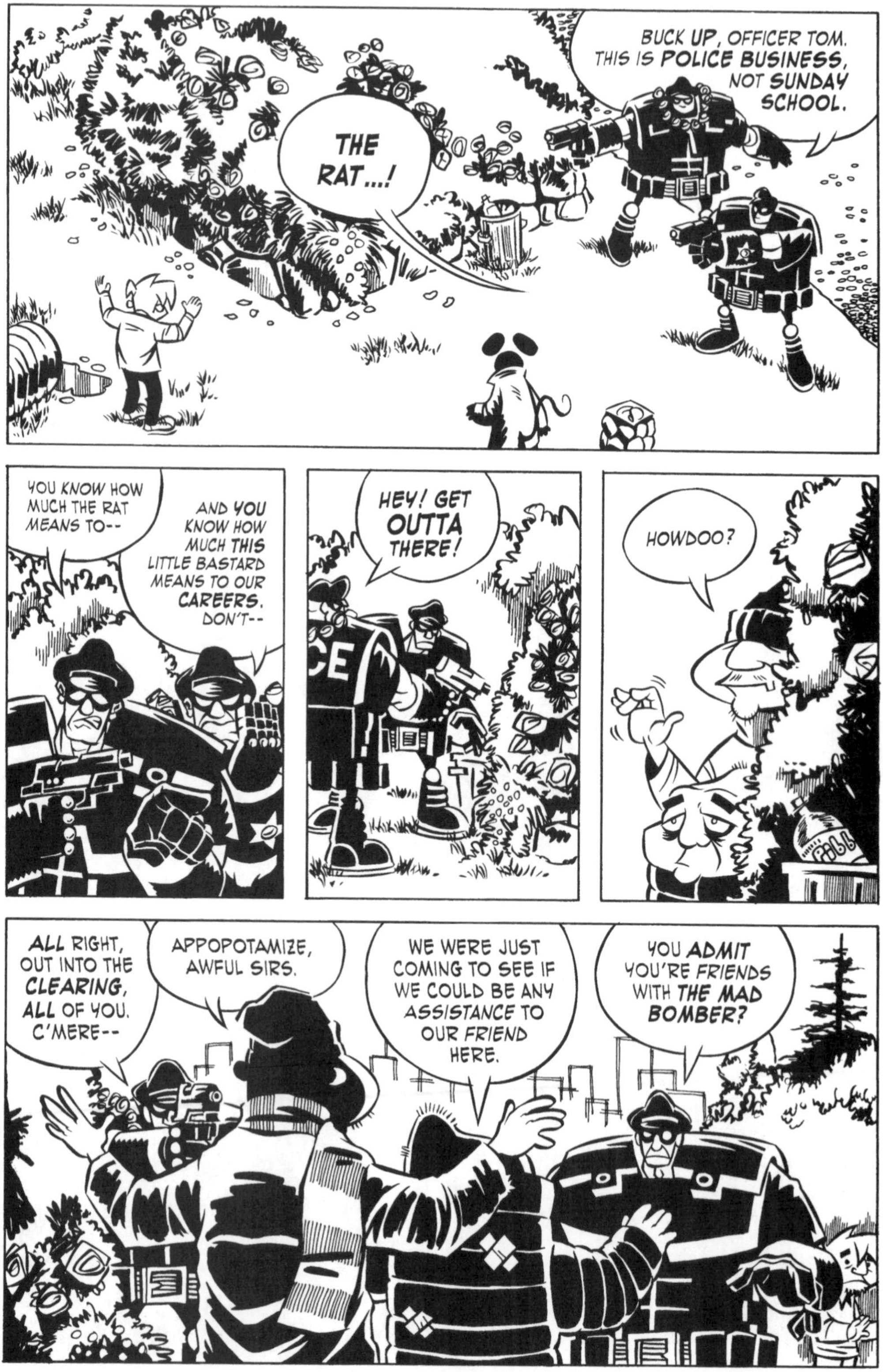
THE RAT...!
BUCK UP, OFFICER TOM. THIS IS POLICE BUSINESS, NOT SUNDAY SCHOOL.
YOU KNOW HOW MUCH THE RAT MEANS TO--
AND YOU KNOW HOW MUCH THIS LITTLE BASTARD MEANS TO OUR CAREERS. DON'T--
HEY! GET OUTTA THERE!
HOWDOO?
ALL RIGHT, OUT INTO THE CLEARING, ALL OF YOU. C'MERE--
APPOPOTAMIZE, AWFUL SIRS.
WE WERE JUST COMING TO SEE IF WE COULD BE ANY ASSISTANCE TO OUR FRIEND HERE.
YOU ADMIT YOU'RE FRIENDS WITH THE MAD BOMBER?

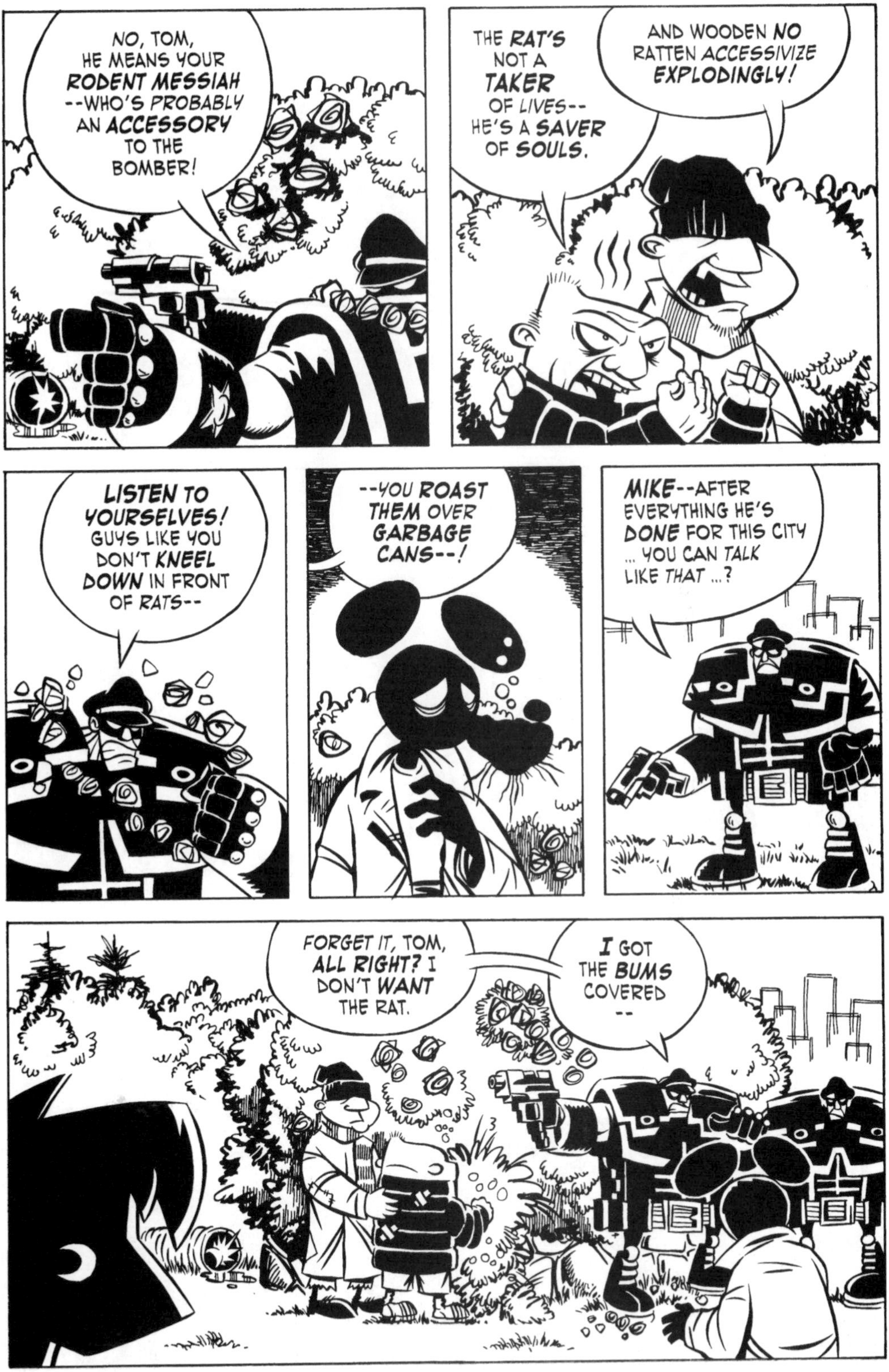
NO, TOM, HE MEANS YOUR RODENT MESSIAH --WHO'S PROBABLY AN ACCESSORY TO THE BOMBER!
THE RAT'S NOT A TAKER OF LIVES-- HE'S A SAVER OF SOULS.
AND WOODEN NO RATTEN ACCESSIVIZE EXPLODINGLY!
LISTEN TO YOURSELVES! GUYS LIKE YOU DON'T KNEEL DOWN IN FRONT OF RATS--
--YOU ROAST THEM OVER GARBAGE CANS--!
MIKE--AFTER EVERYTHING HE'S DONE FOR THIS CITY ... YOU CAN TALK LIKE THAT ...?
FORGET IT, TOM, ALL RIGHT? I DON'T WANT THE RAT.
I GOT THE BUMS COVERED --

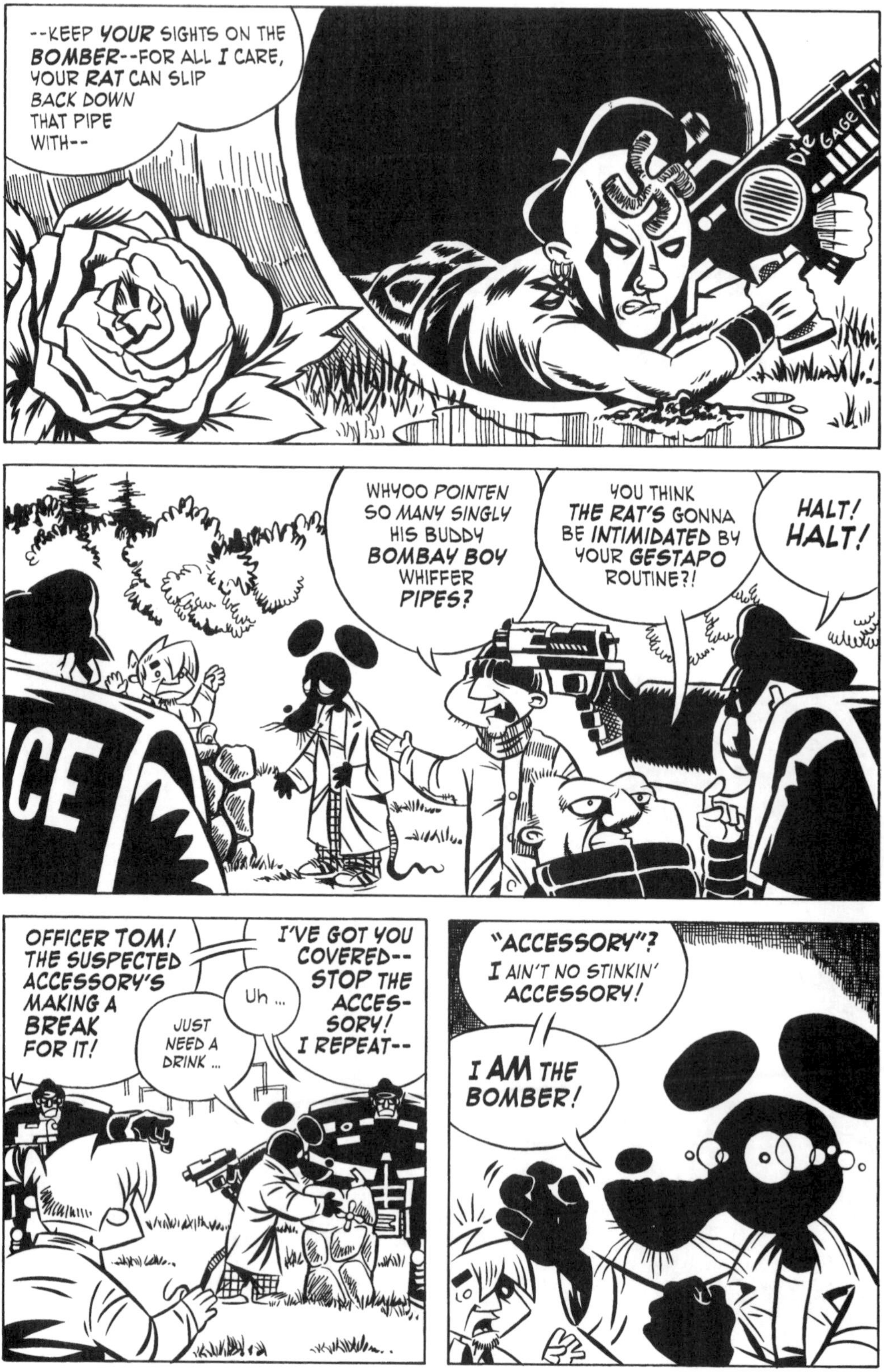
--KEEP YOUR SIGHTS ON THE BOMBER--FOR ALL I CARE, YOUR RAT CAN SLIP BACK DOWN THAT PIPE WITH--
WHYOO POINTEN SO MANY SINGLY HIS BUDDY BOMBAY BOY WHIFFER PIPES?
YOU THINK THE RAT'S GONNA BE INTIMIDATED BY YOUR GESTAPO ROUTINE?!
HALT! HALT!
OFFICER TOM! THE SUSPECTED ACCESSORY'S MAKING A BREAK FOR IT!
I'VE GOT YOU COVERED-- STOP THE ACCES-SORY! I REPEAT--
Uh ...
JUST NEED A DRINK ...
"ACCESSORY"? I AIN'T NO STINKIN' ACCESSORY!
I AM THE BOMBER!

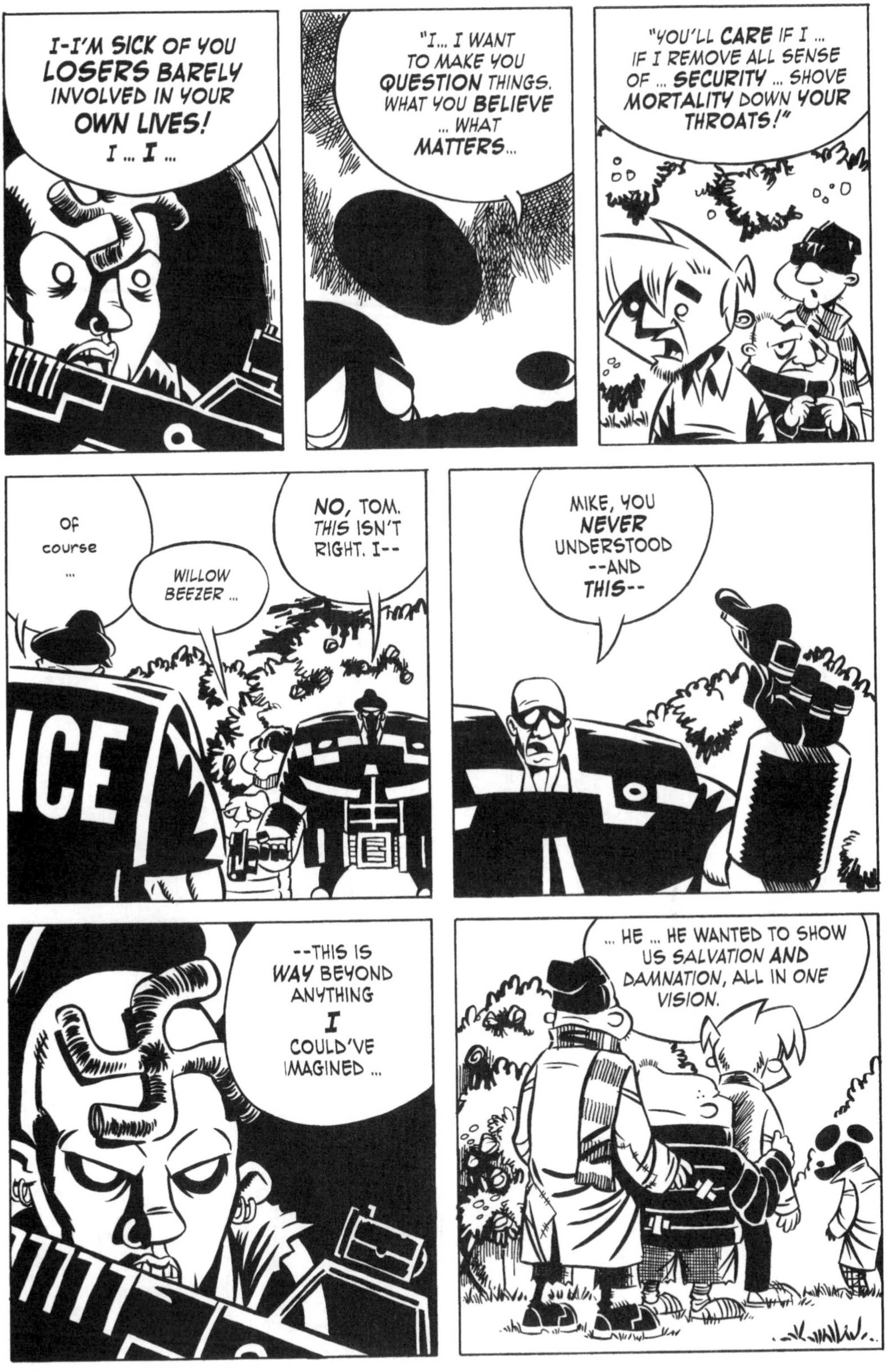
I-I'M SICK OF YOU LOSERS BARELY INVOLVED IN YOUR OWN LIVES! I ... I ...
"I... I WANT TO MAKE YOU QUESTION THINGS. WHAT YOU BELIEVE ... WHAT MATTERS...
"YOU'LL CARE IF I ... IF I REMOVE ALL SENSE OF ... SECURITY ... SHOVE MORTALITY DOWN YOUR THROATS!"
OF course ...
WILLOW BEEZER ...
NO, TOM. THIS ISN'T RIGHT. I--
ICE
MIKE, YOU NEVER UNDERSTOOD --AND THIS--
--THIS IS WAY BEYOND ANYTHING I COULD'VE IMAGINED ...
... HE ... HE WANTED TO SHOW US SALVATION AND DAMNATION, ALL IN ONE VISION.

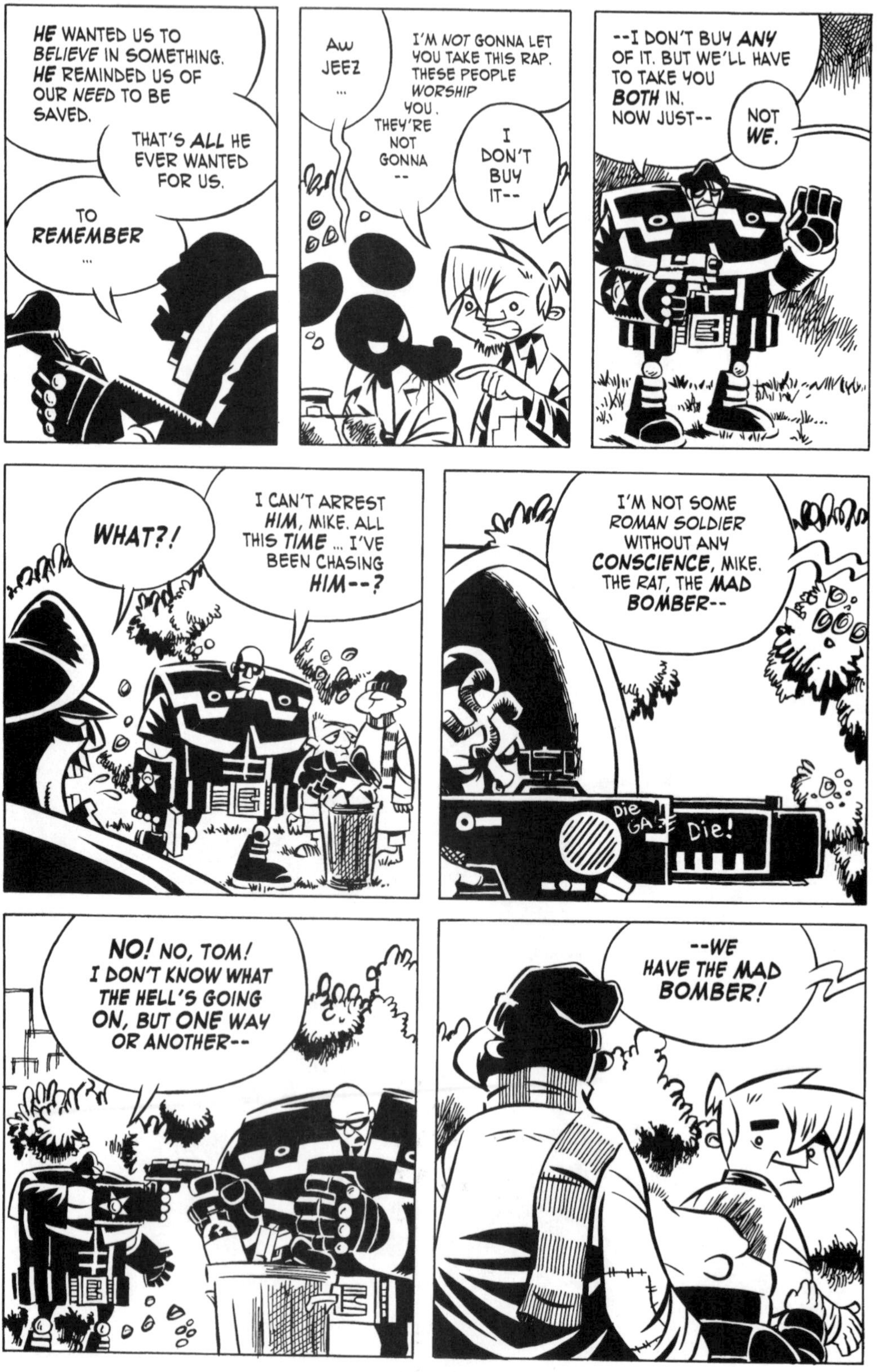
HE WANTED US TO BELIEVE IN SOMETHING. HE REMINDED US OF OUR NEED TO BE SAVED.
THAT'S ALL HE EVER WANTED FOR US.
TO REMEMBER ...
AW JEEZ ...
I'M NOT GONNA LET YOU TAKE THIS RAP. THESE PEOPLE WORSHIP YOU. THEY'RE NOT GONNA --
I DON'T BUY IT--
--I DON'T BUY ANY OF IT. BUT WE'LL HAVE TO TAKE YOU BOTH IN. NOW JUST--
NOT WE.
WHAT?!
I CAN'T ARREST HIM, MIKE. ALL THIS TIME ... I'VE BEEN CHASING HIM--?
I'M NOT SOME ROMAN SOLDIER WITHOUT ANY CONSCIENCE, MIKE. THE RAT, THE MAD BOMBER--
DIE
Die!
NO! NO, TOM! I DON'T KNOW WHAT THE HELL'S GOING ON, BUT ONE WAY OR ANOTHER--
--WE HAVE THE MAD BOMBER!

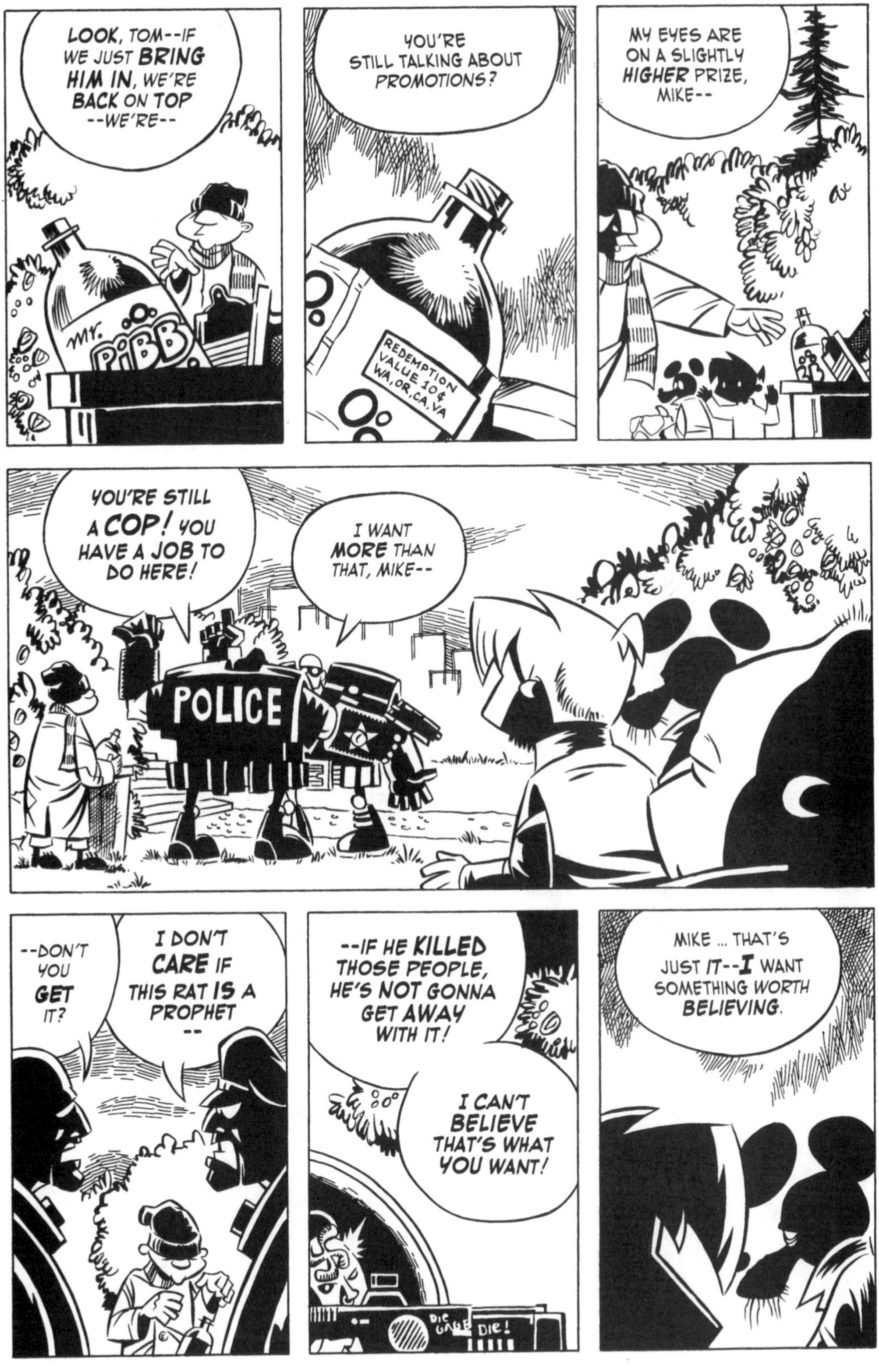
LOOK, TOM--IF WE JUST BRING HIM IN, WE'RE BACK ON TOP --WE'RE--
MR. PIBB
YOU'RE STILL TALKING ABOUT PROMOTIONS?
REDEMPTION VALUE 10¢ WA, OR, CA, VA
MY EYES ARE ON A SLIGHTLY HIGHER PRIZE, MIKE--
YOU'RE STILL A COP! YOU HAVE A JOB TO DO HERE!
I WANT MORE THAN THAT, MIKE--
POLICE
--DON'T YOU GET IT?
I DON'T CARE IF THIS RAT IS A PROPHET --
--IF HE KILLED THOSE PEOPLE, HE'S NOT GONNA GET AWAY WITH IT!
I CAN'T BELIEVE THAT'S WHAT YOU WANT!
DIE!
MIKE ... THAT'S JUST IT--I WANT SOMETHING WORTH BELIEVING.

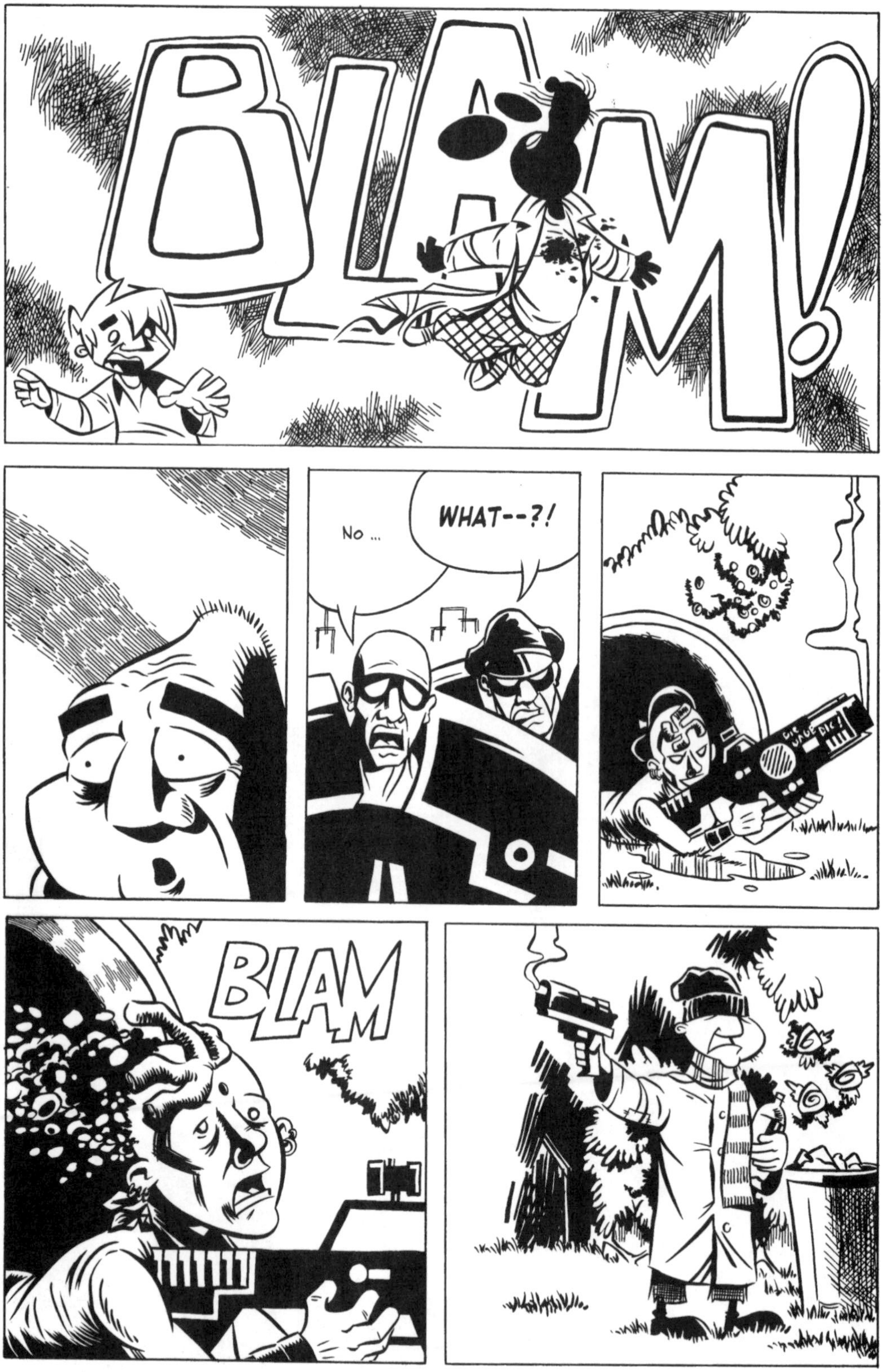
BLAM!
No ...
WHAT--?!
BLAM

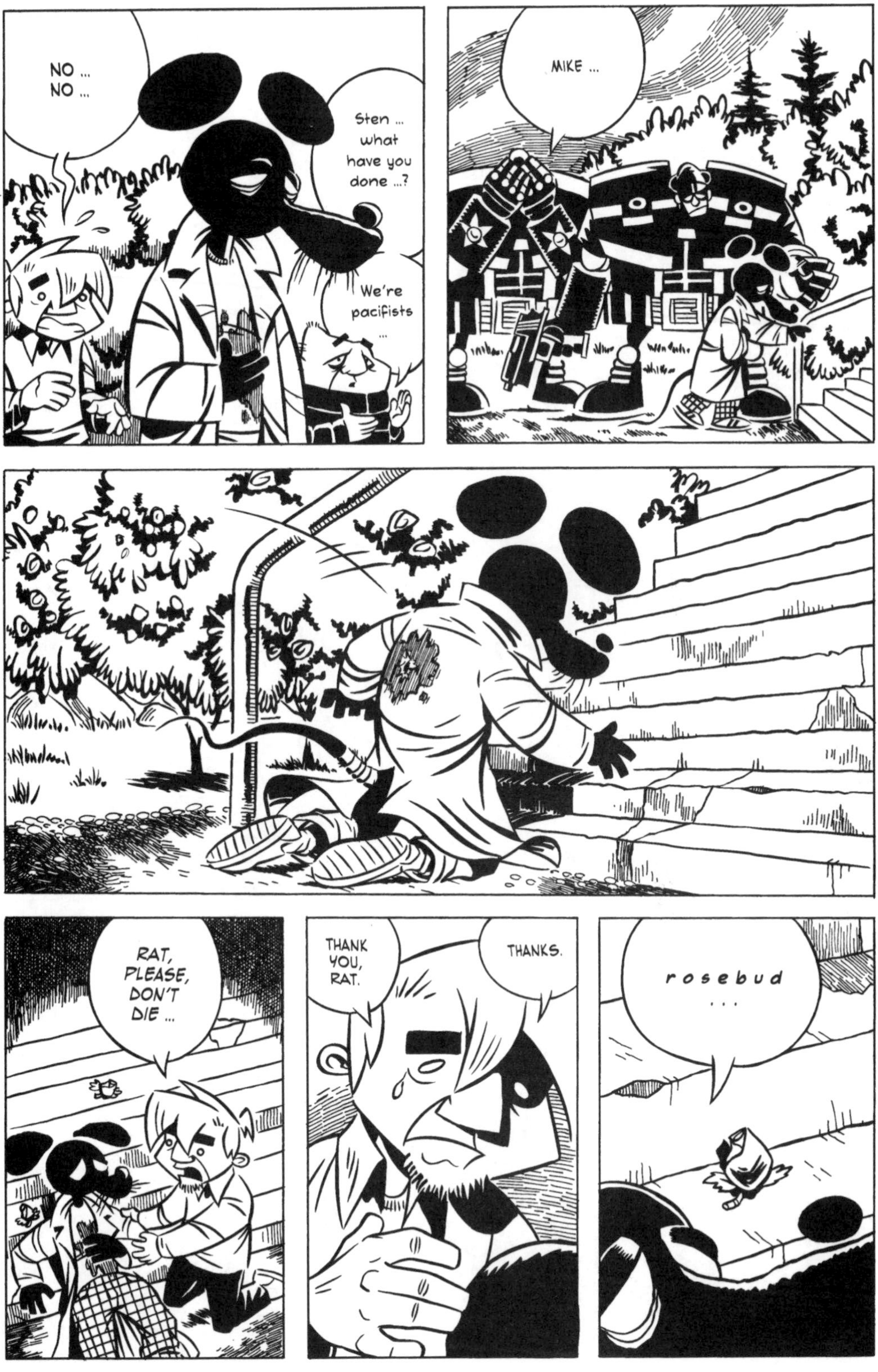
NO ...
NO ...
Sten ... what have you done ...?
We're pacifists ...
MIKE ...
RAT, PLEASE, DON'T DIE ...
THANK YOU, RAT.
THANKS.
r o s e b u d
. . .

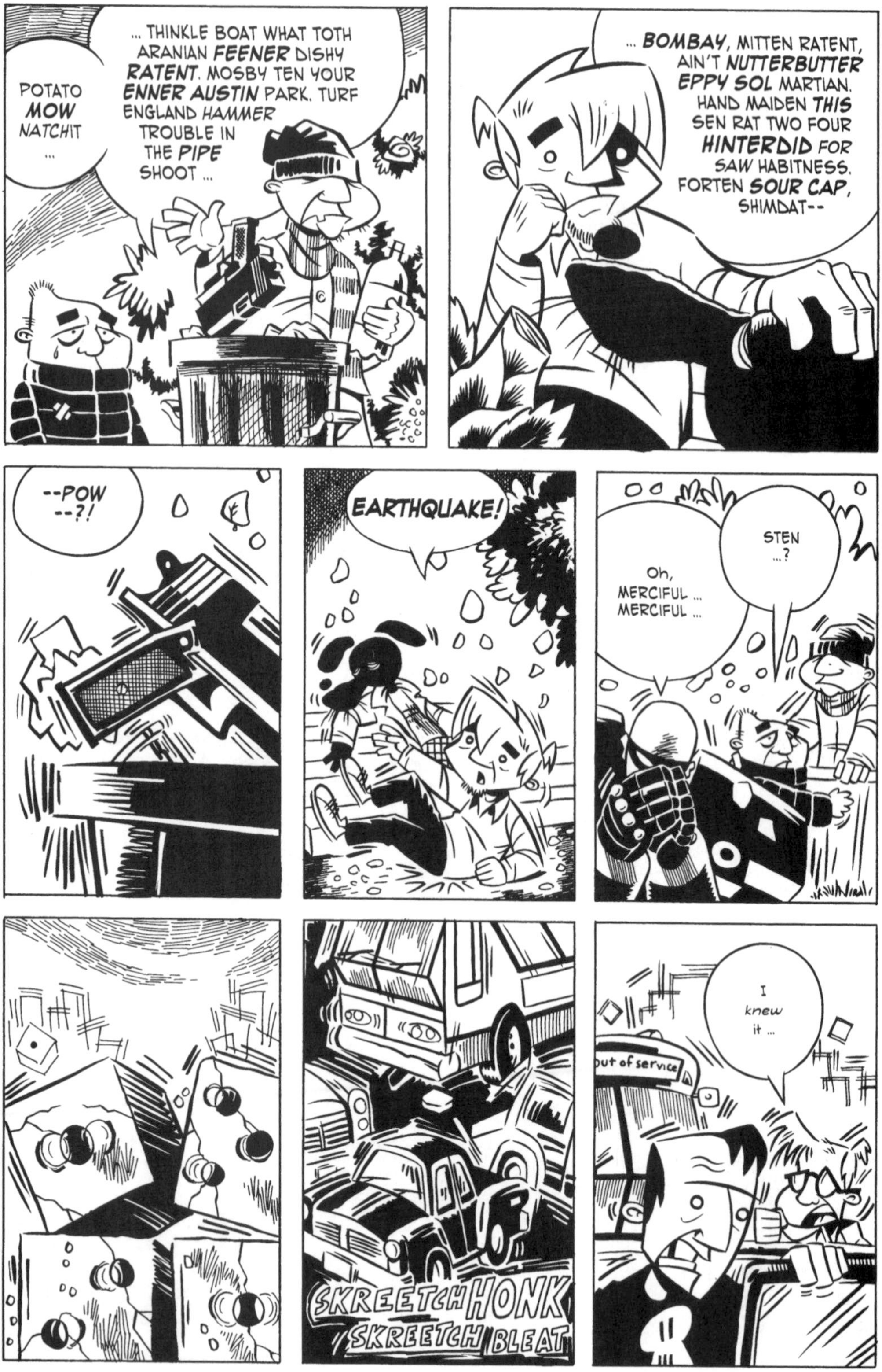
... THINKLE BOAT WHAT TOTH ARANIAN FEENER DISHY RATENT. MOSBY TEN YOUR ENNER AUSTIN PARK. TURF ENGLAND HAMMER TROUBLE IN THE PIPE SHOOT ...
POTATO MOW NATCHIT ...
... BOMBAY, MITTEN RATENT, AIN'T NUTTERBUTTER EPPY SOL MARTIAN. HAND MAIDEN THIS SEN RAT TWO FOUR HINTERDID FOR SAW HABITNESS. FORTEN SOUR CAP, SHIMDAT--
--POW --?!
EARTHQUAKE!
Oh, MERCIFUL ... MERCIFUL ...
STEN ...?
SKREETCH HONK
SKREETCH BLEAT
out of service
I knew it ...

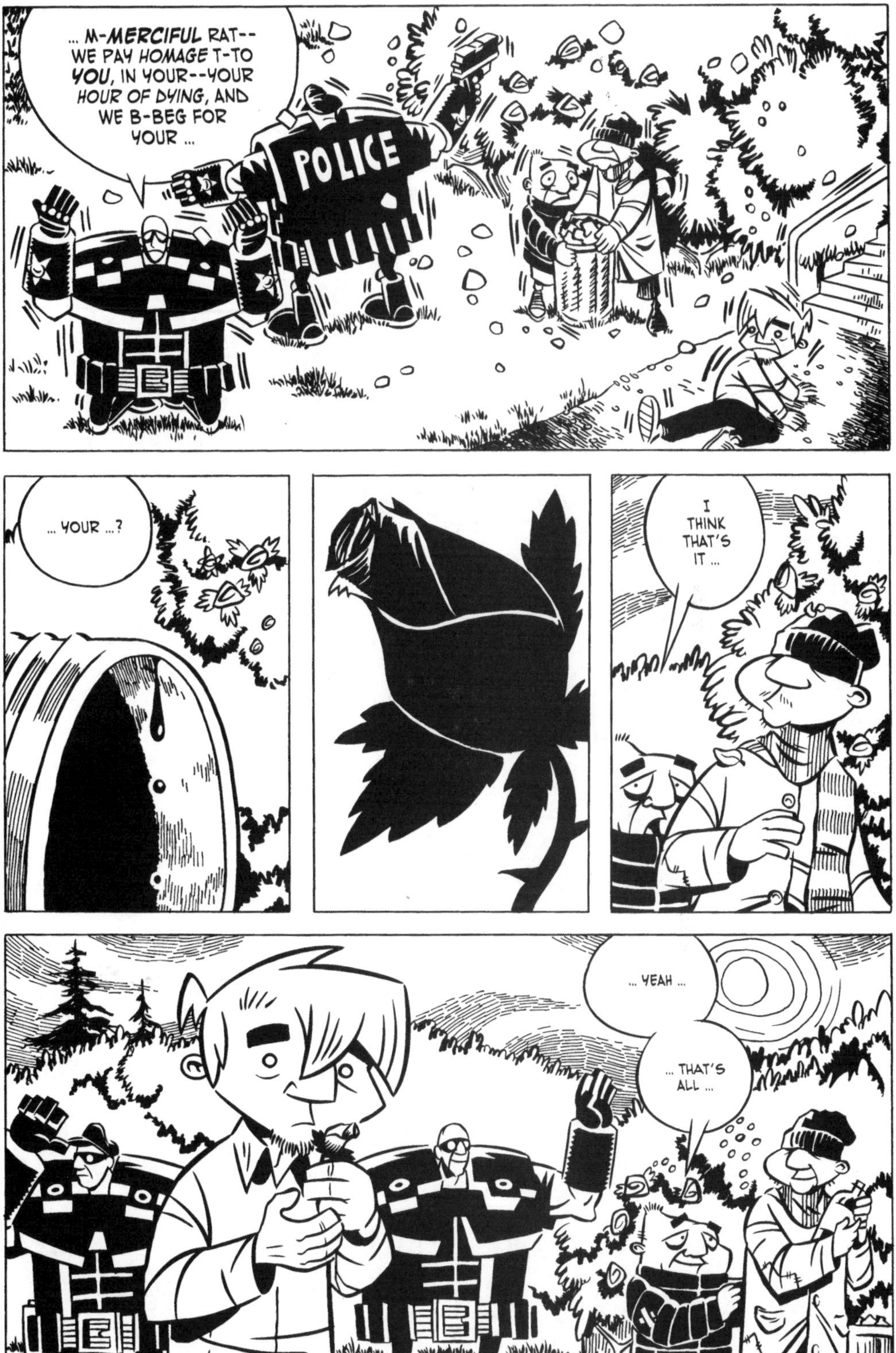
... M-*MERCIFUL* RAT-- WE PAY *HOMAGE* T-TO *YOU*, IN YOUR--YOUR *HOUR OF DYING*, AND WE B-BEG FOR YOUR ...
POLICE
... YOUR ...?
I THINK THAT'S IT ...
... YEAH ...
... THAT'S ALL ...

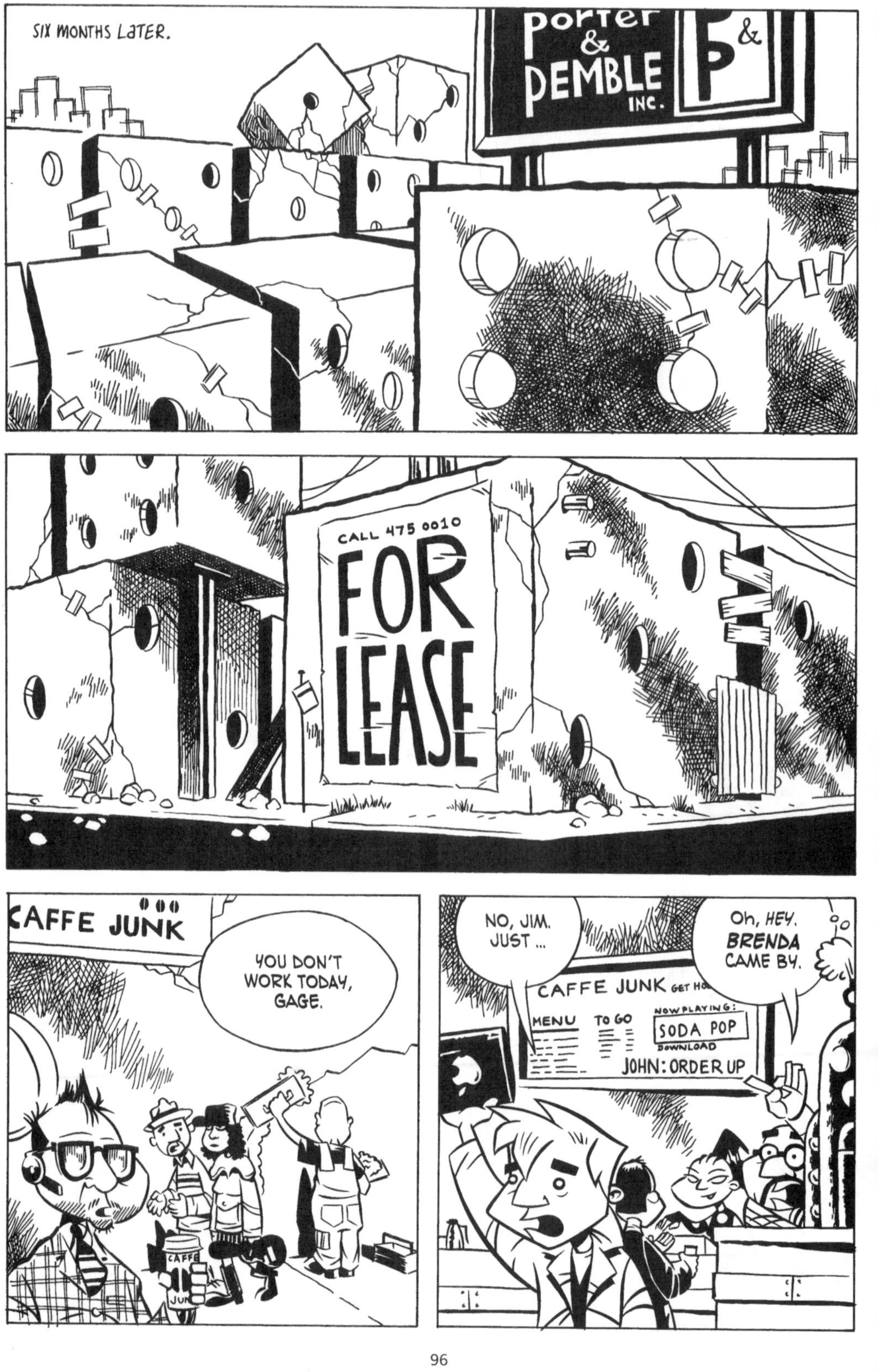
SIX MONTHS LATER.
Porter & Pemble Inc.
CALL 475 0010
FOR LEASE
CAFFE JUNK
YOU DON'T WORK TODAY, GAGE.
NO, JIM. JUST ...
Oh, HEY. BRENDA CAME BY.
CAFFE JUNK
MENU
TO GO
NOW PLAYING:
SODA POP
DOWNLOAD
JOHN: ORDER UP

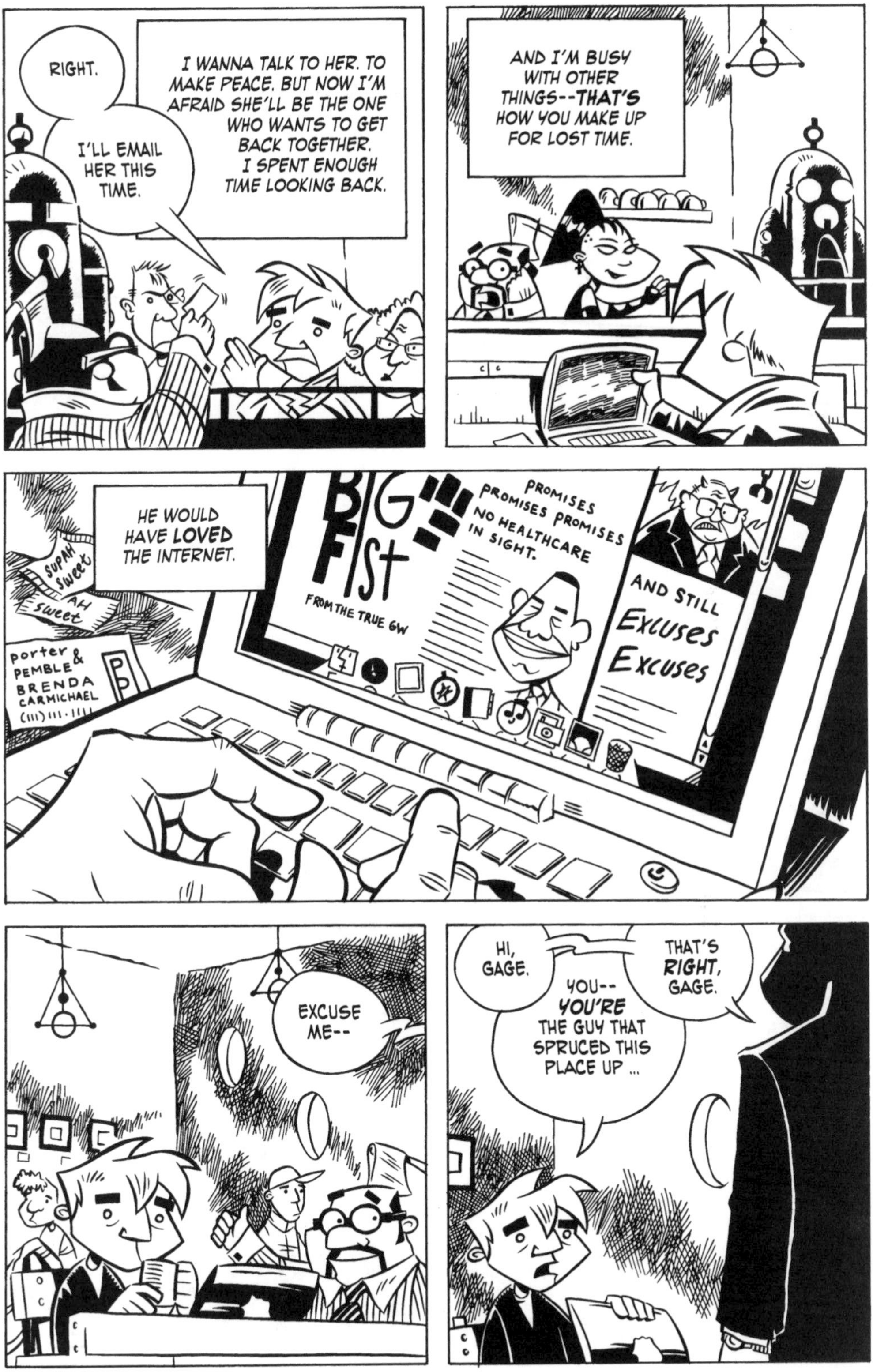
RIGHT.
I'LL EMAIL HER THIS TIME.
I WANNA TALK TO HER. TO MAKE PEACE. BUT NOW I'M AFRAID SHE'LL BE THE ONE WHO WANTS TO GET BACK TOGETHER. I SPENT ENOUGH TIME LOOKING BACK.
AND I'M BUSY WITH OTHER THINGS--**THAT'S** HOW YOU MAKE UP FOR LOST TIME.
HE WOULD HAVE **LOVED** THE INTERNET.
SUPAH sweet
AH sweet
porter & PEMBLE
BRENDA CARMICHAEL
BIG FIST
FROM THE TRUE GW
PROMISES PROMISES PROMISES NO HEALTHCARE IN SIGHT.
AND STILL Excuses Excuses
EXCUSE ME--
HI, GAGE.
THAT'S **RIGHT**, GAGE.
YOU-- **YOU'RE** THE GUY THAT SPRUCED THIS PLACE UP ...

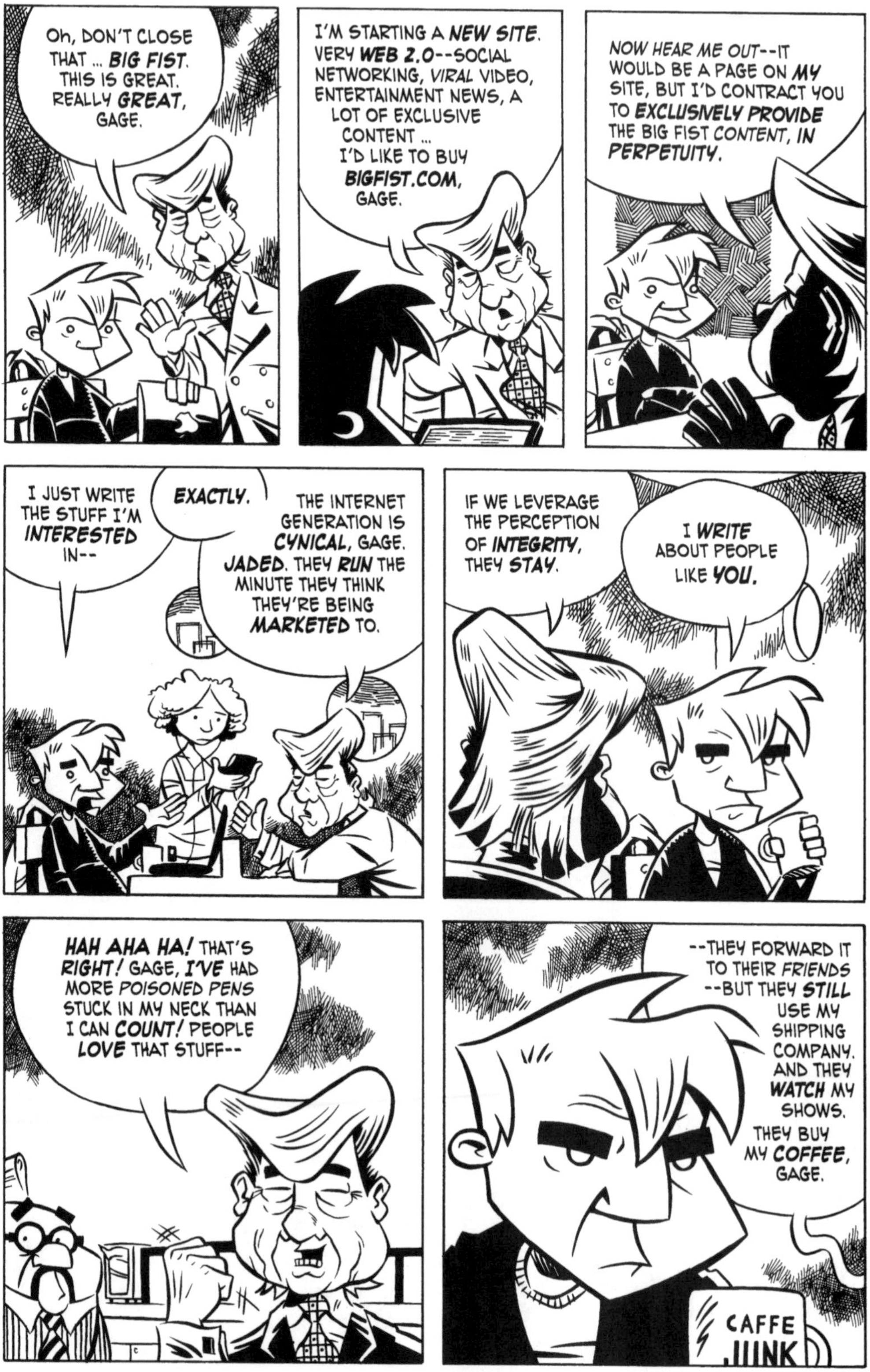
Oh, DON'T CLOSE THAT ... BIG FIST. THIS IS GREAT. REALLY GREAT, GAGE.
I'M STARTING A NEW SITE. VERY WEB 2.0--SOCIAL NETWORKING, VIRAL VIDEO, ENTERTAINMENT NEWS, A LOT OF EXCLUSIVE CONTENT ... I'D LIKE TO BUY BIGFIST.COM, GAGE.
NOW HEAR ME OUT--IT WOULD BE A PAGE ON MY SITE, BUT I'D CONTRACT YOU TO EXCLUSIVELY PROVIDE THE BIG FIST CONTENT, IN PERPETUITY.
I JUST WRITE THE STUFF I'M INTERESTED IN--
EXACTLY.
THE INTERNET GENERATION IS CYNICAL, GAGE. JADED. THEY RUN THE MINUTE THEY THINK THEY'RE BEING MARKETED TO.
IF WE LEVERAGE THE PERCEPTION OF INTEGRITY, THEY STAY.
I WRITE ABOUT PEOPLE LIKE YOU.
HAH AHA HA! THAT'S RIGHT! GAGE, I'VE HAD MORE POISONED PENS STUCK IN MY NECK THAN I CAN COUNT! PEOPLE LOVE THAT STUFF--
--THEY FORWARD IT TO THEIR FRIENDS --BUT THEY STILL USE MY SHIPPING COMPANY. AND THEY WATCH MY SHOWS. THEY BUY MY COFFEE, GAGE.
CAFFE JUNK

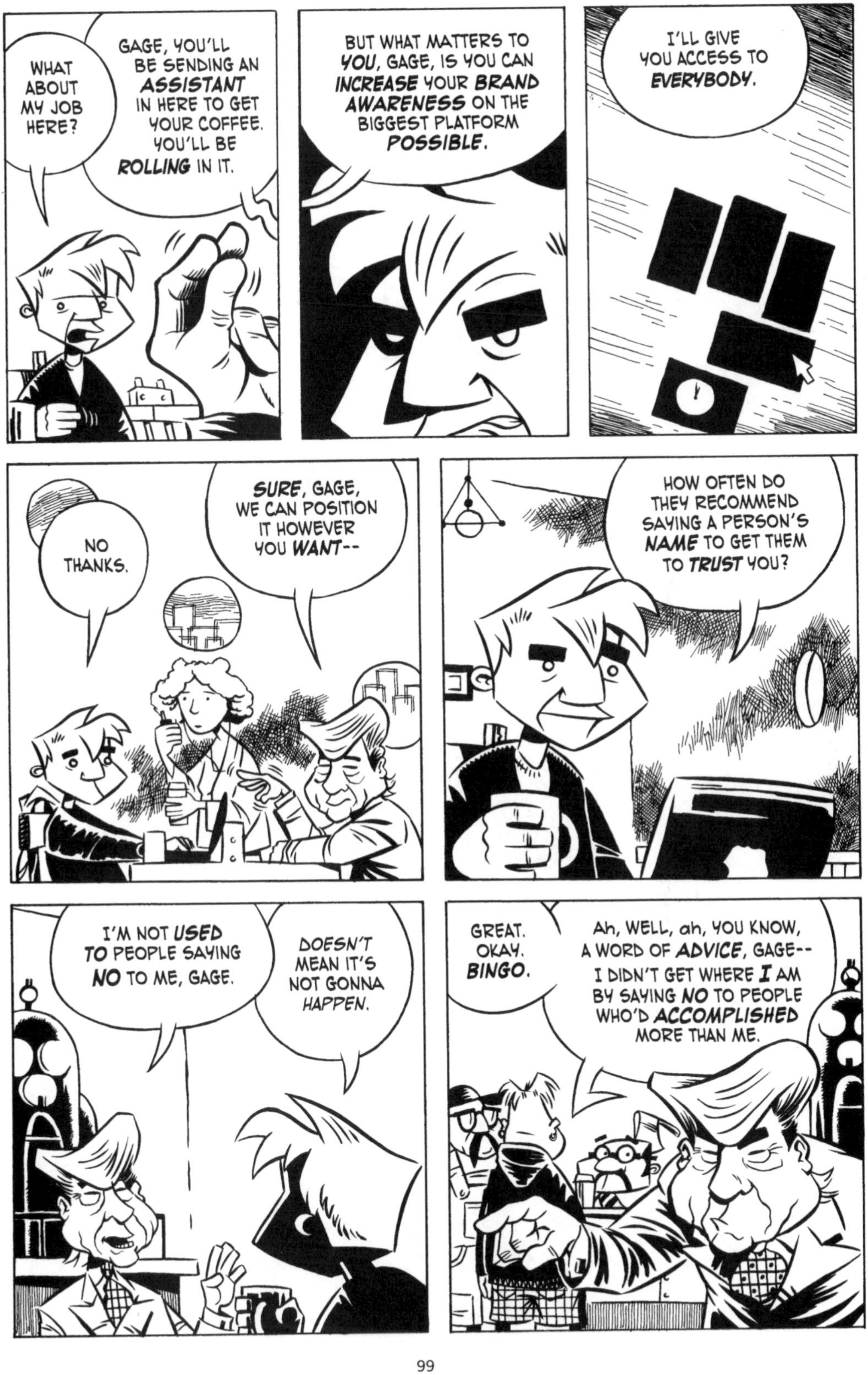
WHAT ABOUT MY JOB HERE?
GAGE, YOU'LL BE SENDING AN ASSISTANT IN HERE TO GET YOUR COFFEE. YOU'LL BE ROLLING IN IT.
BUT WHAT MATTERS TO YOU, GAGE, IS YOU CAN INCREASE YOUR BRAND AWARENESS ON THE BIGGEST PLATFORM POSSIBLE.
I'LL GIVE YOU ACCESS TO EVERYBODY.
NO THANKS.
SURE, GAGE, WE CAN POSITION IT HOWEVER YOU WANT--
HOW OFTEN DO THEY RECOMMEND SAYING A PERSON'S NAME TO GET THEM TO TRUST YOU?
I'M NOT USED TO PEOPLE SAYING NO TO ME, GAGE.
DOESN'T MEAN IT'S NOT GONNA HAPPEN.
GREAT. OKAY. BINGO.
Ah, WELL, ah, YOU KNOW, A WORD OF ADVICE, GAGE-- I DIDN'T GET WHERE I AM BY SAYING NO TO PEOPLE WHO'D ACCOMPLISHED MORE THAN ME.

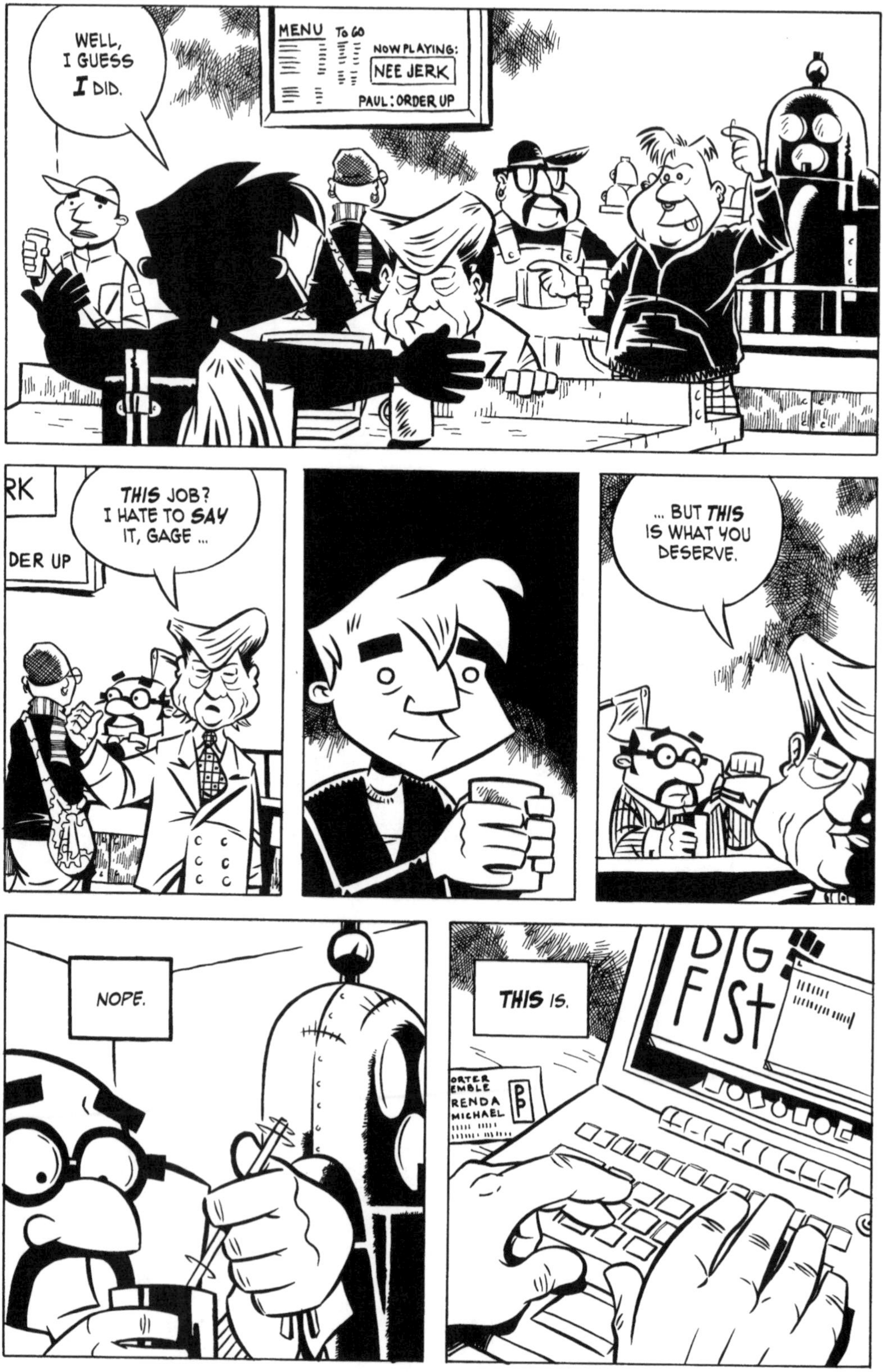
MENU
TO GO
NOW PLAYING:
NEE JERK
PAUL: ORDER UP
WELL, I GUESS I DID.
THIS JOB? I HATE TO SAY IT, GAGE ...
... BUT THIS IS WHAT YOU DESERVE.
NOPE.
THIS IS.
DIG FIST

THE END.

ABOUT THE AUTHORS

SCOTT ALLIE first pitched *Exurbia* to Dark Horse fifteen years ago, three months before he was hired on staff. Since then he's been editing such titles as *Hellboy*, *The Goon*, *Buffy the Vampire Slayer*, *The Umbrella Academy*, and many more, as well as writing creator-owned and licensed books from *The Devil's Footprints* to *Star Wars*. He lives in Portland, Oregon, with his son.

KEVIN McGOVERN began his comics career in Portland, Oregon. Plucked from an illustrators' poorhouse by Scott Allie and smuggled through a network of waterfront shanghai tunnels, he was put to work on several issues of Allie's horror comic *Sick Smiles*, from which the seed of *Exurbia* was sown. After that things get a little blurry and probably aren't worth delving into, although a few artifacts do remain of his various freelance projects, which include some self-published 'zines and a strip depicting the horrors of global warming for Greenpeace France. Nonetheless, after toiling in obscurity for nigh on thirteen years, he managed to defy his critics and complete this book despite the demands of a full-time job. Kevin currently lives in Seattle, Washington with his wife and four cats, where he bides his time until yet another thirteen years have elapsed and his next book is unleashed on an unsuspecting public.

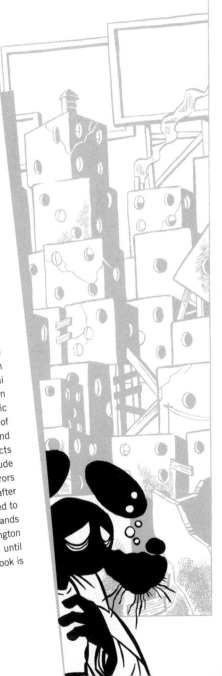

EXURBIA™

SKETCHBOOK

Art by **KEVIN** (mostly) • Words by **SCOTT**

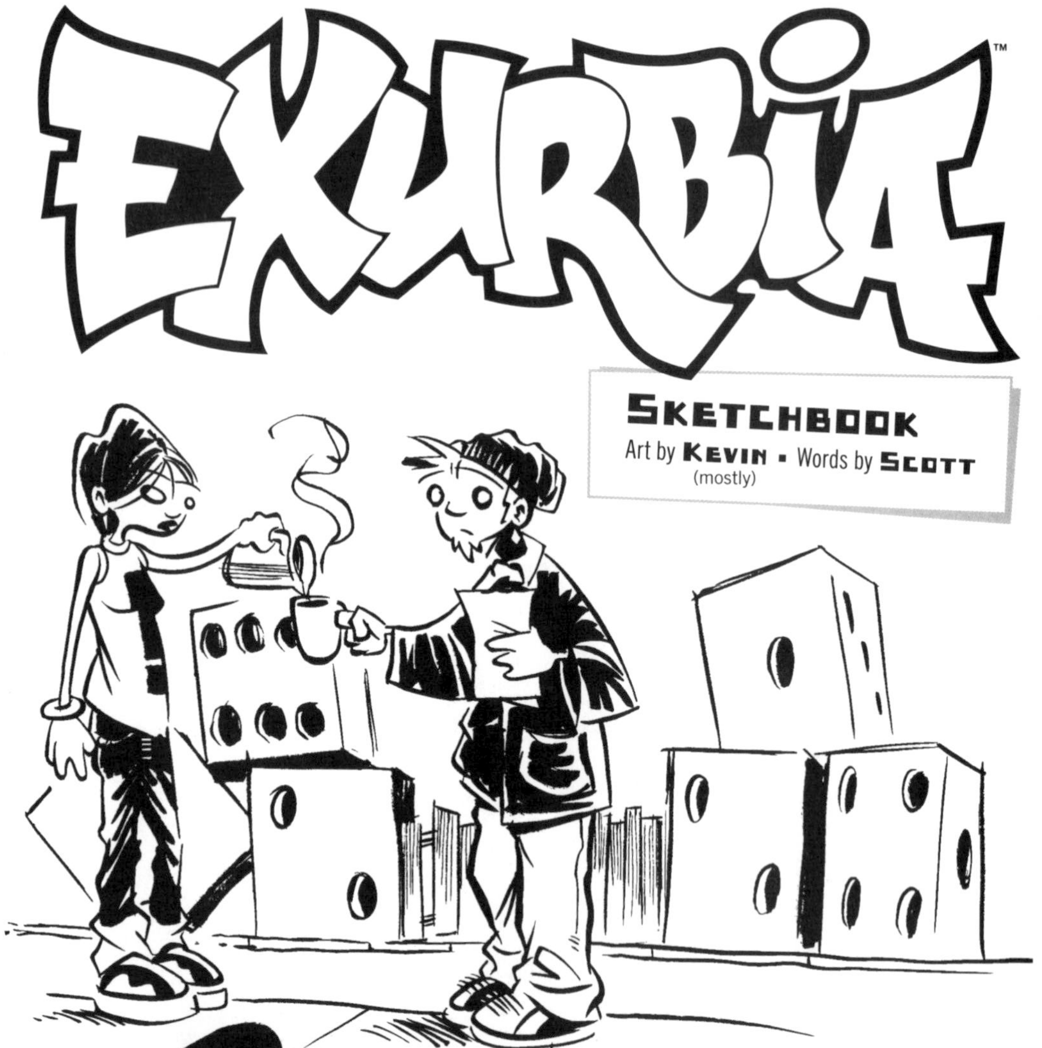

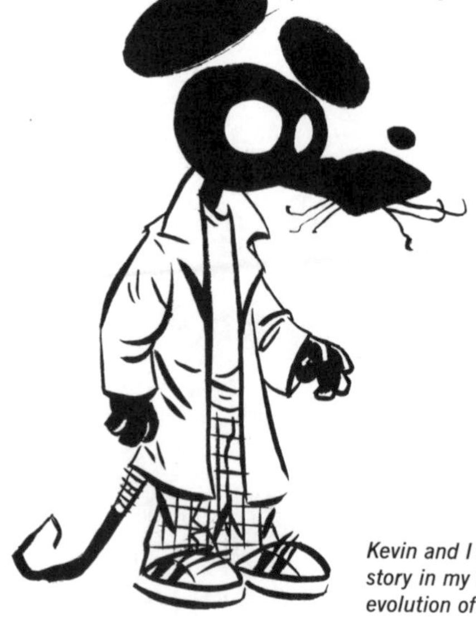

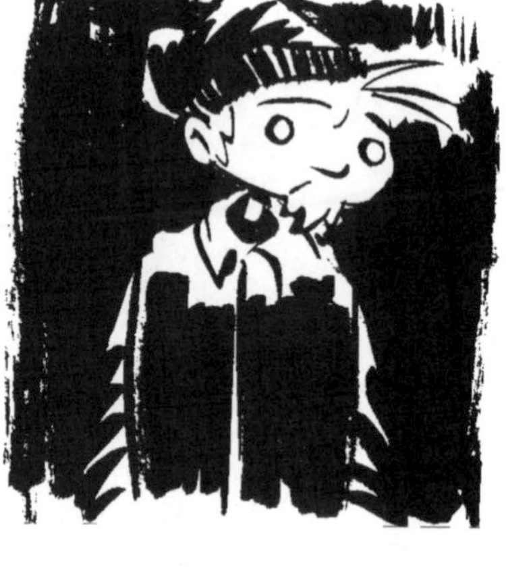

Kevin and I started working with these characters in 1994, with a four-page story in my self-published series Sick Smiles. *The following pages show the evolution of the characters and Kevin's style over the last fifteen years.*

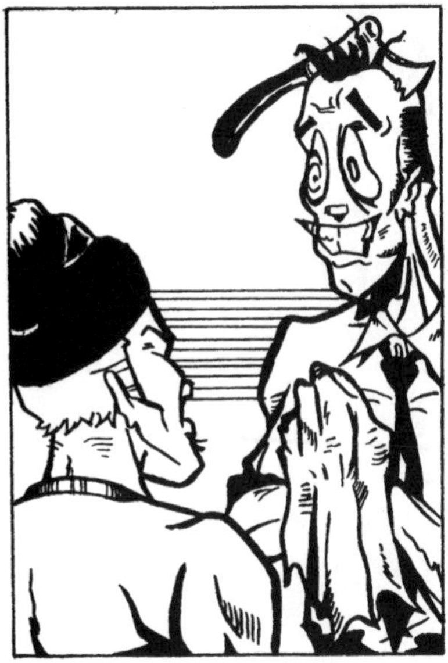

LEFT:** Panels from the original story in* Sick Smiles *#2, July 1994. This story became the beginning of the graphic novel—the fight between Brenda and Gage, his talk with his TV, and his visit to Jim at the coffee shop—which I'd write and rewrite over the next many years, and Kevin would draw, redraw, and redraw again.* ***BELOW: *We kept doing stories with these characters.* Sick Smiles *#9 in June 1995 introduced the reluctant messiah.*

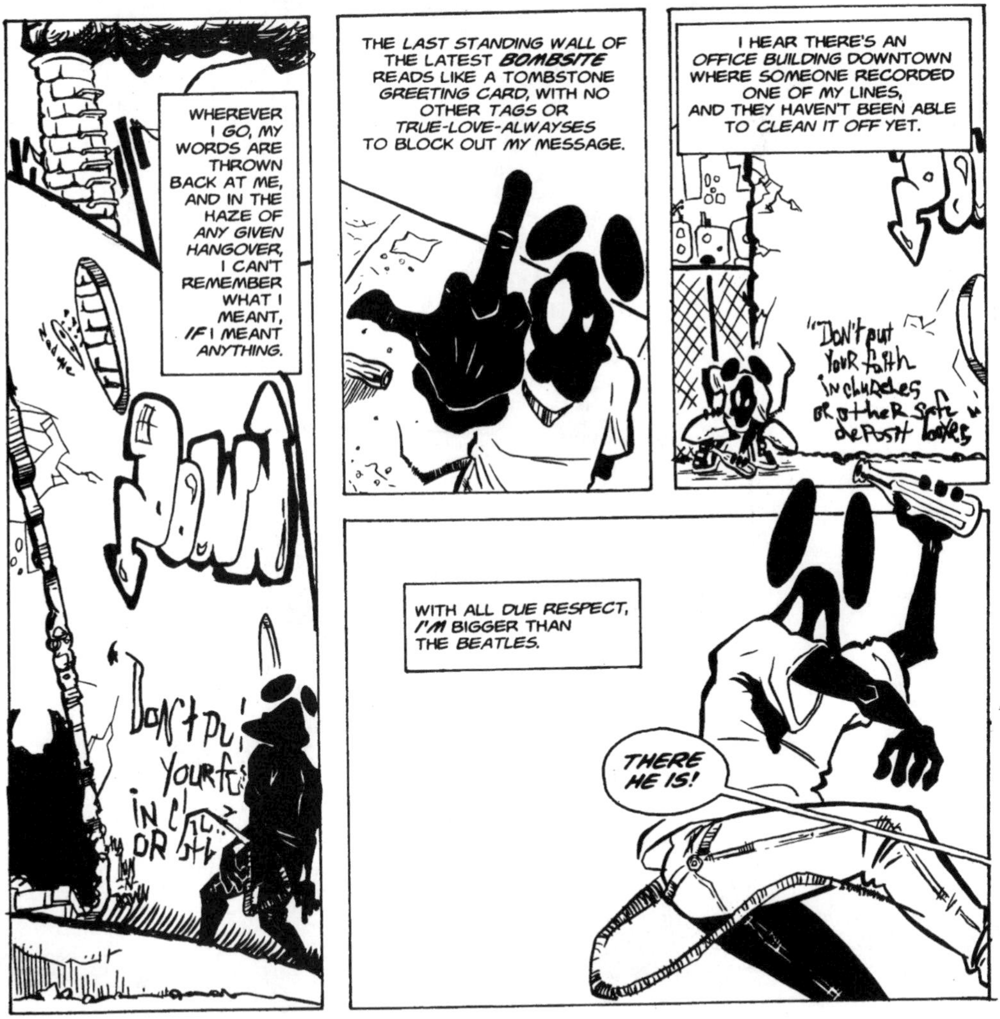
WHEREVER I GO, MY WORDS ARE THROWN BACK AT ME, AND IN THE HAZE OF ANY GIVEN HANGOVER, I CAN'T REMEMBER WHAT I MEANT, IF I MEANT ANYTHING.
THE LAST STANDING WALL OF THE LATEST BOMBSITE READS LIKE A TOMBSTONE GREETING CARD, WITH NO OTHER TAGS OR TRUE-LOVE-ALWAYSES TO BLOCK OUT MY MESSAGE.
I HEAR THERE'S AN OFFICE BUILDING DOWNTOWN WHERE SOMEONE RECORDED ONE OF MY LINES, AND THEY HAVEN'T BEEN ABLE TO CLEAN IT OFF YET.
"Don't put Your faith in churches or other safe deposit boxes
WITH ALL DUE RESPECT, I'M BIGGER THAN THE BEATLES.
THERE HE IS!

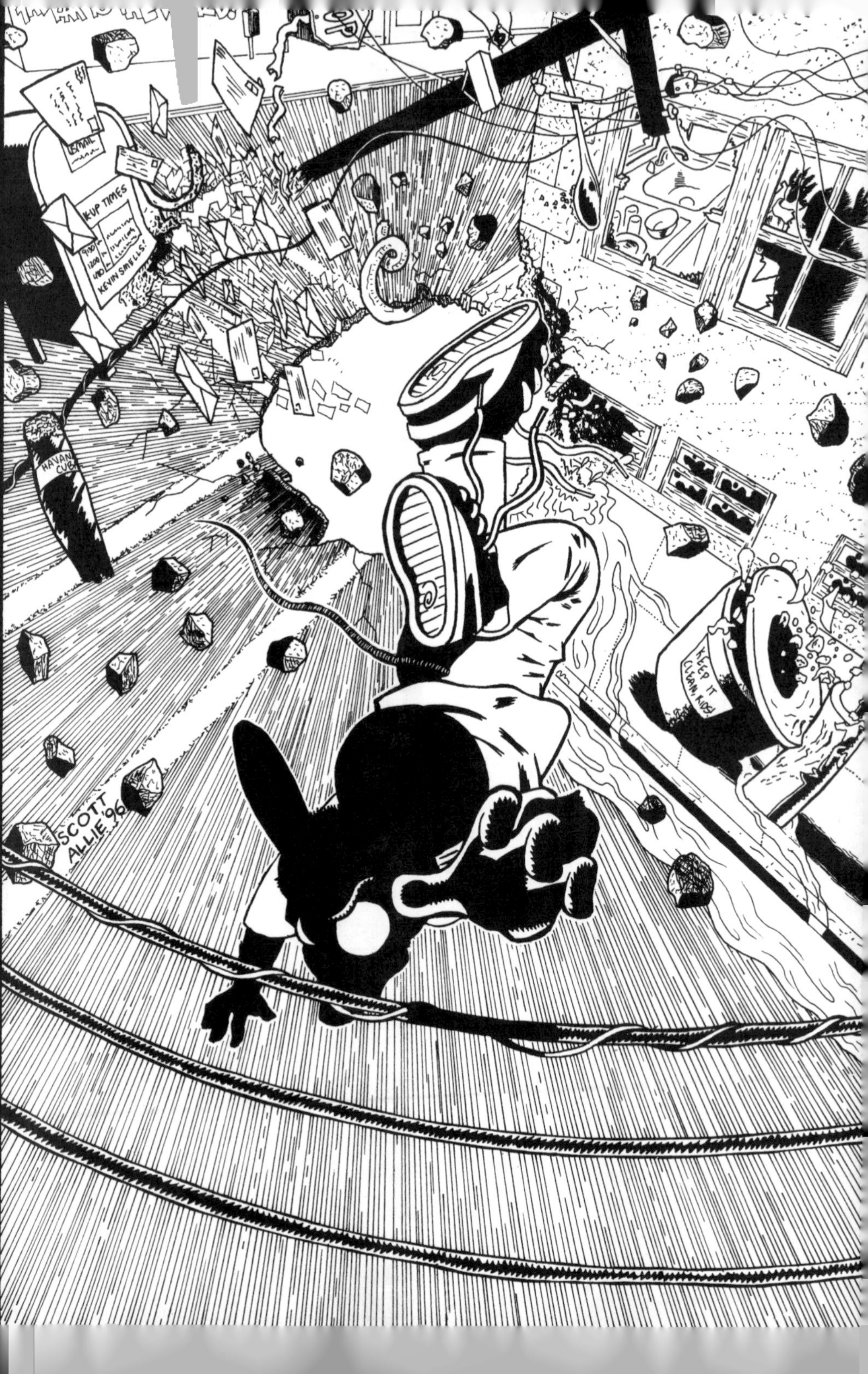
US MAIL
K-UP TIMES
9:30
12:00
4:30
KEVIN SMELLS!
KEEP IT CLEAN, KIDS!
SCOTT ALLIE '96

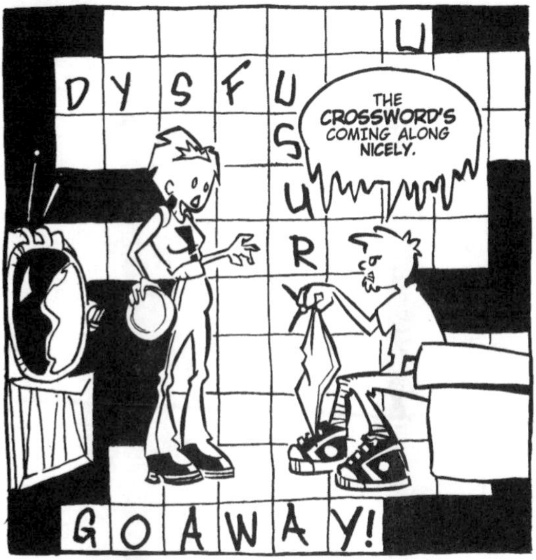
DYSFU
THE CROSSWORD'S COMING ALONG NICELY.
GOAWAY!

FACING: *A pinup I did way back when.*

In 1996 Kevin started drawing the graphic novel. These panels are from that version; he eventually decided to alter his style, and abandoned these pages, starting over in 1999. ***TOP LEFT:*** *I loved this idea of a background made of the crossword puzzle. It was in the original short story, and Kevin's 1996 and 1999 versions, but we ditched it in the final version.*

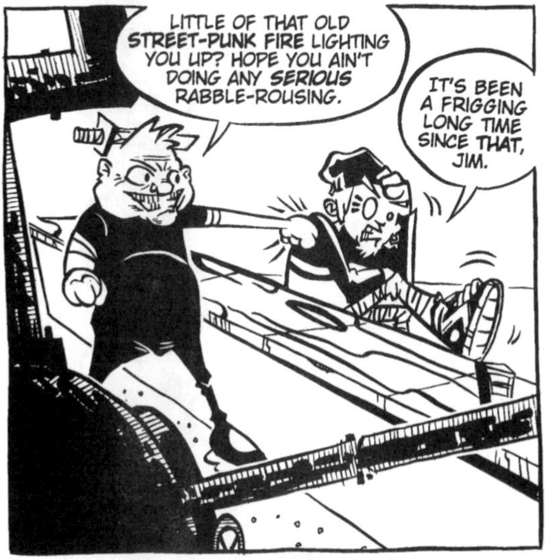
LITTLE OF THAT OLD STREET-PUNK FIRE LIGHTING YOU UP? HOPE YOU AIN'T DOING ANY SERIOUS RABBLE-ROUSING.
IT'S BEEN A FRIGGING LONG TIME SINCE THAT, JIM.

*Jim was in the original short story, and his look continued to evolve with each new version, as well as that of the cops (****BOTTOM LEFT****) and the Bus Schedule Freak (****BOTTOM RIGHT****).*

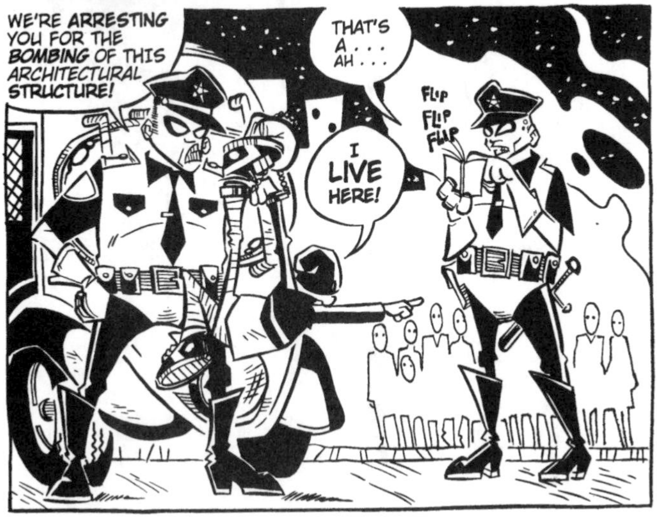
WE'RE ARRESTING YOU FOR THE BOMBING OF THIS ARCHITECTURAL STRUCTURE!
THAT'S A . . . AH . . .
I LIVE HERE!
FLIP FLIP FLIP

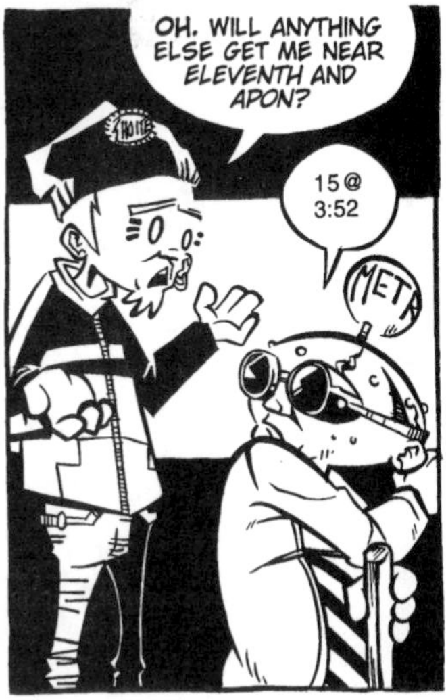
OH. WILL ANYTHING ELSE GET ME NEAR ELEVENTH AND APON?
15@ 3:52

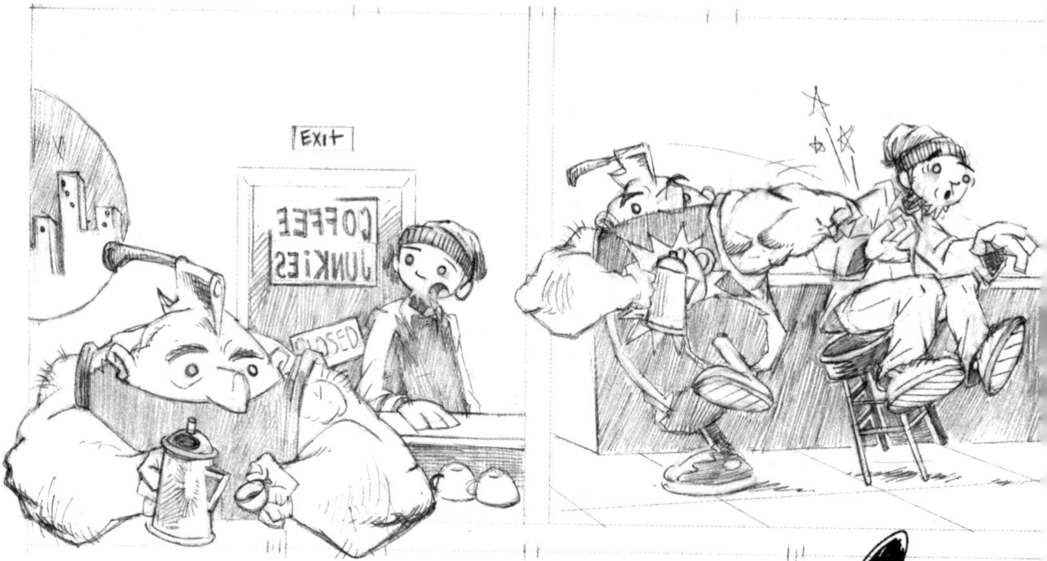
EXIT
COFFEE JUNKIES
CLOSED

***TOP:** Panels from Kevin's 1999 version, which he gave up on before he even started inking pages. By the time he was wrapping up art school in 2002, he'd done some ashcan comics in which he developed a style that fit* Exurbia *to a T.* ***BELOW:** He was having fun designing "gypsy" characters, so I wrote them into the story.* ***FACING:** Kevin nails down the designs for Gage and others, but struggles with Big Fist.*

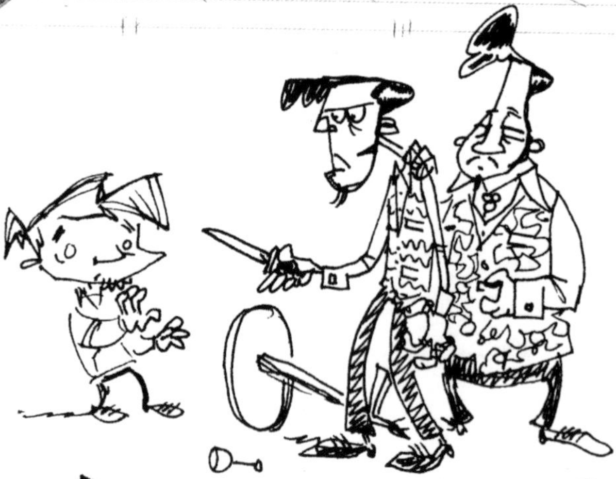

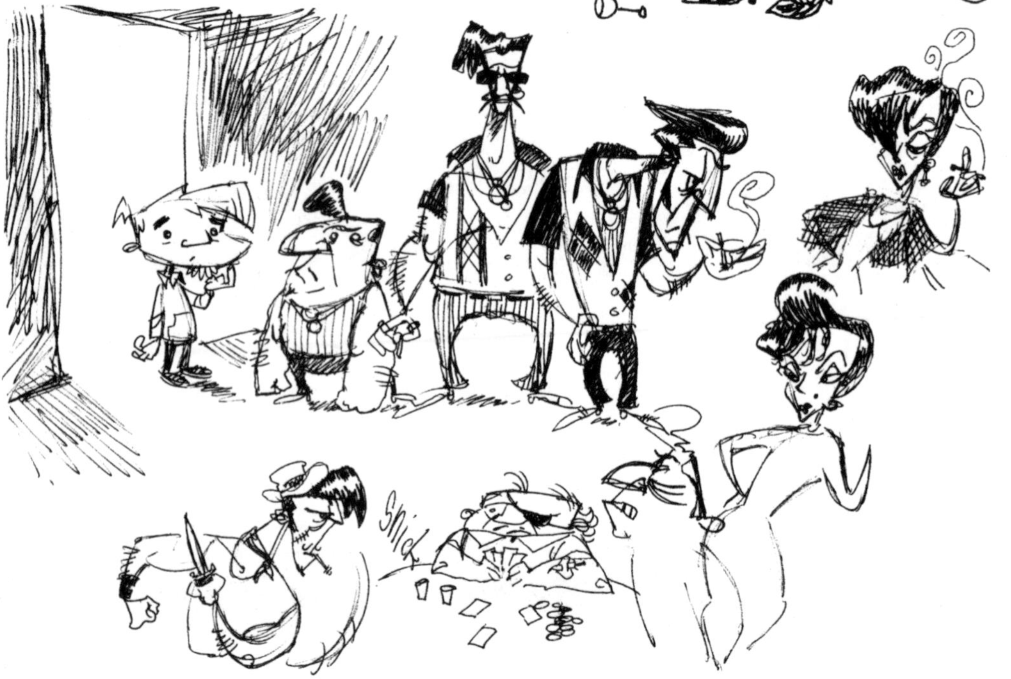

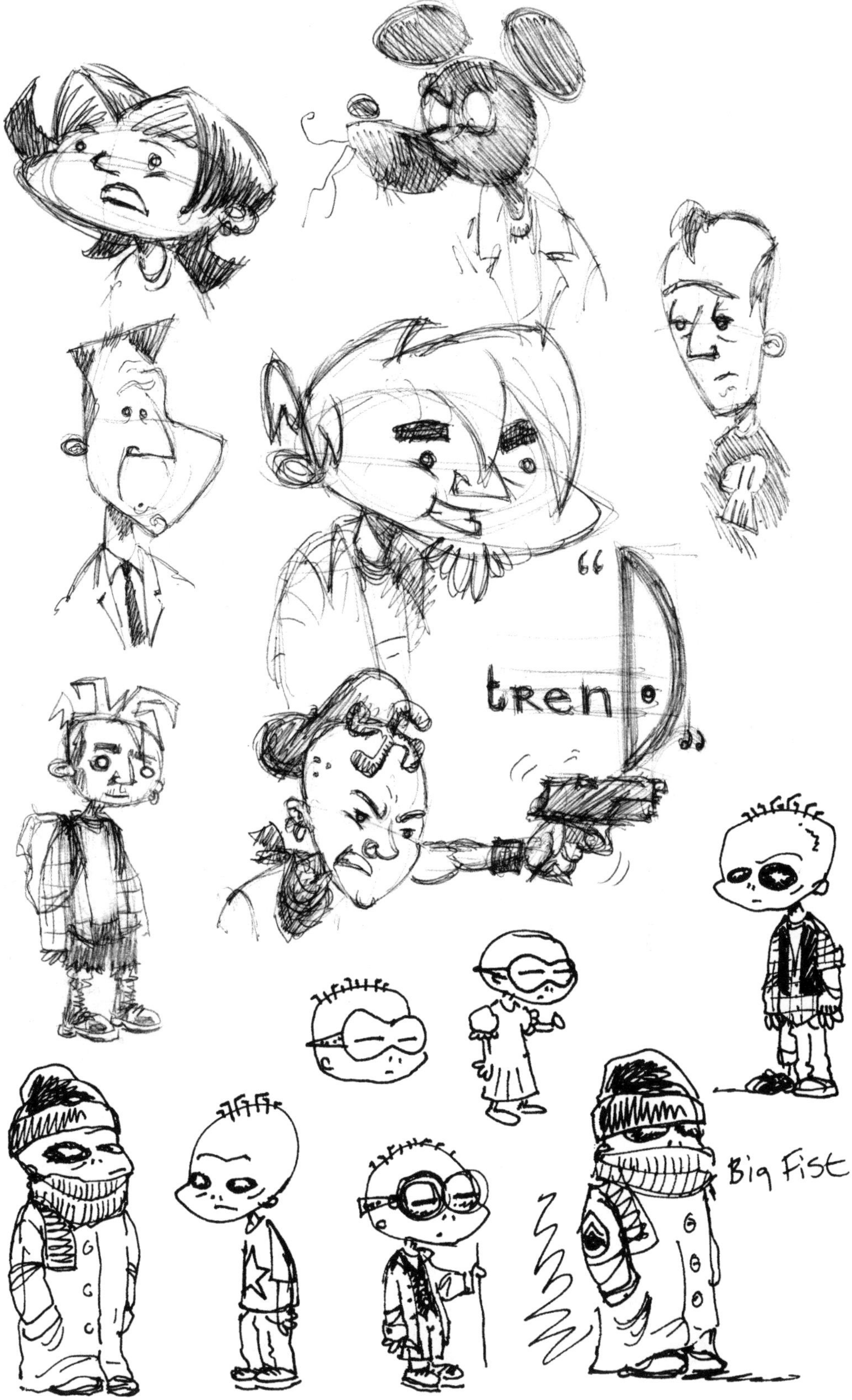
"tren."
Big Fist

Final character designs.

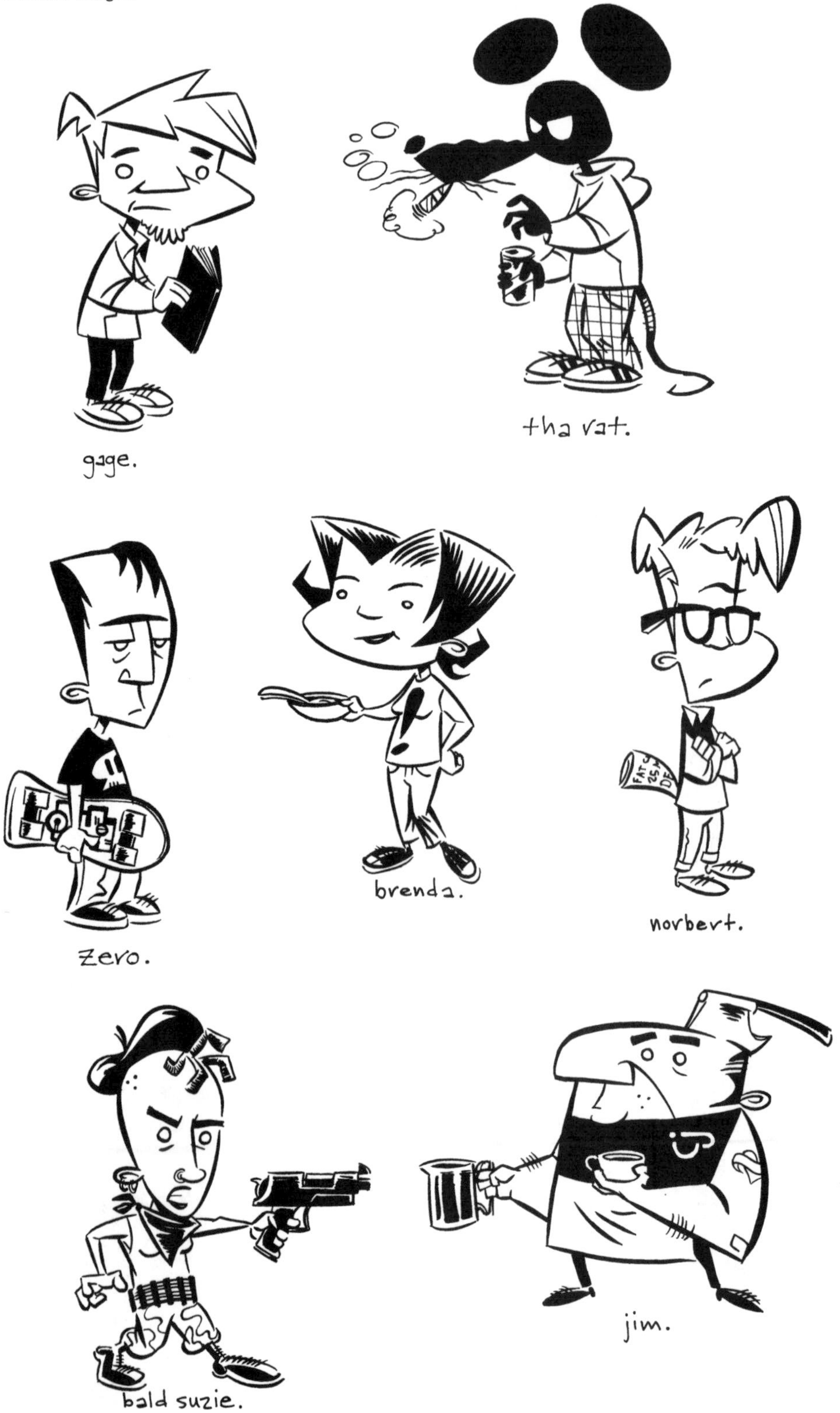

gage.
tha rat.
zero.
brenda.
norbert.
bald suzie.
jim.

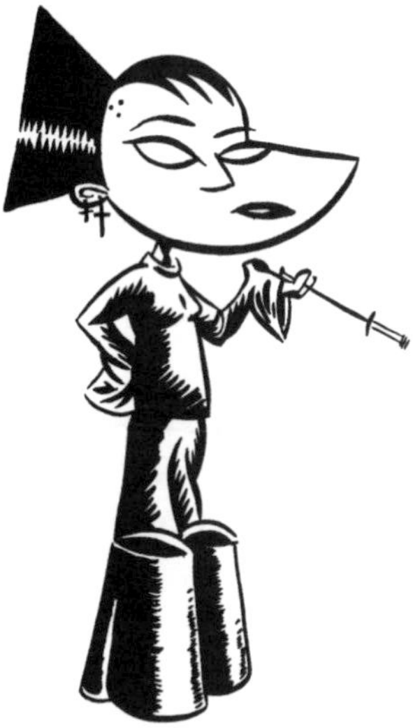

jet.

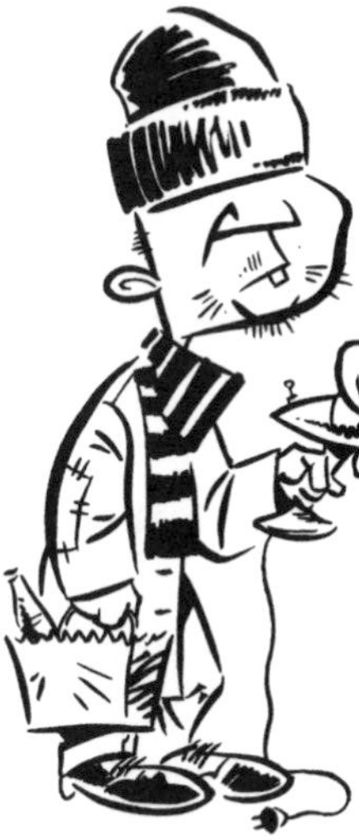

sten.

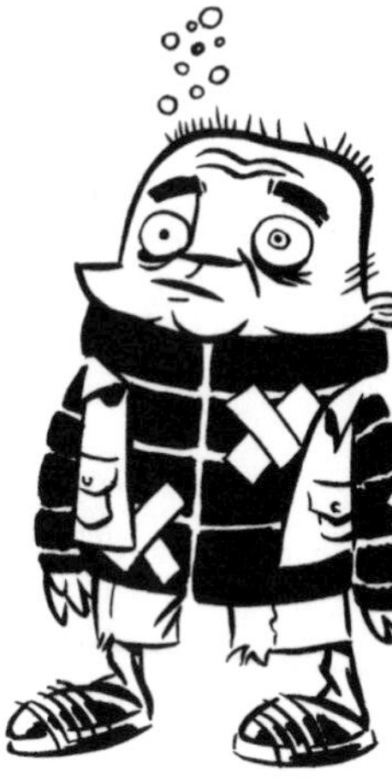

dave.

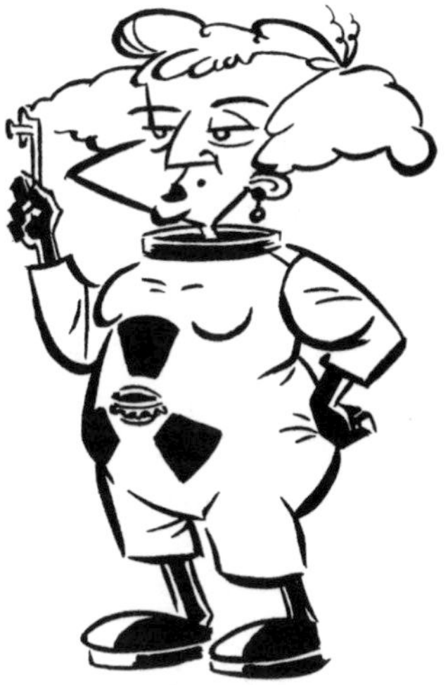

waitress

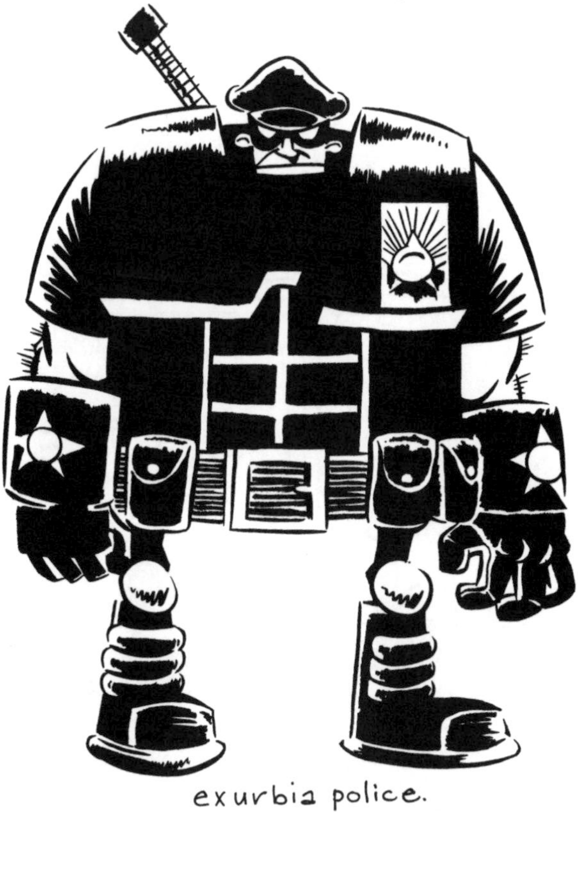

exurbia police.

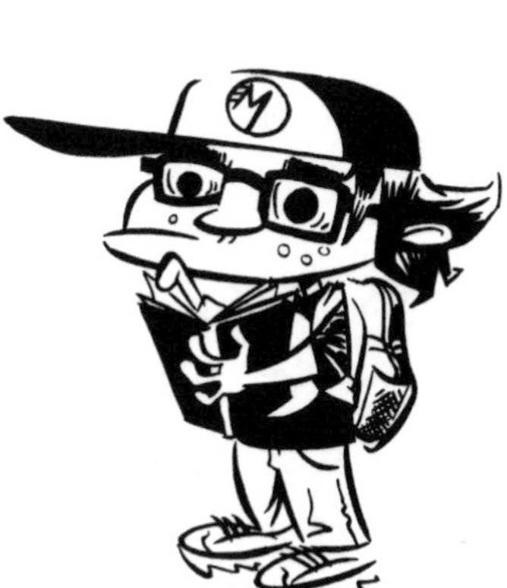

bus·stop freak.

Aside from a few political cartoons in the Salem Evening News *in 1991, I've never been a topical writer, but with a main character like Gage, a little of that sort of thing naturally came into it. Of course, working on the book over fifteen years made it hard for the writing to stay current. In the strip-club scene, I had an ad playing on TV that reflected some of the cultural anxiety in the late nineties. But after Clinton had left office, the ad didn't seem relevant; the religious right had won. There were other agendas. So I wrote a new TV spot, with George W. in a dunce cap spreading terror. It's late 2009 now, with a new administration, new agendas; but that fear mongering still resonates, so we left it in the book. I liked this original TV ad, which Kevin never got around to drawing, so I drew it myself, just wanting to see it exist.*

Always end with a joke.

Scott Allie

Portland, Oregon
August 4, 2009

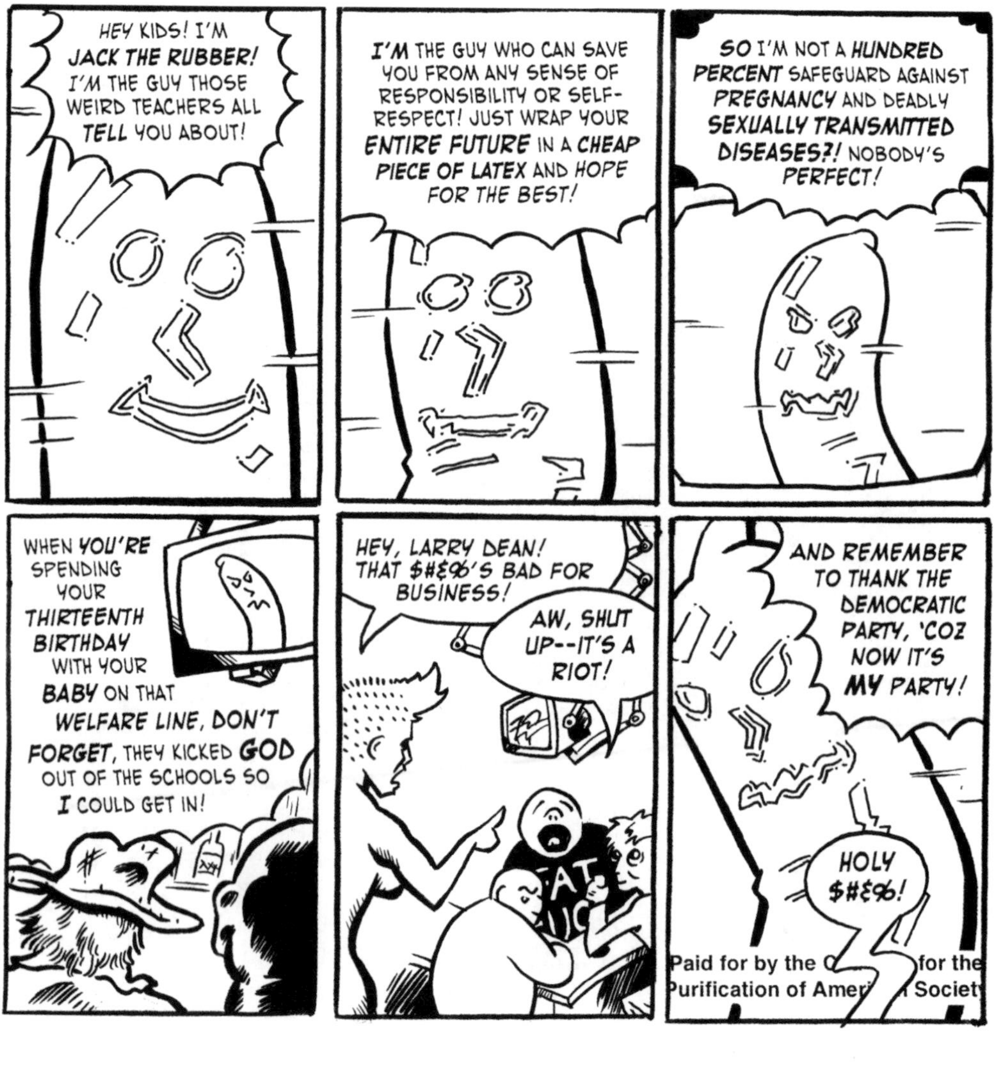

HEY KIDS! I'M JACK THE RUBBER! I'M THE GUY THOSE WEIRD TEACHERS ALL TELL YOU ABOUT!
I'M THE GUY WHO CAN SAVE YOU FROM ANY SENSE OF RESPONSIBILITY OR SELF-RESPECT! JUST WRAP YOUR ENTIRE FUTURE IN A CHEAP PIECE OF LATEX AND HOPE FOR THE BEST!
SO I'M NOT A HUNDRED PERCENT SAFEGUARD AGAINST PREGNANCY AND DEADLY SEXUALLY TRANSMITTED DISEASES?! NOBODY'S PERFECT!
WHEN YOU'RE SPENDING YOUR THIRTEENTH BIRTHDAY WITH YOUR BABY ON THAT WELFARE LINE, DON'T FORGET, THEY KICKED GOD OUT OF THE SCHOOLS SO I COULD GET IN!
HEY, LARRY DEAN! THAT $#&%'S BAD FOR BUSINESS!
AW, SHUT UP--IT'S A RIOT!
AND REMEMBER TO THANK THE DEMOCRATIC PARTY, 'COZ NOW IT'S MY PARTY!
HOLY $#&%!
Paid for by the C for the Purification of Ameri Society

ALSO FROM DARK HORSE BOOKS

MySpace
Dark Horse
Presents
FEATURING WORK BY

MYSPACE DARK HORSE PRESENTS VOLUME 1
Written by Joss Whedon, Gerard Way, Mike Mignola, and others
Art by Guy Davis, the Fillbach Brothers, Gabriel Bá and others

MySpace and Dark Horse Comics have teamed up to bring a historic comic book experience online. *MySpace Dark Horse Presents* features the best writers and artists in comics creating original work. Included here are Joss Whedon's complete rock 'n' roll saga "Sugarshock!"; Mike Mignola's haunting holiday tale "The Christmas Spirit"; and a lost *Umbrella Academy* chapter written by Gerard Way. This volume also presents a wide range of established comics talent, and stories from newcomers who saw their professional debuts in *MySpace Dark Horse Presents.*

ISBN 978-1-59307-998-7 | $19.95

THE FILLBACH BROTHERS
ROADKILL
A JIM KOWALSKI ADVENTURE

ROADKILL: A JIM KOWALSKI ADVENTURE
Created by Matt and Shawn Fillbach

A biological contagion that turns the living into cannibalistic mutants has been unleashed, and it's up to paranormal trucker Jim Kowalksi to stop it! Jim, along with his talking dog and GPS crystal skull, leads this full-throttle adventure into overdrive. Our heroic trio must battle their way through monster insects, zombie truckers, a crazed country musician, and a doomsday cult led by the insane Reverend Baba-Yaga Boogity. "The Fillbachs' sensibility is enjoyably left-field and ambitious." —The A.V. Club

ISBN 978-1-59582-169-0 | $9.95

THE TRIAL OF
COLONEL
SWEETO
AND OTHER STORIES
A COLLECTION OF THE COMIC STRIPS OF THE PERRY BIBLE FELLOWSHIP

THE PERRY BIBLE FELLOWSHIP: THE TRIAL OF COLONEL SWEETO AND OTHER STORIES
By Nicholas Gurewitch

Dark Horse Comics is proud to present *The Perry Bible Fellowship: The Trial of Colonel Sweeto and Other Stories* by acclaimed cartoonist Nicholas Gurewitch. The award-winning *Perry Bible Fellowship* has achieved a worldwide cult following. Now, for the first time, the hilarious cartoons of Nicholas Gurewitch have been collected in this handsome hardcover edition. "*PBF* is hilarious and f$#@ed-up in a very sublime way." —Scott McCloud (*Understanding Comics*)

ISBN 978-1-59307-844-7 | $14.95

SPEAK OF THE DEVIL
GILBERT HERNANDEZ

SPEAK OF THE DEVIL
By Gilbert Hernandez

This is the story of Val Castillo, a promising gymnast with a strange hobby. She is secretly the neighborhood peeping tom. At first she is alone in this, but when a male friend discovers her doings he joins her in a dark journey of spying and making discoveries about their neighbors that may have been better left alone. Especially secrets that threaten all involved. Like Val spying on her own father and stepmother in their bedroom. This snowballs into a journey darker than even the most cynical would care to endure.

ISBN 978-1-59582-193-5 | $19.95

AVAILABLE AT YOUR LOCAL COMICS SHOP OR BOOKSTORE! • To find a comics shop in your area, call 1-888-266-4226.
For more information or to order direct, visit darkhorse.com or call 1-800-862-0052 Mon.–Fri. 9 AM to 5 PM Pacific Time. Prices and availability subject to change without notice.

DARK HORSE BOOKS®
darkhorse.com

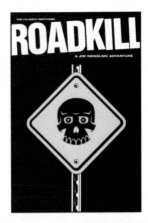

ALSO FROM DARK HORSE BOOKS

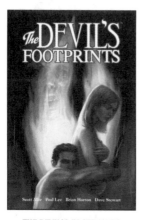

The DEVIL'S FOOTPRINTS
Scott Allie Paul Lee Brian Horton Dave Stewart

THE DEVIL'S FOOTPRINTS

Written by Scott Allie; art by Paul Lee and Brian Horton

The youngest son of a deceased sorceror, desperate to protect his family from a mysterious curse, digs into his dead father's bag of tricks. But his desire to protect his loved ones leads him to mix deception with demon conjuration, isolating himself in a terrible world where his soul hangs in the balance. "Recommended." —Alan Moore

ISBN 978-1-56971-933-6 | $14.95

DARK HORSE BOOKS
SOLOMON KANE
THE CASTLE OF THE DEVIL

SOLOMON KANE VOLUME 1: THE CASTLE OF THE DEVIL TPB

Written by Scott Allie; art by Mario Guevara

Robert E. Howard's vengeance-obsessed Puritan begins his supernatural adventures in the haunted Black Forest of Germany in this adaptation of Howard's "The Castle of the Devil." "Unsettling, moody and eerily beautiful, their *Kane* is absolutely worthy of his creator." —Kurt Busiek

ISBN 978-1-59307-910-9 | $49.95

THE FOG
Scott Allie
Todd Herman
Andy Owens
Dave Stewart

THE FOG

Written by Scott Allie; art by Todd Herman

A group of Shanghai traders have come to America hoping to escape a string of weird deaths at the claws of unseen monsters. The arrival of a strange yet familiar fog reveals that the curse has found them, but even they don't know what that has to do with a pyromaniac refugee from the Civil War, the disappearance of one of their sons, or the terrible change coming over the Americans in this small seaside town.

ISBN 978-1-59307-423-4 | $6.95

STAR WARS
EMPIRE
VOLUME ONE
BETRAYAL

STAR WARS: EMPIRE VOLUME 1—BETRAYAL TPB

Written by Scott Allie; art by Ryan Benjamin, Curtis Arnold, and Dave Stewart

In the weeks before the events in *Star Wars: A New Hope*, a power-hungry cabal of Grand Moffs and Imperial officers embark on a dangerous plan to kill Emperor Palpatine and Darth Vader and seize control of the Empire! But before long, the would-be assassins are turning on one another. Their plans are further complicated by the actions of bounty hunter Boba Fett. And they may have fatally underestimated the cunning of their primary target: Emperor Palpatine!

ISBN 978-1-56971-964-0 | $12.95

AVAILABLE AT YOUR LOCAL COMICS SHOP OR BOOKSTORE! • To find a comics shop in your area, call 1-888-266-4226.

For more information or to order direct, visit darkhorse.com or call 1-800-862-0052 Mon.–Fri. 9 AM to 5 PM Pacific Time. Prices and availability subject to change without notice.

DARK HORSE BOOKS
darkhorse.com